In this exciting new monograph Dr Alison Lui has provided a very timely and contemporary account of the relationship between central banks and financial services regulation. The monograph is extremely well written and illustrates excellent levels of analysis and research. It provides a very unique comparison and comparative commentary between several major economic centres including the United Kingdom and the United States of America. I unhesitatingly recommend this book to students, practitioners, policy makers who have an interest in this area. Dr Lui must be congratulated for producing an excellent piece of work that offers a refreshing and innovative review on a subject that continues to be of significant importance.

Professor Nicholas Ryder, University of the West of England

Financial Stability and Prudential Regulation

Financial stability is one of the key tenets of a central bank's functions. Since the financial crisis of 2007–9, an area of hot debate is the extent to which central banks should be involved with prudential regulation, especially micro-prudential regulation and supervision.

This book examines the macro- and micro-prudential regulatory frameworks and systems of the UK, Australia, the US, Canada and Germany. Drawing on the regulator frameworks of these regions, it book examines the central banks' roles of crisis management and prudential regulation. Alison Lui compares the institutional structure of the new 'twin peaks' model in the UK to the Australian model, the multi-regulatory US model (with some elements of the twin-peaks model) and the single, consolidated regulatory Canadian and German models. The European Banking Union and the impact of the Single Supervisory Regime are also examined.

The book also discusses the extent to which the central bank in these countries, as well as the European Central Bank (ECB), is involved with financial stability. It demonstrates how the Bank of England, ECB and Federal Reserve have gained regulatory and supervisory powers since the global financial crisis. Despite the increase of powers, there is an argument for permitting central banks to have micro-prudential supervisory powers for financial-stability reasons. As a multi-regional, comparative study on the importance and effectiveness of prudential regulation, this book will be of great use and interest to students and researchers in the law of financial regulation, economics and banking.

Alison Lui is a Senior Lecturer in Law at Liverpool John Moores University.

Routledge Research in Finance and Banking Law

Financial Stability and Prudential Regulation

A comparative approach to the UK,
US, Canada, Australia and Germany

Alison Lui

Routledge
Taylor & Francis Group

LONDON AND NEW YORK

British Library Cataloguing in Publication Data
A catalogue record for this book is available from the British Library

Library of Congress Cataloging in Publication Data
Names: Lui, Alison, author.
Title: Financial stability and prudential regulation : a comparative approach to the UK, US, Canada, Australia and Germany / Alison Lui.
Description: Abingdon, Oxon ; New York, NY : Routledge, 2016. | Series: Routledge research in finance and banking law | Includes bibliographical references and index.
Identifiers: LCCN 2016013477| ISBN 9781138899971 (hbk) | ISBN 9781315707563 (ebk)
Subjects: LCSH: Capital market--Law and legislation | Financial institutions--Law and legislation/Classification: LCC K1114 .L85 2016 | DDC 332.1/1--dc23 LC record available at http://lccn.loc.gov/2016013477

ISBN: 978-1-138-89997-1 (hbk)
ISBN: 978-1-138-61435-2 (pbk)

Typeset in Galliard
by Sunrise Setting Ltd, Brixham, UK

To My Father and Mother

Contents

Foreword

Since the global financial crisis, there has been a torrent of national and international legislation aimed at improving the regulation of banks, so as to prevent another crisis: and there has also been much academic commentary on the efficacy (or lack of efficacy) of these measures.

This monograph supplies a gap in the current scholarship, by providing an insightful and measured comparative analysis, by reference to the themes of financial stability, prudential regulation and the increased regulatory role of central banks.

In this work, Alison Lui examines how different jurisdictions have struck the balance between financial innovation and financial stability. She considers the prudential regulatory regimes of the UK, US, Canada, Australia and Germany and discusses how the institutional structures of financial regulation affect the quality of the implementation of financial-stability policies.

In particular, she discusses the impact of the Basel III Accord (particularly the provisions concerning counter-cyclical capital buffers, micro-prudential regulation and supervision) and the impact of the Dodd–Frank Wall Street Reform and Consumer Protection Act 2010 on the US financial regulatory architecture.

Alison Lui also reviews the strengths and weaknesses of the policies adopted by central banks during the global financial crisis and analyses how the Bank of England has carried out its mandate to maintain financial stability since the global financial crisis, before looking to the future.

Financial stability remains a key item on the agenda of central banks. Global threats – the uncertainty surrounding interest rates, emerging market risks and cyber risks – heighten the problem.

Alison Lui's comparative approach, and her critical analysis of the role of central banks, should be of great interest, not just to academics and students, but also to policy makers. I am glad to be able to commend this monograph to everyone with an interest in the topics covered.

Richard Salter QC
Bencher of the Inner Temple, Deputy High Court Judge and Visiting
Fellow in Financial Law, Oxford University Faculty of Law
March 2016

Acknowledgements

Writing a book has always been a goal of mine. In achieving this goal, I wish to personally thank the following people for their assistance and support: Dr Nicholas Ryder, whose help and encouragement throughout the process have been invaluable; Dr Tony Harvey, whose advice and support have been much appreciated; and the publishing team at Routledge for their professional advice and assistance.

Particular thanks go to the Max Planck Institute for Comparative and International Private Law (MPI), Hamburg. With the help of an MPI Fellowship, I was able to work at the MPI on my book for three months. The resources at the MPI library are excellent and I have found them invaluable for my research. Thank you to all the staff at the MPI, particularly the library staff who assisted me a great deal during my stay. Finally, thank you to my family, who have been most patient with me for the duration of this project.

List of abbreviations

American International Group	AIG
Advanced Risk Responsive Operating Framework	ARROW
Asset backed commercial paper	ABCP
Australian Financial Stability Inquiry	AFSI
Australian Prudential Regulatory Authority	APRA
Australian Securities and Investment Commission	ASIC
Bundesanstalt für Finanzdienstleistungsaufsicht	BaFin
Canada Deposit Insurance Corporation	CDIC
Canada Mortgage Housing Corporation	CMHC
Canadian Imperial Bank of Commerce	CIBC
Commodities Futures Trading Commission	CFTC
Council of Federal Regulators	CFR
Domestic Systemically Important Banks	D-SIBs
Euro Interbank Offered Rate	Euribor
European Banking Authority	EBA
European Banking Union	EBU
European Central Bank	ECB
European Financial Stability Facility	EFSF
European Insurance and Occupational Pensions Authority	EIOPA
European Securities and Markets Authority	ESMA
European Stability Mechanism	ESM
European Supervisory Authorities	ESA
European System of Financial Supervision	ESFS
European Systemic Risk Board	ESRB
European Union	EU
Federal Deposit Insurance Corporation	FDIC
Foreign exchange market	Forex
Financial Conduct Authority	FCA
Financial Consumer Agency Canada	FCAC
Financial Regulator Assessment Board	FRAB
Financial Services Authority	FSA
Financial Policy Committee	FPC
Financial Stability Oversight Council	FSOC

Global Systemically Important Banks	G-SIBs
Gross Domestic Product	GDP
Halifax Bank of Scotland	HBOS
Hypovereins Real Estate Aktiengesellschaft	HRE
IKB Deutsche Industriebank	IKB
Landesbank Sachsen Girozentrale	Sachsen LB
Liability Holding Companies	LHC
London inter-bank lending rate	Libor
Monetary Policy Committee	MPC
National Westminster Bank	NatWest
Office of the Comptroller of the Currency	OCC
Office of the Superintendent of Financial Institutions	OSFI
Ontario Securities Commissions	OSC
Orderly Liquidation Authority	OLA
Primary Dealer Credit Facility	PDCF
Probability and Impact Rating System	PAIRS
Prudential Regulatory Authority	PRA
Reserve Bank of Australia	RBA
Royal Bank of Scotland	RBS
Securities and Exchange Commission	SEC
Senior Fraud Office	SFO
Single Supervisory Mechanism	SSM
Special Purpose Vehicles	SPV
Special Resolution Regime	SRR
Standard Chartered Bank	SC Bank
Supervisory Oversight and Response System	SOARS
Supervisory Review and Evaluation Process	SREP
Troubled Asset Relief Programme	TARP
Term Purchase and Resale Agreements	TPRA
Term Securities Lending Facility	TSLF
Treaty on the functioning of the European Union	TFEU
United Kingdom	UK
UK Asset Resolution Limited	UKAR
UK Financial Investments Limited	UKFI
United States	US

Table of legislation

UK Acts of Parliament

Australian Acts of Parliament

US Acts of Parliament

Canadian Acts of Parliament

German Acts of Parliament

European legal materials

Directive 2014/59/EU of the European Parliament and of the Council of 15 May 2014 establishing a framework for the recovery and resolution of credit institutions and investment firms and amending Council Directive 82/891/EEC, and Directives 2001/24/EC, 2002/47/EC, 2004/25/EC, 2005/56/EC, 2007/36/EC, 2011/35/EU, 2012/30/EU and 2013/36/

1 Introduction

Financial stability

Referring to the Capital Requirements Regulation (No. 575/2013) and the Capital Requirements Directive (2013/36/EU) at a Capital Requirements Regulation conference in Brussels in 2015, Jonathan Hill, former Commissioner for Financial Stability, Financial Services and Capital Markets Union at the European Union said that:

> There is a direct link between these technical and detailed pieces of legislation and the everyday lives of our citizens. A direct link between the stability of our banks, the strength of our economy, the resilience of our financial system and the well-being of taxpayers
>
> (Hill 2015)

Hill has made an important point. Legislation on prudential legislation may seem dry on the surface but it is of significance to everyone. A well-designed, proportionate and flexible legal framework can provide the foundation of effective regulation and supervision, desirable factors for financial stability. Challenges remain to construct this legal framework because financial stability is not absolute and it changes with time. Other factors, such as politics, governance and economics, also affect financial stability. Further, financial stability has many dimensions and can include rule-making, policy development and supervision. Harmonisation of legislation at European and international levels posts further challenges due to the diversity in local laws, history and culture. As seen in the financial crisis of 2007–9, hegemony of financial innovation since the early 1980s led to the near collapse of several banks in the UK, US and Germany. Low interest rates at the beginning of 2000 and a search for greater profits led banks to adopt an 'originate to distribute' model. This model allowed banks to sell loans (including corporate loans) in the secondary loan market, giving greater liquidity, more borrowing capacity and the ability to transfer risks to ultimate investors. It also allowed banks to circumvent banking regulations, such as the Basel II Accord on capital requirements (Acharya *et al.* 2009).

Derivatives became popular and investment banking became highly desirable and profitable. Banking became complicated, due to the use of securitization and lax lending requirements. Securitized products such as American sub-prime mortgages were repackaged and sold on to investors with very little due diligence conducted. Not many bankers fully analysed the risks or realised that risks were not actually passed to the ultimate investors. With profit being the ultimate goal, the business models of banks such as Northern Rock and Royal Bank of Scotland were risky and aggressive (Onado 2009; Financial Services Authority 2011). Short-term targets combined with large salaries and bonuses incentivised some bankers to take uncalculated risks. The banking model evolved from 'relationship banking' to 'sales banking' (Moore 2010). Banking was no longer seen as a personal service. Rather, it was about selling as many financial products as possible. Banker bashing and the Occupy movement in the UK following the global financial crisis represent the anger and frustration of taxpayers at the damage that certain banks caused. Greed and recklessness prevailed over sensible, conservative banking models.

Yet the banks were too big and important to fail. A number of banks in the UK, US and Germany were rescued, nationalised or bailed out. Rancière *et al.* (2008) suggest that countries that have experienced occasional financial crises have, on average, demonstrated higher economic growth than countries that have shown more stable financial conditions. Whilst Rancière *et al.* (2008) are not suggesting that financial crises are good for economic growth, they suggest that the systemic risk-taking that overcomes financial hindrances to economic growth is associated with occasional financial crises. In brief, the unique systemic nature of the financial system as a result of the use of credit and securitisation is here to stay. The risk of contagion when a bank is struggling financially is high due to the interconnectedness of the financial system. Financial crises are inevitable. The ultimate aim of macro-prudential regulation is to internalise regulatory costs. Macro-prudential regulation and supervision contribute towards financial stability because they involve the relevant regulatory authority monitoring systemic risks holistically. Macro-prudential regulation was neglected during the period before the global financial crisis at the expense of micro-prudential regulation. Central banks such as the Bank of England lacked the necessary tools to tackle the financial crisis. Central banks were not able to curb excessive leverage built up by banks through the use of the capital-adequacy ratio, the principal regulatory instrument of central banks (Goodhart 2009). Without appropriate regulation to tackle excessive leverage during the global financial crisis, central banks had to widen their range of collateral, as well as creating special liquidity schemes to stabilise the global financial system. The first part of each chapter therefore focuses on how central banks in the UK, US, Australia, Canada and Germany carried out their crisis management roles. The second part critically analyses the macro- and micro-prudential regulatory and supervisory weaknesses in the countries mentioned.

Central banks

Chapter 2 focuses on the role of central banks. With a Canadian governor at the Bank of England, this monograph is timely and adopts a comparative legal analysis of the UK, Australia, the US, Canada and Germany. This book will examine central banks' roles of crisis management, resolution and prudential regulation. Both the World Bank and the Bank of International Settlements agree that since the financial crisis of 2007–9, one of the areas of debate is the extent to which the central bank should be involved with prudential regulation. This includes both macro- and micro-prudential regulation. Financial stability is one of the key tenets of a central bank's functions. Apart from its role as lender of last resort, 90 per cent of central banks across the world considered that they have responsibility for financial stability and regulatory issues (Bank for International Settlements 2009). It will be seen that central banks, such as the Bank of England, Federal Reserve and the European Central Bank (ECB), lacked appropriate tools – for example, counter-cyclical capital buffers – to tackle excessive leverage as a result of economic booms. Without such tools and appropriate regulation, these central banks had to widen their range of collateral, as well creating new liquidity schemes to stabilise the global financial system. The lender-of-last-resort role of central banks widened during the global financial crisis to tackle the interbank market and rescue non-bank institutions. Bagehot's principle thus has to be amended to take into account the complexity and interconnectedness of modern financial markets. Whether giving central banks new macro-prudential regulatory tools is a wise decision can only be known when they are utilised in the next financial crisis. However, past experiences, such as the Japanese financial crisis in the late 1980s, revealed that achieving financial stability through macro-prudential regulation is possible because having more stringent micro-prudential regulation tends to lead to lower efficiency in financial intermediation.

Two questions follow from this observation. Should central banks also have a role in micro-prudential regulation? If so, does the regulatory architecture of the authorities affect the effectiveness of financial regulation if central banks can become too powerful? Regulatory architecture can facilitate effective supervision, especially if the regulators have clear mandates. Good co-ordination between the financial regulatory agencies is also very important to effective prudential regulation. This is dependent on the institutional structure of the financial regulatory model of each country. The author has chosen to focus on common-law jurisdictions, such as the UK, US, Canada and Australia. In addition, she has chosen Germany because it is the largest economic power in the EU and because its financial regulatory regime is similar to the UK's previous regulator, the Financial Services Authority (FSA).

The institutional structure of the new 'twin peaks' model in the UK will be compared with the Australian twin-peaks model, the multi-regulatory US model and the single regulatory Canadian model. The US model of multiple supervisory regulatory authorities is in contrast to the twin-peaks model. The strengths and weaknesses of these different institutional regulatory models will be analysed. The author's study reveals that there are similarities between the German and UK regulatory models, especially the relationship between the central bank and financial regulator. The relationships between the financial prudential regulator and the central bank in these countries will be discussed. Some scholars fear that the Bank of England might have too much power and is thus a super single financial regulator in the twin-peaks model. It will be revealed that early indications suggest that this fear is premature, although the Bank of England needs to improve its accountability and transparency through several channels, as the author will reveal in Chapter 8.

UK

The UK provides a good example how the tripartite system failed during the global financial crisis, and Chapter 3 focuses on the UK. The Bank of England has admitted that it focused too much on macro-prudential regulation. It realises that it needs to establish a better link between monetary policy and micro-prudential regulation (Bank of England 2008, Bank of England 2009). Following the US's 'Greenspan put' policy, the Bank of England was reluctant to act upon the continued growth of asset prices and was too preoccupied with the present rather than the future. This was exacerbated by the long period of low interest rates and credit growth. As a result, the Bank of England was ill-prepared for the global financial crisis. The lack of suitable UK insolvency legislation to deal with distressed banks further hampered the effectiveness of the Bank of England's role as the macro-prudential regulator. The Banking Act 2009 was thus passed to provide emergency measures such as the Special Resolution Regime to deal with distressed banks.

The FSA, as the single regulator, failed in its role as a micro-prudential regulator. Communication between the FSA and the Bank of England was poor. The FSA was also weak in its capacities as a regulator and supervisor. The case studies of Northern Rock and Halifax Bank of Scotland (HBOS) in Chapter 3 provide detailed analysis of the FSA's failings. In particular, an interview with Paul Moore, the former Head of Group Regulatory Risk at HBOS, provided useful insight into the weaknesses of the FSA and at HBOS. The legal framework, namely in the form of the Financial Markets and Services Act 2000, did not help since it was complex and conflicting. The FSA was unable to determine whether financial innovation or consumer protection should be prioritised. The risk-based supervisory approach of the FSA proved to be a far cry from reality because lobbying from banks persuaded the FSA that they were able to use their own bank models. Regulatory capture meant that the FSA took a hands-off, reactive supervisory approach. Together with cuts in staff at the FSA, the supervisory approach proved to be a disaster.

The change from a single regulatory model to a twin-peaks model was primarily political. With a coalition government in power in 2010, George

Osborne recommended a shift from the single regulator to a twin-peaks model on the grounds that the tripartite system 'failed spectacularly' in ensuring financial stability (BBC 2010). The HM Treasury document 'A new approach to financial regulation: judgement, focus and stability' (2010) explained that the single regulatory model failed to identify debt-related risks and that primary legislation was needed to reform the regulatory architecture, hence the Financial Services Act 2012 setting out the responsibilities of the regulators under the twin-peaks model. The Financial Policy Committee (FPC) is responsible for macro-prudential regulation and the Prudential Regulatory Authority (PRA) is responsible for micro-prudential regulation. The Financial Conduct Authority (FCA) is responsible for regulating the business conduct of all financial-services firms, as well as prudential regulation of firms not regulated by the PRA. Legislation and handbooks have been amended so that the regulators have more powers, especially under the Financial Services Reform Act 2012. The supervisory style of both the PRA and FCA has changed to a more proactive and judgement-based approach. They co-operate and communicate well. Enforcement actions have also been more frequent and tougher.

Australia

The UK took inspiration from Australia when the former adopted the twin-peaks model in 2010. Australia has been called the 'lucky country' as it emerged relatively unscathed from the global financial crisis. Abundance of natural resources and commodities protected Australia to a certain degree. Its financial regulatory structure, supervisory approach and the 'four pillars' policy served the country well. The Wallis Inquiry of 1997 reviewed the regulatory structure of Australia and recommended the twin-peaks model. The Reserve Bank of Australia (RBA) is the macro-prudential regulator, with the Australian Prudential Regulatory Authority (APRA) the micro-prudential regulator. The Australian Securities and Investment Commission (ASIC) is responsible for conduct of business regulation. The three regulatory agencies communicated and worked well during the global financial crisis. The RBA was decisive in making several interest-rate decisions which boosted the economy (Hill 2012). It was also original in creating new liquidity mechanisms when there was a liquidity shortage. The RBA widened its collateral framework to include residential mortgage-backed securities for repurchase agreements (Brown and Davis 2010). However, the ASIC and the Australian Securities Exchange were criticised for imposing a long and strict ban on short-selling during the global financial crisis. Although empirical research into a short-selling ban and liquidity is mixed, Australia's ban is the longest and harshest in comparison to those in the US, UK, Canada and Germany.

The Australian Financial Stability Inquiry (AFSI) did not recommend any changes to the twin-peaks model after the global financial crisis. The APRA's interventionist and proactive supervisory style proved to be effective. Similar to the UK, however, the APRA lacked powers to deal with distressed banks.

New legislation was passed to strengthen the APRA's powers in bank resolution. Further, the relationship between the APRA and the RBA became closer when new legislation was enacted to enable the APRA to assist the RBA to respond to any financial threats. The APRA had the advantage of being funded by industry players. The ASIC however, did not have this benefit. Moreover, its enforcement powers were weak. Therefore, the ASIC was not as successful as the APRA. Therefore, the AFSI recommended some improvements to these areas. Chapter 4 will analyse these recommendations.

The four-pillar policy is a unique feature of the Australian financial system. The four major banks in Australia are not permitted to merge with each other, yet they can merge with second-tier banks and foreign banks. The debate on the relationship between competition law and financial stability is inconclusive to date. In Australia, the four-pillars policy and the conservative business model of the banks provided financial stability, but the AFSI advised the regulators to review the competitiveness of the Australian financial system every three years. This is because the regulators must be able to demonstrate how they can balance competition with other regulatory objectives. This seems sensible in the light of a slump in demand for commodities such as coal and iron ore as well as a fall in commodity prices at the end of 2015 (Critchlow 2015). The economic outlook for Australia is difficult for two reasons. First, Australia is currently relying on its foreign reserves due to a fall in commodity prices. However, it does not have a bottomless amount of foreign reserves, which means that Australia has to borrow more to maintain its living standards. Second, its net foreign debt was 60 per cent in the first quarter of 2015. Compared to a net foreign debt of 175 per cent in Greece, Australia's net foreign debt seems not too bad. However, the percentage will only increase if the Australian economy weakens further (Critchlow 2015). Australia needs to be ready for the next financial challenge.

US

If Australia's financial regulatory structure is defined by simplicity, America's is the antithesis. Of the five countries studied in this book, the US has the most complicated regulatory architecture. The decentralised, multi-regulatory model with overlaps between federal and state regulators is so complex that 'if it did not exist already, no one would invent it' (Kushmeider 2005). Yet Gadinis (2013) argues that the American model of multiple regulatory agencies has the advantage of being highly independent, an indicator of good-quality financial regulation. Within the American financial system, there are four prudential bank regulators. They include the Federal Reserve Board, Office of the Comptroller of the Currency, Federal Deposit Insurance Corporation and National Credit Union Administration. The two regulatory agencies which protect consumers are the Securities and Exchange Commission (SEC) and the Commodities Futures Trading Commission. As the world's largest economy, the Federal Reserve is arguably the leader of the central banks. Naturally, other central banks do not have to follow but they will be affected by the Federal Reserve's decisions in interest rates to a certain extent (*Financial Times* 2015). Its decision to keep interest rates low for a long period prior to the global financial crisis has been criticised. However, the Federal Reserve was bold and innovative when new liquidity mechanisms were required during the global financial crisis. The Federal Reserve created the Term Auction Facility, Term Securities Lending Facility and Primary Dealer Credit Facility. The use of the emergency powers under section 13(3) of the Federal Reserve Act 1913 to lend to non-banks had not been utilised since the 1930s, but the Federal Reserve used them to rescue Bear Stearns. The rescue of Bear Stearns is significant because it is the first investment bank which was rescued. Chapter 5 provides a discussion of why the US regulators bailed out Bear Stearns but not Lehman Brothers. In particular, the use of a guarantee by the US Treasury under the Emergency Economic Stabilisation Act 2008 was instrumental to the rescue of Bear Stearns.

Consumer protection was weak in the US prior to the global financial crisis. The regulators failed to protect consumers: 87 per cent of borrowers could not identify the total cost of loans and 51 per cent could not identify the loan amount from their documents. Although some borrowers were guilty of lying about their credit history, the regulators failed in their supervisory roles. Information asymmetry led to a reliance on credit ratings by the regulators, especially the SEC. A discussion on how information asymmetry can be improved in financial markets can be found in Chapter 5. Another problem demonstrated by the US financial market is that of 'too big to fail'. In 2007, the US had approximately 8,000 financial institutions, including 20 bank holding companies. It also had a larger range of non-bank financial institutions, such as securities firms and money-market mutual funds, than Canada (Knight 2012). The Dodd–Frank Wall Street Reform and Consumer Protection Act 2010 ('the Dodd–Frank Act') was passed with the intention of reducing moral hazard associated with the too-big-to-fail concept. It will be argued that the Dodd–Frank Act does not fully achieve this. It does not resolve the problem of interconnectedness, either. The author will discuss potential solutions to these issues. Finally, the interesting relationship between deposit-insurance schemes and financial stability will also be analysed.

Canada

When the US was heavily hit by the global financial crisis, Canada did not suffer the same fate. In fact, Canada has not had a financial crisis since 1840 (Breydo 2015). This difference can be explained by their different historical backgrounds. Canada's smaller population and reliance on commodities have led to a simpler and smaller financial system than that of the US. The influx of immigrants to the US between the 1880s and 1920s saw an increase in small banks for different ethnicities, hence there are around 8,000 financial institutions in the US. Part of a safe, reliable and conservative financial sector, Canadian banks were less complex and relied less on whole-sale funding when they entered the global financial crisis (Knight 2012). Does this mean that Canadian banks are risk averse and dull? Not at all. It will be seen in Chapter 6 that some Canadian banks were rather aggressive in their business strategies. Breydo (2015) submits that Canada's resilience is down to one single factor: its superior financial regulatory architecture. He believes that the simple yet modern financial regulatory structure of Canada delivered effective macro-prudential supervision, which is crucial to financial stability. The Office of the Superintendent of Financial Institutions (OSFI) has the clear mandate of being the sole macro-prudential regulator for all financial services. By contrast, there are more than 100 regulatory agencies for this in the US. The other Canadian regulatory agencies (the Bank of Canada, Canada Deposit Insurance Corporation and Department of Finance) also have unambiguous mandates.

Other factors contributing to the robust Canadian financial market include the structure of the Canadian residential-mortgage market and the central banks. The Bank of Canada provided minimal but decisive, aggressive yet flexible support to banks during the financial crisis. The most successful factor was the Canadian Mortgage Housing Corporation (CHMC). The extension of the CMHC programme to purchase government-insured mortgages pro-vided much needed liquidity in the financial market. However, the asset-backed commercial paper ('ABCP') crisis in the early stage of the financial crisis proved to be a challenge for the regulators, especially the OSFI. It was criticised for not regulating and supervising non-banks which created ABCP. Otherwise, the OSFI was commended and praised for its strict yet effec-tive regulatory approach. The FCAC protected consumers well. Canada's financial sector is popular and highly trusted by Canadians, evidenced by 90 per cent of Canadians having a very good impression of their personal banks (Canadian Bankers Association 2014). This is a true sign of a success-ful financial sector, particularly when only 21 per cent of US citizens said the same for the US financial sector.

At a macro-prudential level, the Canadian philosophy of prevention is bet-ter than cure can be found in the supervisory framework and the OSFI's style of supervision. The ABCP crisis demonstrated that the OSFI and the provin-cial securities regulators lacked a co-ordinated response. Scholars, academics and politicians have discussed over the years whether Canada should have a single, national securities regulator to deal with systemic risks. Systemic risks are particularly prevalent in modern banking, primarily because of the reliance on securitisation and the interconnectedness of financial institutions. Further, Canadian banks are highly concentrated and there is a danger of too-big-to-fail. Chapter 6 will focus particularly on two macro-prudential issues: first, whether Canada needs a single national securities regulator and, second, whether the tight oligopoly of Canadian banks intensifies the too-big-to-fail problem and the concentration of the banking sector. The best kept secret of the global financial crisis will also be revealed.

Germany

German Chancellor Angela Merkel and Finance Minister Peer Steinbrück made no secret of the fact that they opposed the Anglo-American model of self-regulation and laissez-faire regulatory style. For Merkel and Steinbrück, the global financial crisis was an *Epochenwende*, an epoch-changing moment confirming the German government's view that reliance on and trust in the financial market was misguided. German regulators had a tight rein on the German financial system, ranging from strict control over tax havens through tight capital requirements to restricted bonus payments (Schirm 2015). The German regulatory architecture is based on a single regulator, the Federal Financial Supervisory Authority (Bundesanstalt für Finanzdienstleistungsaufsicht (BaFin)). BaFin, as the micro-prudential regulator, regulates and supervises all financial-services providers. Meanwhile, the German central bank (Deutsche Bundesbank) is the macro-prudential regulator and shares banking supervisory duties with BaFin. The Ministry of Finance has control over the federal fiscal budget and market supervision. Having lost its monetary policy powers to the ECB in January 1999, under European Economic and Monetary Union, the Bundesbank merely implements the ECB's monetary decisions. Therefore, Chapter 7 will examine the ECB's policies during the global financial crisis in detail. Similar to the Federal Reserve and the Bank of England, the ECB had to be creative with its fiscal measures. In particular, the Securities Markets Programme is controversial since it bailed out government deficits by allowing commercial banks to sell sovereign debts to the ECB (Belke 2010). The Bundesbank too was not keen on the Securities Markets Programme initially, since it thought the programme was trying to circumvent Article 123 of the Treaty of the Freedom of the European Union (TFEU) (Sester 2012). Article 123 of the TFEU bans central banks from financing governments.

The Bundesbank and BaFin received mixed reviews for their performances during the global financial crisis. The former was criticised for its supervision of two banks: IKB Deutsche Industriebank (IKB) and Landesbank Sachsen Girozentrale (Sachsen LB). The former is a small, specialised public bank, whilst the latter is a regional, state-owned bank, but they shared similar business models. Both banks invested heavily in asset-backed securities (Marinova 2009). BaFin did not take any action after a special audit into Sachsen LB revealed that the bank's management was unaware of the amount of asset-backed securities it had created in its Dublin branch. Further, Sachsen LB was aware of the potential losses it could incur (Marinova 2009). Having learnt from these two scenarios, the Bundesbank and BaFin performed better in the rescue of Hypovereins Real Estate Aktiengesellschaft (HRE). Saving HRE was a complicated matter since it still required help after two rescue packages. The German Parliament passed the Financial Market Stabilisation Act in October 2008 and gave HRE a guarantee line of €52 billion in separate tranches. In return, the German government took over HRE. The Ministry of Finance was criticised for its poor performance in the HRE incident, primarily because it was understaffed and therefore became heavily dependent on BaFin.

The rescue of the above three banks demonstrates a fundamental weakness of the German banking system, namely an inefficient political regulatory framework for regulating state-owned banks. State-owned banks are a hybrid because, although they are regional and avoid competing with each other, in cities they compete with private, commercial banks (Hackethal 2004). The state-owned banks became vulnerable during the global financial crisis because they operated risky business models as part of their competitiveness. Further, an interesting but not ideal feature of state-owned banks is that they share an auditing firm with their regional associations, and external auditors at state-owned banks do not produce external auditors' reports. External auditors' reports are useful because they provide an assessment of a bank's risk profile (Fischer and Pfeil 2004). Without external auditors' reports, questions about the quality of audits may be raised. There is thus an argument that state-owned banks should produce reports by external auditors because the business model of state-owned banks is similar to commercial banks. This means that the risk profiles of state-owned banks can then be closely scrutinised. There is now more political will then ever for politicians in Germany to merge state-owned banks and savings/co-operative banks. Chapter 7 will discuss the reasons and will feature ask two macro-prudential regulatory questions. First, is it likely that the German state-owned banks will merge with savings/co-operative banks? Second, if this is the case and the de facto boundaries within these banks disappear, what are the implications for the German regulators to ensure financial stability?

In relation to micro-prudential regulation, BaFin's powers increased after the global financial crisis so that it can intervene earlier when banks have insufficient capital and/or liquidity. BaFin has been working with the three European Supervisory Authorities since 1 January 2011, when the European financial supervisory framework came into force. BaFin is still responsible for day-to-day supervision of financial institutions but it works with the European supervisory authorities ('ESAs') to ensure that there is greater harmonisation of financial supervision in the EU. Early indications from the Supervisory Convergence Report of the European Banking Authority bodes well for the future. There has been convergence in supervisory frameworks but more work needs to be done to achieve convergence in supervisory methodologies, practices and outcomes (European Banking Authority 2015).

Conclusion

Regulation is required to deal with market failures (World Bank 2013) but it is not a panacea for financial crises. Executive authorities, in particular the financial regulatory authorities, play an important part in oversight and enforcement. When both are successful, public confidence is sustained. Both retail and wholesale depositors' confidence in the financial sector is therefore crucial

(Chari and Jagannathan 1988). In the period leading up to the global financial crisis, business decisions by some banks were inadequately challenged. Nor were moral questions asked of decisions such as selling unnecessary and complex financial products to customers or paying huge bonuses to top bankers. Even when the FSA found that banks were guilty of malpractice, the penalty was usually a financial fine. Although the fines imposed on banks in the UK have increased since the global financial crisis, it was evident that the public wanted to hold senior managers of banks accountable (Financial Services Authority 2002; McDermott 2013; Financial Conduct Authority 2015).

In the financial world, prosecuting individuals involves a great deal of complex investigations since large banks make gathering evidence difficult. Regulators also want to ensure fairness and objectivity at the same time (McDermott 2013). Iceland has imprisoned 26 financiers for their actions leading up to the global financial crisis. Individual accountability in the UK is still lacking, especially at senior management level. However, the new Senior Managers Regime and Certification Regime, which came into force in March 2016, is encouraging. These regimes increase individual accountability and create a new offence of being involved in a reckless decision causing a financial institution to fail, subject to the normal criminal standard of proof. Further, Tom Hayes, the first trader to be convicted of manipulating the London inter-bank lending rate (Libor), has been sentenced to 11 years in prison. The tide is turning: UK courts are firmer on financial crimes, as are the regulators following the introduction of the twin-peaks model and 'credible deterrence'.

The difficulty in achieving justice in regulating the financial world is due to a number of factors: the close relationship between politics and finance; regulatory capture in the form of lobbying; the importance of the financial industry, especially in the UK; and the size and interconnectedness of banking. It is generally recognised that the US is more captured than the UK in financial regulation since American banks had more access to Hank Paulson, the US Treasury Secretary (Paulson was formerly the CEO of Goldman Sachs (Hacker and Pierson 2011)). American banks thus had huge instrumental power in influencing regulators but they lacked structural power to defy them. In the UK, HSBC bank demonstrated that it was able to reject the Labour government's recapitalisation programme in 2008, and the government had no power to force HSBC to take part. HSBC even threatened to take the UK government to court if they tried to force them to enter into the recapitalisation programme (Culpepper and Reinke 2014).

Chapter 8 discusses methods of tackling regulatory capture, an ongoing issue in the world of banking. In particular, the Warwick Commission has made two recommendations for dealing with lobbying. Using the Bank of England as a case study, Chapter 8 critically analyses how the Bank of England is using its new macro-prudential regulatory tools to sustain financial stability. The twin-peaks model vests a great deal of power in the Bank of England, so it is important that it is transparent and accountable in all aspects of its work. This is particularly true in relation to the Bank of

England's lender-of-last-resort role during the global financial crisis. With more vertical co-operation between the Bank of England, the European Supervisory Authorities and the ECB due to the centralisation of monetary policy and supervision, there will be more information sharing. Adequate resources, good communication and co-operation at a vertical level are thus essential for effective supervision.

Bibliography

Acharya, V. V., Philippon, T. and Richardson, M. (2009) 'The Financial Crisis of 2007–2009: Causes and Remedies' in Acharya, V. V. and Richardson, M., eds, *Restoring Financial Stability: How to Repair a Failed System*, Hoboken, NJ: John Wiley & Sons, pp. 1–56.

Bank for International Settlements (2009) *Roles and Objectives of Modern Central Banks*, Switzerland: Bank for International Settlements.

Bank of England (2008) *Bank of England Court of Directors' Minutes 2007–2009*, 2008 B2, London: Bank of England.

Bank of England (2009) *Bank of England Court of Directors' Minutes 2007–2009*, London: Bank of England.

BBC (2010) 'Q&A: Osborne's Financial Regulation Reforms' [online], available: http://www.bbc.co.uk/news/10343900 [accessed 10 January 2015].

Belke, A. (2010) 'Driven by the Markets? ECB Sovereign Bond Purchases and the Securities Markets Programme', *Intereconomics*, 45(6), pp. 357–63.

Breydo, L. (2015) 'Structural Foundations of Financial Stability: What Canada Can Teach America about Building a Better Regulatory System', *University of Pennsylvania Journal of Business Law*, 17(3), pp. 973–1082.

Brown, C. and Davis, K. (2010) 'Australia's Experience in the Global Financial Crisis' in Kolb, Robert W., ed., *Lessons from the Financial Crisis: Causes, Consequences, and Our Economic Future, Kolb Series in Finance*, Hoboken, NJ: John Wiley & Sons, pp. 537–44.

Canadian Bankers Association (2014) 'What Canadians Think about Their Banks', available: http://www.cba.ca/contents/files/backgrounders/bkg_annualpoll_en.pdf.

Chari, V. and Jagannathan, R. (1988) 'Banking Panics, Information, and Rational Expectations Equilibrium', *Journal of Finance*, 43, pp. 749–60.

Critchlow, A. (2015) 'Commodities Crash Could Turn Australia into a New Greece', *The Telegraph* [online], available: http://www.telegraph.co.uk/finance/newsby-sector/industry/mining/11749706/Commodities-crash-could-turn-Australia-into-a-new-Greece.html [accessed 28 December 2015].

Culpepper, P. and Reinke, R. (2014) 'Structural Power and Bank Bailouts in the United Kingdom and the United States', *Politics & Society*, 42(4), pp. 427–54.

European Banking Authority (2015) 'EBA Report on Convergence of Supervisory Practices' [online], available: http://www.eba.europa.eu/supervisory-convergence;jsessionid=C4710DF6F0F9482C7C2DEA760E2AB7CE [accessed 27 December 2015].

Financial Conduct Authority (2015) *FCA Fines Table* [online], available: http://www.fca.org.uk/firms/being-regulated/enforcement/fines [accessed 26 December 2015].

Financial Services Authority (2002) *FSA Fines Table* [online], available: http://www.fsa.gov.uk/about/press/facts/fines/2013 [accessed 26 December 2015].

Financial Services Authority (2011) *The Failure of the Royal Bank of Scotland: Financial Services Authority Board Report*, London: Financial Services Authority.

Financial Times (2015) 'Other Central Banks Are Not Obliged to Follow the Fed's Lead' [online], available: http://www.ft.com/cms/s/0/a3cf25d4-a579-11e5-a91e-162b86790c58.html [accessed 28 December 2015].

Fischer, K.-H. and Pfeil, C. (2004) 'Regulation and Competition in German Banking: An Assessment' in Krahnen, J. and Schmidt, R., eds, *The German Financial System*, New York: Oxford University Press, pp. 291–343.

Gadinis, S. (2013) 'From Independence to Politics in Financial Regulation', *California Law Review*, 101, pp. 327–406.

Goodhart, C. (2009) 'Liquidity and Money Operations: A Proposal' in Goodhart, C., ed., *The Regulatory Response to the Financial Crisis*, Cheltenham: Edward Elgar.

Hacker, J. and Pierson, P., eds (2011) *Winner-Take-All Politics: How Washington Made the Rich Richer – And Turned Its Back on the Middle Class*, New York: Simon & Schuster.

Hackethal, A. (2004) 'German Banks and Banking Structure' in Krahnen, J. and Schmidt, R., eds, *The German Financial System*, New York: Oxford University Press, chapter 3.

Hill, J. (2012) 'Why Did Australia Fare So Well in the Global Financial Crisis?' in Ferran, E., Moloney, N., Hill, J. and Coffee, J., eds, *The Regulatory Aftermath of the Global Financial Crisis*, Cambridge: Cambridge University Press, pp. 203–300.

Hill, J. (2015) 'The Impact of the CRR and CRD IV on Bank Financing of the Economy', in *Speech by Commissioner Jonathan Hill at the CRR Review Conference, DG FISMA*, Brussels.

HM Treasury (2010) *A New Approach to Financial Regulation: Judgment, Focus and Stability*, Cn 7874, London: HMSO.

Knight, M. (2012) 'Surmounting the Financial Crisis: Contrasts between Canadian and American Banks', *American Review of Canadian Studies*, 42(3), pp. 311–20.

Kushmeider, R. (2005) 'The U.S. Federal Financial Regulatory System: Restructuring Federal Bank Regulation', *FDIC Banking Review*, 17(4), pp. 1–29.

McDermott, T. (2013) *Enforcement and Credible Deterrence in the FCA*, London: Financial Conduct Authority.

Marinova, M. (2009) 'Can Capital Ratios Be the Centre of Banking Regulation – A Case Study', *European Financial and Accounting Journal*, 4(4), pp. 8–34.

Moore, P. (2010) 'Interview: Corporate Governance and Regulation of Banks', interview, Thirsk, Yorkshire, 10 July.

Onado, M. (2009) 'The Rise and Fall of Northern Rock' in Bruni, F. and Llewellyn, D., eds, *The Failure of Northern Rock: A Multi-dimensional Case Study*. European Money and Finance Forum, Vienna.

Rancière, R., Tornell, A. and Westermann, F. (2008) 'Systemic Crises and Growth', *Quarterly Journal of Economics*, 123(1), pp. 359–406.

Schirm, S. (2015) 'Varieties of Strategies: Societal Influences on British and German Responses to the Global Economic Crisis', *Journal of Contemporary European Studies*, 19(1), pp. 47–62.

Sester, P. (2012) 'The ECB's Controversial Securities Market Programme (SMP) and Its Role in Relation to the Modified EFSF and the Future ESM', *European Company & Financial Law Review*, 9(2), pp. 156–78.

World Bank (2013) *Global Financial Development Report 2013*, Washington, DC: World Bank.

2 The roles of central banks and financial regulatory agencies

Introduction

Established in 1668, the Swedish National Bank is the oldest modern central bank in the world (Riksbank 2015). Prior to 1668, King Karl X of Gustav of Sweden had appointed Johan Palmstruch to run the Bank of Palmstruch. Palmstruch was innovative for two reasons. First, he began to use deposits to fund loans. Second, he printed the first European banknotes as an answer to bulky copper coins and more valuable silver coins hoarded by Swedes. The Bank of Palmstruch ultimately failed due to the issuance of too many bank notes without the requisite collateral. A bank run followed. The Sven Court of Appeal convicted Palmstruch of mismanagement and subsequently ordered him to be executed. King Karl X of Gustav later pardoned Palmstruch (Chaudhuri 2014).

This historical incident has two significant implications. First, the bank run on the Bank of Palmstruch illustrates the concept of lending by a central bank. Central banks are the bankers' bank. The lender-of-last-resort role overlaps with monetary policy, financial supervision and regulation. Freixas and Parigi (2014) argue that the role of lender of last resort has been broadened by the global financial crisis. This is because central banks have to monitor the interbank market as well as bail out non-bank institutions. Indeed, the Bank of England, Federal Reserve, Bank of Canada, Reserve Bank of Australia and ECB all widened their range of acceptable collateral during the global financial crisis to stabilise the financial system.

Second, the banknotes issued by the Bank of Palmstruch were not supported by collateral. To address this vulnerability of central banks in a crisis, Bagehot's principle of providing liquidity support against good-quality collateral at a penalty rate became a general rule of thumb (Bagehot 1873). Therefore, banks which are illiquid but still solvent can receive help from central banks (Campbell and Lastra 2010). The global financial crisis highlighted the need for Bagehot's principle to be modernised in light of the more complex, securitised world of finance. The Federal Reserve, Bank of England and ECB have been criticised for lending to banks against collateral of inferior quality. The new paradigm of providing liquidity by central banks such as the ECB and the Federal Reserve in a crisis fuses monetary and fiscal policies. This is a heated topic since it has implications for liquidity provision and the institutional structure of banking supervision, especially between the Treasury and central banks.

Since the global financial crisis, the role of financial stability of central banks has increased in prominence. Financial stability – or systemic stability, to be more precise – is important since securitisation and globalisation have made financial institutions more interconnected. The growth of large, complex financial institutions has turned into a system risk (Herring and Carmassi 2014). The International Monetary Fund's Global Financial Stability Report of October 2015 (International Monetary Fund 2015) made it clear that the global financial market is still vulnerable due to liquidity issues – in particular, the threat of non-performing loans in the Euro area. Further, interest rates have been very low since the onset of the financial crisis, and the UK leaving the EU is creating uncertainty in the UK's monetary policy. Monetary policy and financial stability are linked, and more emphasis should be put on co-ordinating these two objectives, which Adrian and Shin (2009) describe as 'inseparable'. Balancing monetary policy with financial stability can be difficult, especially during a crisis. This chapter will discuss central banks' lender-of-last-resort function since it is one method of dealing with financial stability. It will reveal that central banks lacked the requisite tools to deal with liquidity and solvency risks during the crisis and that as a result their actions to firefight systemic risks were limited.

In a 2008 survey by the Bank of International Settlements, 90 per cent of central banks responded that they have either full or partial oversight responsibility for banks and financial stability (Bank for International Settlements 2009). Financial supervisory and regulatory agencies in the UK, US, Germany and Canada have been criticised for weak supervision of financial institutions prior to the global financial crisis. Structural reforms have taken place in the UK, US and at European level to improve micro-prudential regulation and supervision. The latest scholarship suggests that central banks have been given too much power since the crisis, so there is a fear of us living in an era of 'central bank diktat' (Halligan 2015). Meanwhile, Whalen (2011) is of the view that the Federal Reserve suffers from a 'superman complex'. Should central banks regulate and supervise in addition to other mandates such as monetary policy and financial stability? If so, what is a suitable regulatory and supervisory structure for the countries studied in this book? This chapter is not about finding the ideal or superior model – there is no such concept (Masciandaro 2012). Rather, each country is unique and lessons should be learnt from past mistakes from across the world. The focus of this chapter is on national and supranational central banks such as the ECB to reflect the comparative-law approach of this book. One of the most significant reforms in financial stability is the creation of the European Banking Union. This consists of three pillars: the single rulebook, the Single Supervisory Mechanism, where the ECB became the single macro-prudential regulator of banks in the Eurozone, and a single resolution mechanism. The European Banking

Union, in particular the Single Supervisory Mechanism, has centralised the European supervisory system with regard to capital requirements. Convergence in supervision contributes to harmonisation at the European level, but flexibility is required to reflect national factors.

The rest of this chapter begins by discussing the mandate of financial stability. The change in central banks' role as lender of last resort is then examined. The following sections discuss the dual roles of monetary policy and banking supervision, before considering the institutional architecture of regulators in the UK, Australia, Germany, EU, US and Canada. Particular attention will be paid to the UK, Germany, EU and US since Australia and Canada fared better in the global financial crisis (the relatively new regulatory framework of the European Systemic Risk Board deserves closer examination); and the final section offers a conclusion. It will be seen that central banks such as the Bank of England, the ECB and the Federal Reserve have become powerful since the global financial crisis primarily because they were ill-equipped entering the crisis. The lender-of-last-resort role and micro-prudential supervision are crucial in a crisis, and it is justifiable for central banks to have more interest in financial supervision since they usually increase and widen their range of acceptable collateral in a crisis. Whether the twin functions of financial stability and prudential regulation should co-exist under the same roof depends to a certain degree on each country's culture, politics and legal system. However, clear communication and co-operation are necessary to ensure that central banks and regulatory agencies sustain the synergy effectively.

Financial stability and central banks

Central banks are government organisations shaped by public law (Meade 2012). In Fischer's lecture of 1994, he sets out the principles of the new central-bank doctrine whereby central banks must have a clear mandate to maintain price stability, exercise independence in using monetary tools such as setting interest rates and be accountable for their actions (Liikanen 2013). Modern central banks are primarily occupied with monetary-policy matters (Bank for International Settlements 2009) since confidence in price stability and the currency is crucial for a healthy economy. With time, the combination of economic crises, wars and the breakdown of the gold standard transformed central banks from government banks into public agencies. This shift to a public-policy dimension meant that central banks are now working towards the interests of the financial system as a whole, rather than for commercial objectives. Like most concepts in finance, financial stability is not absolute and it changes with time. It has many facets, embracing rule-making, policy development and supervision. The lender-of-last-resort role is a way for central banks to sustain financial stability by assisting individual banks rather than monitoring liquidity for the general financial system. In exceptional circumstances such as the global financial crisis, the general liquidity and specific liquidity lending under the lender-of-last-resort principle merge. It is interesting to note that only 20 per cent of the 146 central banks have express objectives *for* financial stability and that around 50 per cent of the world's central banks have more generic objectives *regarding* financial stability. Since the global financial crisis, the Reserve Bank of Australia, Federal Reserve, Bank of Canada, Bank of England and ECB have all had the wide objective of promoting, enhancing and contributing to financial stability.

Macro-prudential regulation and supervision contribute to financial stability by involving the relevant regulatory authority in monitoring systemic risks holistically. Effective central-bank regulation is of practical importance because it can affect the quality of bank regulation and supervision (Koetter *et al.* 2014). The ultimate aim of macro-prudential regulation is to avoid macro-economic costs linked to financial stability (Galati and Moessner 2010). There is a distinction between macro-prudential tools and other macro-economic tools such as fiscal policy to sustain financial stability (Borio 2009; Blanchard *et al.* 2010). The major macro-prudential regulatory tool for central banks is counter-cyclical capital requirements (Galati and Moessner 2010), which, according to Goodhart (2009), was missing prior to the global financial crisis. The literature on the effectiveness of macro-prudential tools has been limited so far as data is very difficult to obtain. Nonetheless, research by Nadauld and Sherlund (2009) into sub-prime-mortgage-backed securitised deals in the US reveals that raising capital requirements might constrain the growth of asset prices. In Canada, Gauthier *et al.* (2010) analysed banks' loan books and risk exposures. Their results show that capital buffers can substantially improve financial stability by reducing the probability of bank defaults and a systemic crisis by up to 25 per cent, showing the usefulness of capital requirements in designing capital regulation.

The Basel III Accord introduces the counter-cyclical capital buffer to deal with issues such as excessive leverage and maturity mismatch. The buffer will then absorb the losses. The counter-cyclical capital buffer is implemented as part of core Tier 1 capital and will range between 0–2.5 per cent of risk-weighted assets. If a bank cannot meet the requirement, it will face restrictions on the distribution of dividends. Although Basel III provides some flexibility in determining the calculation of the buffer, one of the biggest challenges in macro-prudential policy is the problem of different credit cycles in various economies. Also, the definition of 'excessive' credit growth is uncertain. Will the concept of 'this time is different' apply next time (Reinhart and Rogoff 2011)? The next section will highlight how central banks, especially in the UK and US, did not have the right tools to deal with liquidity problems. In particular, the controversial role of lender of last resort will be analysed, as will the European and US legislation on countercyclical and capital-conservation buffers. These buffers should contribute towards financial stability, but, as liquidity is still a major global concern (International Monetary Fund 2015), regulators should also focus on the asset quality of loans to ensure that there is sufficient liquidity in the financial system.

Liquidity management: the change in central banks' function as lender of last resort

The global financial crisis revealed that the central banks studied in this book did not have the necessary tools to deal with complex liquidity and solvency issues. The prevailing philosophy in the US and UK prior to the global financial crisis was one of neoliberalism and laissez-faire. Two decades of accommodative interest rates, deregulation and financial safety nets increased risk-taking through the use of excessive leverage, lower liquidity and capital requirements. Asset quality was ignored in some cases, affecting the effectiveness of capital in absorbing losses. De-regulation promoted 'competition in laxity' (Sinn 2010) and a race to the bottom with regards to regulatory standards. A French regulator captured this nicely:

> We had resolved to approve a financial product only if at least one of us understood it worked. We were unable to adhere to this principle however, as we always had to hear that it would then be approved by the English or German authorities. So we closed our eyes and gave the approval.
>
> (quoted in Sinn 2010: 157)

This perverse incentive can only be rectified by international agreements such as Basel I and II. However, Basel II regulations meant that individual banks were able to self-regulate (Sinn 2010; Whalen 2011). This is a serious issue since the capital-adequacy ratio is the main instrument for central banks to deal with liquidity problems (Goodhart 2009).

The scale and depth of the global financial crisis were a shock to many governments. Crisis management involves central banks, supervisory authorities and fiscal authorities (Hartmann *et al.* 2015). This section will examine the difficulties central banks, especially in the UK and the US, faced in relation to liquidity and solvency problems. Goodhart (2009) explained that central banks were unable to curb excessive leverage built up by banks through the use of the capital-adequacy ratio, the principal regulatory instrument of central banks. The capital-adequacy ratio failed to curb excessive leverage because it is pro-cyclical. It did not discourage growth of house prices or credit expansion (Goodhart 2009). Ultimately, the financial market did not seize up due to lack of cash. On the contrary, the real problems were 'financial dislocation and re-intermediation' (Goodhart 2009). Financial institutions realised that they could not sell their loans at reasonable prices because money-market managers were reluctant to do so. The use of Special Investment Vehicles backed by ABCP by financial institutions proved to be disastrous when there was a loss of market liquidity in the US sub-prime-mortgage crisis. Investors became risk averse and ABCP issuers were unable to roll their ABCP.

Goodhart's view is that central banks should have more rule-based tools to deal with financial stability such as counter-cyclical capital requirements to stem the exuberance in economic booms (Goodhart 2009). He is aware of the difficulties in operating counter-cyclical capital requirements, the main one being that it takes a very brave regulator to spoil the party and apply the brakes. Cooper (2010) compares this with the analogy of regulators trying to find out who is swimming naked. Naturally, this is not a problem on a nudist beach, but generally 'the impetus of the animal spirits driving a boom puts a lot of pressure on the resources of a regulator seeking to use the enforcement tool to be overtly counter-cyclical'. Walker (2010) is sceptical of counter-cyclical capital requirements for several reasons. First, difficulties may arise regarding the complexity of such requirements, since several distinct models and metrics can be employed. Second, potential additional costs may be imposed on banks as a result of the complexity of the models. Finally, it may be difficult to reach an international or European agreement on the required standard for counter-cyclical capital requirements.

Despite these concerns, the Basel Committee (2010) has laid down the counter-cyclical capital buffer requirements in the Basel III Accord. In calculating the buffer, the credit-to-Gross Domestic Product (GDP) gap ratio is used. Bonfim and Monteiro (2013) agree that the credit-to-GDP gap ratio is a one of the best indicators to predict banking crises. However, a wide range of indicators should be used, including house-price indicators, equity-price growth and credit growth to provide an even more accurate prediction. Further, Repullo and Saurina (2011) submit that the credit-to-GDP gap ratio might actually enhance pro-cyclicality. This is because credit usually lags behind a business cycle and the results of Repullo and Saurina reveal that GDP growth and the credit-to-GDP gap ratio are negatively correlated. They believe that a better indicator is credit growth in relation to its long-term average (Bonfim and Monteiro 2013). Since the use of a counter-cyclical capital buffer is a relatively new macro-prudential tool and there is little empirical evidence of its success, legislation has to reflect this. Flexibility has to be built into the system to reflect local culture and factors. Kowalik (2011) argues that it is better for regulators to adopt a rules-based approach to setting the counter-cyclical capital buffer. This is because regulators need less information to decide how much and when capital requirements need to be changed. Communication problems would thus be avoided. Further, regulators do not have room to pursue different goals and therefore adverse incentives could be minimised (Kowalik 2011). This study believes that strict adherence to uniform rules on counter-cyclical capital requirements is likely to have undesirable consequences since this approach cannot reflect the unique characteristics of a legal system or culture. The example of the UK will be discussed later in the chapter. It will be seen that regulatory and supervisory convergence contribute towards international harmonisation, but flexibility has to be retained for financial-stability purposes.

Research has shown that the asset quality of loans affects economic recovery. Data from Wheelock and Wilson (2000) revealed that banks with little capital and low-quality and illiquid assets are more likely to fail. They also found that banks with relatively high non-performing loan ratios are less attractive takeover targets. Jin *et al.* (2011) conducted research into the factors leading to bank failures during the financial crisis of 2007. They obtained data from the Federal Reserve Bank of Chicago's Bank Holding Company, using several variables to predict bank failure such as proportion of securitised assets to total assets, level of non-performing loans, growth in various loan categories and loan-portfolio mix. Their results show that non-performing loans have a positive correlation with bank failures. From the experience of the Japanese financial crisis in the late 1980s, we know that economic recovery is delayed when the level of non-performing loans increases. This is because banks which are constrained by capital tend to discourage credit growth (Fujii and Kawai 2009). Statistics reveal that during 2004–14, Germany had the worst non-performing-to-performing-loan ratio amongst the five countries studied in this book (World Bank 2015). This can be explained by German banks' exposure to the real-estate sector and to the sovereign-debt crisis. As a result of this, the Financial Stability Committee in Germany (2015) made some recommendations giving the German financial regulator powers to regulate residential-property loans. These recommendations included a cap on the loan-to-value and debt-to-income ratios, as well as compulsory amortisation requirements. Relevant country-specific legislation is thus required to tackle liquidity and solvency issues.

Without appropriate regulation to tackle excessive leverage during the global financial crisis, central banks had to widen their range of collateral, as well as creating special liquidity schemes to stabilise the global financial system. The Eurosystem's collateral framework was more prepared for the global financial crisis than those in the UK and the US. It only had to make minor adjustments to its collateral framework. This can be explained on two grounds. First, the UK and US were more heavily affected by the global financial crisis – certainly in the initial phase of it. The Bank of England and the Federal Reserve entered the global financial crisis with a narrower range of collateral, so they had to expand their collateral frameworks as the crisis worsened. This was particularly so for the Bank of England, which had the narrowest eligible collateral compared to the Federal Reserve and the Eurosystem (Cheun *et al.* 2009; Bank for International Settlements 2013).

Second, the banking structures in EU member states are more diverse and the Eurosystem's collateral framework has to reflect this. The collateral frameworks of the Bank of England, the Federal Reserve and the Eurosystem are different. For example, the US Term Auction Facility and the Primary Credit Facility have a broader range of collateral. Apart from the collateral available in the Eurosystem, the Federal Reserve allowed unsecuritised residential-mortgage loans and consumer-credit loans, although it did not permit asset-backed securities (Cheun *et al.* 2009). In addition, the list of counterparties eligible for financial assistance is wider than in the Eurosystem. The Federal Reserve provided financial assistance to non-bank institutions such as money-market mutual funds, government-sponsored entities and one large insurance company. The Federal Reserve also provided dollar liquidity swap lines to several central banks such as the Bank of England, ECB and Bank of Canada (Johnson 2011). Yet the Federal Reserve's broadening range of collateral was temporary whilst the Eurosystem's was permanent. Although Australia and Canada were not as seriously affected as the UK and US by the global financial crisis at the beginning, both countries expanded their collateral frameworks as it continued. Australia added foreign-currency assets and covered bonds to its list of collateral. Australia's collateral framework is wide and so it did not need to increase its collateral parameters too much. The Reserve Bank of Australia enjoys a degree of discretion in accepting additional types of collateral. In 'extraordinary circumstances', the Reserve Bank of Australia will accept related-party asset-backed securities. Canada added bank-sponsored ABCP and non-mortgage loan portfolios to its range of collateral (Bank for International Settlements 2013). When the Bank of Canada accepted asset-backed commercial paper, the combination of the eligibility criteria and more disclosure requirements promoted transparency and boosted confidence in the ABCP market.

Cheun *et al.* (2009) argue that the expansion of the range of collateral and counter-parties are useful tools for crisis management. Freixas and Perigi (2014) believe that central banks gained more responsibility and powers as they had to tackle the interbank market as well as bailing out non-bank institutions during the global financial crisis. Other scholars agree. Campbell and Lastra (2010) submit that central banks continue to have a lender-of-last-resort responsibility to the market and the entire financial sector, rather than to any specific financial institution. Since time is of the essence in a financial crisis, it was necessary for certain banks to receive financial help, even though they were insolvent, to reduce systemic risks. Walker (2010) is of the view that Bagehot's principle is therefore dated and needs to be amended to reflect interbank markets. Technology has made modern financial products more complicated and less transparent. Central banks' decisions to widen the range of collateral is unprecedented. Although this path diverges from Bagehot's principle, it can only be seen as justified in light of the central banks' lack of macro-prudential regulatory tools.

Central banks as micro-supervisors and monetary-policy makers?

Goodhart (2009) believes that central banks should retain their macro-prudential regulatory role since they are strong on monitoring market relationships and economic issues. Adrian and Shin (2009) submit that monetary policy and prudential regulation are connected because the monetary-policy transmission mechanism runs through the balance sheets of financial institutions. However, there might be a trade-off between the two roles of monetary policy and maintaining financial stability as they may require action in different directions. King (2013) argues that macro-prudential policy can be one tool in tackling financial-stability risks. Like many policy issues, there is no clear empirical evidence that it is better for central banks to retain macro-prudential regulation (Green 2012; Jackson 2013). Nevertheless, the boundary between macro- and micro-prudential policy is grey and the two areas will often share similar interests. From the Japanese financial crisis in the late 1980s, evidence shows that monetary stability and financial stability are complementary in the medium to long term; therefore, central banks need to plan their policy frameworks in the medium to long term (Shiratsuka 2011). Further, the Japanese experience showed that it is right to focus on macro-prudential regulation since trying to achieve financial stability by stricter micro-prudential regulation tends to result in lower efficiency in financial intermediation. The controversial issue now is whether central banks should have micro-prudential supervisory roles to sustain financial stability. If they should, will the regulatory architecture affect the effectiveness of financial regulation, given that central banks may become too powerful? The traditional arguments for and against combining the dual roles within central banks will be presented first, and then the specific regulatory weaknesses of the UK, US and German central banks will be analysed.

There are advantages and disadvantages of placing the roles of micro-prudential supervision and monetary policy within a central bank. Advantages include the fact that the central bank can synergise information and provide better focus on reducing systemic risks (Ferran 2011). Goodhart (2002) argues that 'micro-level supervisory information may be a valuable input into macro-level monetary decisions, certainly during periods of financial instability'. Peek *et al.* (1999) submit that deciding on monetary-policy issues is more efficient due to better information. Another advantage of combining prudential regulation with monetary policy within the central bank is its capacity as lender of last resort. The new emphasis on financial stability in, for example, section 2(2)(a)(b) of the Financial Services Act 2010 in the UK, lends weight to the argument that the Bank of England, as the lender of last resort, should have increased powers for financial stability. Bernanke (2011) supports the creation of the Financial Policy Committee within the Bank of England, the creation of the European Systemic Risk Board in Europe and the revamped Federal Reserve, where the focus on systemic stability has been broadened. The Federal Reserve has been given new responsibilities for financial stability, including supervisory authority over non-bank financial institutions. A central bank can only provide liquidity assistance in times of crises if it has the relevant information. As Eichengreen and Dincer (2011) explain: 'the central bank is the ultimate guarantor of financial stability, and it cannot make good on that guarantee in the absence of the kind of information that can only be obtained through hands-on supervision'. Blinder (2010) argues that the central bank should be the macro-prudential regulator because maintaining financial stability links well with the aims of monetary policy and being the lender of last resort.

Empirical research from Čihák and Podpiera (2008) reveals that banking supervision under the 'twin peaks' model produces better quality of supervision, even after adjusting for cross-country differences. The twin-peaks model allocates prudential regulation to one regulatory agency and conduct of business to another. The twin-peaks model's impact on supervisory quality in insurance and securities is not entirely different to that of other models. The twin-peaks model relies on better prudential regulatory frameworks and practices (Čihák and Podpiera 2008). Čihák and Podpiera's research is extensive, covering 84 countries in the period of 2000–5. The main advantage of the twin-peaks model is that both macro- and micro-prudential regulation is brought within the central bank. Taylor (2009) asserts that the twin-peaks model is better in times of crises. Bringing together the lender of last resort and the gatherer of information as the banking regulator should accelerate the decision-making process.

A disadvantage of combining prudential regulation with monetary policy within the central bank is that potential conflicts of interest can arise between policy independence and prudential supervision (Goodhart 2002; Ferran 2011) For example, the central bank may be reluctant to control inflation when it is concerned that higher interest rates may lead to bank failures (Čihák and Podpiera 2008). Potential conflicts of interest can lead to less time being dedicated to monetary policy since supervision is a time-consuming and thankless task (Goodhart 2002). On the other hand, the central bank will find it easier to gain credibility through implementing monetary policy than through supervision since banking supervision is mainly about the prevention of financial crises. Regulators will only be mentioned in the press for supervisory failures. Therefore, 'if an independent central bank feels the need to achieve credibility and a good reputation, then being yoked with simultaneous credibility for banking supervision may not be advisable' (Goodhart 2002).

The skills utilised in monetary policy and financial supervision are different, according to some scholars (Goodhart 2009; Green 2012). Monetary policy is more holistic. It involves officials collecting and analysing a great deal of data to set interest rates and consider the composition of the balance sheets of central banks. Financial supervision on the other hand is more microscopic in its routine tasks of on-site visits, dialogues and checking systems and controls. Green (2012) is of the view that these two roles should be separate but encourages close co-operation and exchange of knowledge. However, Green acknowledges the increased recognition that the dual roles of monetary policy and financial supervision are complementary (Borio 2003), not least the view that it is natural and justifiable for central banks to have more interest in financial supervision in a crisis, when they usually increase the amount of lending and widen their range of collateral (Athanassiou 2014). Central banks will be more involved in financial supervision during a crisis because they are firefighters, stepping in to provide assistance to banks in the form of liquidity and minimising the damage to financial stability (Cukierman 2011).

There is a strong argument for permitting central banks to have micro-prudential supervisory powers for financial stability reasons. Central banks use a combination of factors, such as haircuts, eligibility criteria for collateral, wide or narrow frameworks and market environments, to design their collateral framework. If a country's liquidity rules are similar or narrower than the Basel III Accord then the country is less concerned with the possibility of regulatory arbitrage. If a country's liquidity rules are wider than the Basel III Accord then it is possible for its central bank to restrict undesirable behaviour through higher haircuts or widening the range of acceptable collateral. The latter is more favourable from a risk-management perspective, since it is safer for central banks to accept less-risky assets (Cheun *et al.* 2009). However, in emergency cases, central banks may well have to accept less-risky assets and raise haircuts. The global financial crisis has demonstrated this scenario. In this instance, central banks will need more information from the counterparties regarding the type, maturity, credit and liquidity of collateral assets. The Bank of Australia's haircuts during the global financial crisis were granular, reflecting the different factors affecting the collateral. The collateral portfolios of the UK, US and Eurosystem varied significantly as the crisis developed. Therefore, central banks would benefit from having micro-prudential supervisory powers to deal with liquidity issues.

Analysis of the financial regulatory architecture in the UK, Australia, Germany, EU, US and Canada

Having analysed the general arguments for and against central banks combining the roles of prudential regulation and monetary policy, it is only appropriate to examine concrete examples from the global financial crisis. As Whalen (2011) commented, countries which separated the two roles before the crisis now want to combine them and vice versa. The involvement of a central bank in supervision is a hot topic because it concerns power, politics and legitimacy (Green 2012). Statistics from Masciandaro and Quintyn (2009) provide an interesting insight into global regulatory architecture. They researched the regulatory structures of 102 advanced countries. Prior to the global financial crisis, 35 per cent of the sampled countries adopted the institutional model; 24 per cent followed the consolidated, integrated model; 2 per cent adopted the twin-peaks model; and 39 per cent had the functional model. After the crisis, 33 per cent of the sample had the institutional model; 30 per cent adopted the consolidated, integrated model; 4 per cent adopted the twin-peaks model; and 33 per cent had the functional model. Although some countries' structures did not fit neatly into a category, it is apparent that since the crisis there have been more countries adopting the consolidated and twin-peaks models, although the latter remains the least popular. Despite the lack of conclusive correlation between regulatory structure and supervisory effectiveness, the clear trend since the financial crisis is an increase in central banks' roles in prudential supervision (Barth *et al.* 2002; Čihák and Podpiera 2007; Eichengreen and Dincer 2011).

The twin-peaks model in the UK

The UK moved away from a single regulator to a twin-peaks model in 2013. The tripartite system in the UK failed for several reasons. Under this system, the Financial Services Authority (FSA) was the micro-prudential regulator and supervised financial institutions; the Treasury was responsible for legislation; and the Bank of England was the macro-prudential regulator for financial stability. Legal instruments such as the Bank of England Act 1998 and the Memorandum of Understanding attempted to set out the boundaries and responsibilities of each organisation. The Bank of England Act 1998 established the principle that the FSA was the sole regulator and had banking-supervision powers. The Bank of England had the right of sole decision and action with regards to interest-rate matters. The Memorandum of Understanding prescribed how the three organisations should work together. However, the memorandum did not define the role of the lender-of-last-resort function nor 'systemic damage' (Singh 2007). Nor did it state when the lender-of-last-resort function would operate. The absence of such definitions proved disastrous in the financial crisis of 2007–9: the failures of Northern Rock and HBOS demonstrated the confusion as to the regulators' roles and responsibilities in the tripartite system.

In Goodhart's opinion, the FSA and the Bank of England had different outlooks. The FSA was driven by lawyers and accountants who paid more attention to conduct-of-business regulatory issues than to prudential regulation. Lord Turner (2009) agrees. The FSA spent a great deal of time on conduct-of-business initiatives, such as the Retail Distribution Review and the Treating Customers Fairly Initiative (MacNeil 2010). The Retail Distribution Review aims to raise professional standards in the financial advisory industry and provide clearer information to clients about costs and services. The Treating Customers Fairly Initiative aims to protect consumers by highlighting the benefits and risks of the products that they are buying. These are both attempts to uphold the principle of acting in the clients' best interests in clause 2.1 of the Conduct of Business Obligations. Although no amount of regulation can fully protect consumers, MacNeil (2010) disagrees with Lord Turner and argues that it is right to focus on conduct-of-business regulation. This is because increased pressure on banks to raise capital and boost profits may lead to unfair treatment of customers.

A change of government led to a reform of the UK financial regulatory landscape in 2010. Chancellor of the Exchequer George Osborne recommended a shift from the single regulator to a twin-peaks model on grounds that the tripartite system 'failed spectacularly' in ensuring financial stability (BBC 2010). Looking at the twin-peaks model, it is apparent that the Financial Policy Committee (FPC), which is part of the Bank of England, can make recommendations and give directions to the Prudential Regulatory Authority (PRA) and the Financial Conduct Authority (FCA) so that its objectives of reducing systemic risks and supporting the government's economy policy are pursued. The relationship of the Bank of England, PRA and FPC is close. This is demonstrated by the fact that the Chief Executive Officer of the PRA is also a member of the FPC and a deputy governor of the Bank of England; but the fact that the FPC can direct both PRA and the FCA is worrying. This is because the main principle of the twin-peaks model is to separate prudential regulation from consumer protection, where the regulatory strategy is different. The National Audit Office's Report (National Audit Office 2014) also found that the PRA is dependent on the Bank of England for financial purposes. The PRA does not have its own finance role, so it relies on the Bank of England for access to information. There are thus concerns that the Bank of England is too powerful under the new regulatory structure and will become a single super-regulator (Scott 2010; Ferran 2011). Interestingly, the FSA had more powers than those given to any single Australian financial regulatory body (Primikiris 2004). It performed functions equivalent to those of three out of four regulatory agencies in Australia.

With prudential regulation, the regulator relies upon a co-operative relationship with the financial institutions, whereas the regulator responsible for consumer protection is more adversarial since it protects consumers from financial institutions (Taylor 1995). Therefore, the Bank of England's powers over both the PRA and FCA would seem to be in conflict with the supervisory strategy. In practice, the PRA and FCA have conflict-resolution meetings to resolve any disagreements. Further, when regulatory conflicts arise, under the Memorandum of Understanding between the Bank of England, the Financial Conduct Authority, the Payment Systems Regulator and the Prudential Regulation Authority (Bank of England 2015), the respective authorities have a power of veto under sections 33–7. The authorities have to produce a Memorandum of Understanding under section 99(5) of the Financial Services (Banking Reform) Act 2013. To date, neither the PRA nor the FCA has exercised this veto power (National Audit Office 2014). This may be interpreted as a sign of effective co-operation and communication, and there is further evidence that this is the case. The National Audit Office (2014) cited an example of a board appointment which is regulated by both the PRA and FCA. The former wanted to approve the appointment and the latter to reject it. The FCA Regulatory Transactions Committee examined the evidence and decided that there was insufficient evidence to reject the appointment and so the FCA agreed to the appointment. The PRA and FCA expressed the view that this was an unusual incident and that they have learnt to co-operate with each other.

The twin-peaks model cost £127 million, 24 per cent more than the FSA (National Audit Office 2014). The costs are funded by banks but ultimately by customers. Running two separate regulatory agencies will inevitably increase the operational costs of more staff and IT equipment. Although the costs seem high at first sight, they can be explained by the potential benefits which the forward-looking and proactive regulatory approach can bring. The UK twin-peaks model aims to avoid the FSA's mistakes, thus reducing potential harm and costs to taxpayers. Time will tell whether the investment made in restructuring pays off.

The twin-peaks model in Australia

The restructuring of the financial regulatory architecture in Australia followed the recommendations of the Wallis Inquiry, in 1997 (Financial System Inquiry Final Report 1997), which was not a consequence of a scandal or crisis. Therefore, it could be argued that the Wallis Inquiry was free from political pressure when reviewing the regulatory structure (Cooper 2006). Bakir (2009) challenges this: he believes that the Howard government influenced the members of the Wallis Inquiry. The Howard government wanted to change the financial regulatory architecture in order to pursue its regulatory reforms. Bakir (2003) argues that the Wallis Inquiry 'was used as a "venue" to generate industry and public support for the regulatory changes, and was used to build a network of alliances within and outside the parliament'.

Prior to the twin-peaks model, Australia had 11 regulators at state and federal levels. The Reserve Bank of Australia enjoyed regulatory powers. In 1998, Australia was the first country to adopt the twin-peaks model of financial regulation (Bakir 2009). Under the twin-peaks model, the prudential regulator is the Australia Prudential Regulatory Authority (APRA) and the regulator for conduct of business is the Australian Securities and Investments Commission (ASIC). The Reserve Bank of Australia has oversight for macro-prudential regulatory matters and pursues the objective of financial stability. Considering that Australia did not have any bank runs or government bailouts, the country performed well during the global financial crisis. The APRA was subject to reviews by the International Monetary Fund and the Financial Stability Board, which were both very positive about the APRA's performance as an effective prudential regulator during the global financial crisis (Australia Prudential Regulatory Authority 2014). Further, praise from an officer of the Reserve Bank of Australia regarding the APRA's excellent prudential regime and co-ordination with the Council of the Financial Regulators confirmed that the twin-peaks model worked well. The APRA was commended by the financial industry itself, highlighting that the regulator was well-managed and used international best practice to sustain prudent standards (Australian Bankers' Association 2011). Praise from industry stakeholders is not easy to come by. The most valuable and enduring contribution made by the APRA is its counter-cyclical implementation of tough rules on financial institutions. Specific regulatory examples include stricter capital requirements for equivalent overseas financial institutions and a risk-based capital framework for insurers. The APRA's proactive supervisory oversight was also commended. In particular, the supervision was continuous and the APRA was able to identify weaknesses and problems of specific institutions before the global financial crisis (Australian Financial Stability Inquiry 2013). Overall, the APRA was able and willing to act as an effective prudential regulator.

High ratings in the APRA's stakeholder survey (Australia Prudential Regulatory Authority 2015) in areas such as staff, prudential framework and supervisory approaches confirm that these are strengths. Nevertheless, the survey indicates some areas for improvement, mainly to do with business and the Direct 2 APRA data-reporting mechanisms, as well as regulatory and compliance costs. In light of the APRA's robust and proactive supervisory style, high compliance costs are understandable. Some institutions are not convinced that the Direct 2 APRA data-collection mechanism is a beneficial source, but an evident positive point is greater acceptance of the APRA's regulatory framework. This is important since prudential regulation and supervision are easier if industry stakeholders accept the framework.

The ASIC also received generally very positive ratings for conduct-of-business regulation. Particular strengths include market supervision and oversight; holding relevant parties to account; transparency; and providing useful, user-friendly guidance and an easy registration and licensing system (Australian Securities and Investments Commission 2013). Tony D'Alonsio, ASIC Chairman, explained that the objective of conduct-of-business regulation was achieved for several reasons. First, the Financial Services Reform Act 2001 provided a strong regulatory and licensing framework for financial sales and advice. Market integrity was thus possible under the 2001 Act. Second, Ponzi-type schemes had to be registered and faced more risk-management hurdles before they were offered to consumers. Finally, regulatory oversight for auditors offered important protection (D'Alonsio 2010). As always, however, there are some weaknesses, as pointed out in the ASIC survey of 2013. They relate to enforcement, communication, bureaucracy and resources. The ASIC has responded to these weaknesses by providing action plans for each of them. For example, it will communicate more about the procedural side of investigations and reduce bureaucracy by examining whether certain class orders are necessary (Australian Securities and Investments Commission 2013). The Senate Inquiry into the ASIC's performance in 2013 (Industry Super Australia 2013) provides a positive report overall. The Senate Inquiry was triggered by the Commonwealth Financial Planning Limited Scandal, where poor advice was given to clients, where there was inadequate auditing and where an internal compliance team was used rather than an external one. Since the scandal, the ASIC has banned seven advisers at Commonwealth Financial Planning Limited (Industry Super Australia 2013). The Inquiry recommended that the ASIC should review its funding model to support its increased responsibilities. It cited the FCA in the UK as a good funding model since it charges fees from authorised firms and does not rely on the government. The ASIC has increased its breadth of regulated organisations, which includes superannuation, insurance and credit markets (Industry Super Australia 2013). It would be sensible for industry stakeholders rather than taxpayers to fund the costs of financial regulation.

The consolidated regulatory model in Germany

Political ideology and interests can shape the financial regulatory architecture of a country. This can be illustrated in the consolidated regulatory model of Germany. Interestingly, Germany modelled its financial regulatory architecture on the integrated FSA structure. The prevailing political philosophy in Europe in 2000 was against central-bank oversight. The German single integrated regulator was part of the European Lamfalussy Process and its decentralised financial supervisors were accountable to elected governments (Engelen 2010). When the Social Democrats lost the election in 2009, BaFin suddenly became vulnerable to a 'tear down BaFin' campaign by the centre-right majority. With the support of pro-business politicians, the new government pushed for a more powerful Bundesbank. Axel Weber, the Bundesbank President at the time, proposed that the Bundesbank should have fully integrated solvency supervision and not just market supervision. The Bundesbank Board supported Weber's proposal since they blamed BaFin for their late intervention and failure of proper supervision during the global financial crisis. They also pointed to the failure of the FSA model in the UK and argued that a twin-peaks model would avoid a conflict of interest arising from having market supervision and solvency supervision under one roof (Engelen 2011). However, BaFin's defence was robust: their late intervention was due to a lack of legal power to intervene early and not to an inherent supervisory weakness. BaFin could only step in when banks could not meet capital and solvency standards, by which time it was too late. The tear-down-BaFin campaign ultimately failed and the law was amended so that BaFin now has the power to intervene earlier under sections 10(b), 11(2) and 45(1) of the German Banking Act 1961.

The German financial regulatory architecture is interesting for three reasons. First, the German Bundesbank has a long history of independence. Despite the federal government's attempt to eradicate BaFin in favour of the Bundesbank in 2008, the strong tradition of independence within the Bundesbank meant that there were no changes. If the Bundesbank was given more supervisory powers, this would have brought it under closer scrutiny of the Treasury, which would compromise the independence of the Bundesbank (Athanassiou 2014). In fact, the Bundesbank realised the importance of independence and decided to resist the temptation of more supervisory powers (Hellwig 2014). A compromise was reached whereby the Bundesbank retained its supervisory role and BaFin had micro-prudential regulatory powers (Zimmermann 2012). Vletter-van Dort (2012) categorises the German financial regulatory model as a twin-peaks model with an autonomous central bank. The independence of the Bundesbank is not disputed, since Article 12 of the German Banking Act 1961 clearly stipulates that the Bundesbank is free from interference and instructions from the federal government. The description of the German regulatory system as a twin-peaks model is more interesting. Although the Bundesbank has macro-prudential regulatory powers, BaFin and the supervisory authorities at state level are responsible for supervising the insurance and securities sectors, not the Bundesbank. Further, the Bundesbank has more than one objective. In addition to prudential regulation, it has responsibilities in relation to the monetary and payment systems. Therefore, the German regulatory model is a hybrid of the consolidated and twin-peaks models.

Second, the structure of the German model is conducive to efficient co-operation between the regulatory authorities. The risk committee and ongoing supervision committee in the German regulatory model are very useful. These committees should help to reduce the possibility of overlaps of responsibilities and the problem of information sharing. The Bank of England does not have such committees. The Governor of the Bank of England, the Deputy Governor for Financial Stability and the Chief Executive Officer of the PRA sit on the boards of both the PRA and FPC. The PRA and FCA are also parties to the Memorandum of Understanding with the Bank of England as a whole. These measures are insufficient to ensure that there is healthy information exchange and co-operation between the PRA and FPC, and a PRA risk committee and ongoing supervision committee should be established, similar to the German regulatory structure.

Third, although the UK and Germany have a similar single, integrated regulatory model, national legislation and culture explain their different supervisory strengths and weaknesses. To cite Primikiris (2004) once more, the FSA had more powers than those given to any single Australian financial regulatory body, performing functions equivalent to those of three out of four regulatory agencies in Australia – and it had too much power in comparison to BaFin. Further, the main piece of legislation in the UK, the Financial Services Markets Act 2000, was complex and conflicting. The objective of consumer protection was at odds with the principle of the FSA facilitating financial innovation and competition. Lord Turner (2009) argues that the FSA spent too much time on conduct-of-business regulation and insufficient time on prudential regulation. The poor supervision of HBOS Bank, as discussed in detail in Chapter 3, is an illustration of this. Further, the FSA (mistakenly) put too much faith and trust in the market and market players. The supervisors at the FSA believed that it is the responsibility of bank management to anticipate potential problems. The FSA would only intervene if a bank had breached the technical standards of liquidity and capital requirements (Bank of England and Financial Services Authority 2011). The FSA should have intervened earlier but its supervisory philosophy and assumptions led to it taking a relaxed and reactive approach.

In Germany, this is not the case. The real problems are the administrative-law culture and lack of legal power for BaFin to intervene early (Hellwig 2014). German law was influenced by the predominantly Anglo-American push for securitisation and the drive for profits in the early 1990s. As a result of this, the assumption is that BaFin cannot intervene unless an action is banned. This is demonstrated by the inability of a German supervisor, who could not stop regulated banks from holding large amounts of asset-backed securities and collateralised debt obligations in offshore special-purpose vehicles. This is particularly risky because the debts are short-term but the assets being funded have long-term maturities (Hellwig 2014). According to Hellwig (2014), officers in administrative authorities are not encouraged to exercise much judgement under German administrative law. It is therefore apparent that local legislation and culture will influence institutional architecture. This is particularly important to bear in mind because of Germany's membership of the European Banking Union, where there is more convergence on financial regulation. Balancing harmonisation with flexibility for local customs is difficult to achieve.

Financial regulation in the EU

The regulatory and supervisory framework of the EU was reformed following the De Larosière report in 2009 (De Larosiere 2009). In brief, the report created a decentralised network of micro-prudential supervisory regulators. The principles of subsidiarity and proportionality were taken into consideration so that national supervisors were given the day-to-day supervisory roles. However, authorities are needed at the European level to deal with more complex, cross-border issues affecting financial stability, which led to the creation of the European System of Financial Supervision (ESFS). The ESFS comprises three European Supervisory Authorities (ESAs) to ensure greater harmonisation of financial supervision in the EU. The European Systemic Risk Board (ESRB) is in charge of macro-prudential supervision and will work with national authorities. Three ESAs – the European Banking Authority (EBA), the European Securities and Markets Authority (ESMA) and the European Insurance and Occupational Pensions Authority (EIOPA) – are responsible for micro-prudential supervision. The three ESAs work under the ESFS together with the existing national supervisory authorities. This has resulted in more vertical co-operation between national supervisors and the ESAs.

During the global financial crisis, it was evident that reforming the financial regulatory structure was insufficient, especially when the banking crisis turned into a sovereign-debt crisis. A more integrated banking union was needed. Sabine Lautenschläger, the former Vice-President of the German Bundesbank and currently an executive board member of the ECB, said that 'almost everything that could be reformed has been reformed' when the European Banking Union (EBU) was launched in 2012 (Kaetzler and Ronken 2015). The EBU has certainly been extensive in reforming the regulatory and supervisory framework of the EU. The EBU aims to provide a more integrated approach to a single-currency area. The three key elements to the EBU include, first, a single rulebook to ensure common standards on capital requirements (Capital Requirements Directive 2013/36/EU) and a common bank-resolution mechanism based on a bail-in concept (Directive on Bank Recovery and Resolution 2014/59/EU). EU depositors will also be reassured that their deposits of up to €100,000 (per depositor per bank) will be guaranteed everywhere in the EU (Directive on Deposit Guarantee Scheme 2014/49/EU). Second, the Single Supervisory Mechanism (SSM) gives the ECB direct supervisory powers over approximately 130 'systematically important' banks in the EU, with assets of more than €30 billion or constituting at least 20 per cent of the home country's GDP or which have requested or received direct public financial assistance from the European Financial Stability Facility (EFSF) or the European Stability Mechanism (ESM). Although national supervisory authorities retain day-to-day micro-prudential supervisory powers, the ECB can directly supervise a bank to ensure that it complies with the single-rulebook standards. However, this authority is subject to specific tasks under Article 127(6) of the Treaty on the functioning of the EU (TFEU). This means that the ECB has control over specific key supervisory tasks regarding the financial stability of credit institutions (but not insurance institutions), and national supervisors have authority on matters not expressly mentioned in the TFEU, such as consumer protection issues (European Commission 2013). Finally, the third key element of the EBU is the Single Resolution Mechanism. With the assistance of a Single Resolution Board and Single Resolution Fund, ailing banks will be wound up in an orderly manner. Most importantly, shareholders and creditors will pay for the costs of a bank's failure, not taxpayers.

Looking at the European Commission's report on the operation of the ESAs and the ESFS, it appears that in the first year of running the EBU the ESAs spent more time on regulation than supervision (European Commission 2014). This can be explained by the necessity of drafting technical standards and rules for harmonisation purposes. Further, resources were scarce, so priority was given to regulation (European Commission 2014). The report suggests that the ESAs spend more time on supervision through peer reviews and follow-ups since there is convergence in supervisory practices. In terms of financial stability, the report commends the ESAs for developing useful tools for identifying systemic risks. Overall, the verdict by the European Commission on the ESAs and the ESFS is positive, with room for more improvement in certain areas. The positive report is encouraging, although two issues concerning European financial regulation and supervision need to be discussed here.

First, some scholars have concerns about the ECB's macro- and micro-prudential regulatory powers under the EBU. Article 3 of the SSM Regulation (Council Regulation No. 1024/2013) calls for the ECB and the ESRB to work closely together. The fear is that with more supervisory convergence on European supervision, the ECB may increase its macro-prudential supervisory powers within the ESRB. Andenas and Chiu (2014) are concerned that the ECB will dominate the ESRB, where the ESRB focuses on monitoring systemic risks (macro-prudential regulation) and the ECB on financial stability. Athanassiou (2014) submits that the ECB's supervisory powers under the Capital Requirements Directive (2013/36/EU) and Article 5 of the SSM Regulation (Council Regulation No. 1024/2013) to apply higher capital buffers to credit institutions and impose stricter capital requirements, subject to close co-operation with national supervisors, go beyond the position established under Council Regulation (EU) No. 1096/2010. The latter conferred specific tasks on the ECB with regards to its co-operation with the ESRB, the macro-prudential supervisor. Ferran and Babis (2013) argue that there may be a conflict of interest between the ECB's micro-prudential supervisory power under Article 5 of the SSM Regulation and its role as a systemic-risk supervisor. The effectiveness of the ECB may thus be compromised. The ECB also has wide investigatory and enforcement powers under Articles 64–6 of the Capital Requirements Directive (2013/36/EU). It can ask relevant persons (natural and legal) to provide information and carry out investigations and inspections for supervisory purposes.

These concerns are valid. Under Council Regulation No. 1096/2010, although it is clear in the preamble that the ECB can make a significant contribution to macro-prudential oversight, Article 2 states that the ECB's task is to provide statistical, informational and administrative support to the ESRB. The ECB is thus a source of assistance under Council Regulation No. 1096/2010. Article 5 of the SSM Regulation (Council Regulation No. 1024/2013), however, has given the ECB micro-prudential supervisory powers. This also goes against the De Larosière Report, where the consensus in 2009 was not to give the ECB micro-prudential supervisory powers since the ECB should carry out its mandate of monetary policy. Further, the De Larosière group was worried that the ECB would have to deal with a multitude of national supervisors. It would appear therefore that the SSM gives less weight to the principles of proportionality and subsidiarity in light of the ECB's increased role in micro-prudential supervision.

Yet it may be argued that the increase in ECB's micro-prudential supervisory power is a response to increased harmonisation of European financial supervision. The current trend is increased consolidation in European financial supervision, although European regulation remains sectoral (Jackson 2009). EU directives distinguish legislation between the banking, securities and insurance sectors, which is similar to the US approach. Consolidated financial supervision is demonstrated by gradual supervisory convergence in the EBU, especially in supervisory frameworks. Ferran and Babis (2013) argue that EU regulation is only partially harmonised, as demonstrated in the single rulebook. However, there are signs in European regulation that there is increased harmonisation. The ESMA states that by 2016 there should also be convergence in the implementation of the Markets in Financial Instruments Directive II (DeWaal 2015).

Whilst regulatory and financial convergence contributes to harmonisation of European financial regulatory law, a certain amount of flexibility is required to reflect local factors. Arguably, there is some flexibility in the current single rulebook. For example, the amount of capital can be increased for real-estate lending to tackle the issue of asset bubbles. Further, member states are responsible for adjusting their counter-cyclical buffers according to their economic cycles. The EU legislation provides some scope for flexibility. This is demonstrated in Articles 81 and 82 of the Capital Requirements Directive (2013/36/EU) when determining the counter-cyclical capital buffer: 'the buffer rate should take into account the growth of credit levels and changes to the ratio of credit to GDP in that Member State, and *any other variables relevant to the risks to the stability of the financial system*'. Article 82 of the Capital Requirements Directive says that: 'The buffer rate should reflect, in a meaningful way, the credit cycle and the risks due to excess credit growth in the Member State and should duly take into account *specificities of the national economy*'. The Bank of England will decide the buffer rate, although the ESRB and EBA will work with the Bank of England to ensure there is consistency under Article 88 of the Capital Requirements Directive (2013/36/EU).

Although the UK is not part of the EBU, it is a member of the EU and is thus affected by EU law. Mark Carney (2015) has made it clear that there needs to be flexibility within the European regulatory framework:

> Ensuring the Bank of England has the instruments necessary to achieve its financial stability objective will depend on the EU continuing to have regulations of the highest standards, which strike the appropriate balance between harmonisation and flexibility, and which accommodate necessary national responsibilities, including for supervision.

The UK has more cross-border lending, OTC derivatives and foreign-exchange activities than France or Germany. The UK's financial system constitutes almost 800 per cent of its GDP, whilst France's is less than 60 per cent (Carney 2015). Therefore, these specific details are arguably reflected in the calculation of the counter-cyclical buffer under the Capital Requirements Directive (2013/36/EU). Since the ESRB and EBA will work together with the Bank of England, the latter should communicate clearly and effectively if it is concerned about the fact that unique features of the UK financial system are not being taken into account. Otherwise, the fear of regulatory arbitrage may materialise and financial institutions will move headquarters to a more favourable regulatory environment. With the implementation of the EBU, there is more supervisory convergence under the SSM. There is also more regulatory convergence under the single rulebook. The future direction is likely to be more reliance on the co-operation between national supervisors and the ESAs and the ESAs with the ECB. There will be a shift from the traditionally perceived decentralised supervisory structure to a more centralised system (Ferran and Babis 2013).

In relation to micro-prudential supervision, emphasis should be paid to the asset quality of loans. The International Monetary Fund said in 2015 that:

> Further strengthening of euro area banks by comprehensively tackling nonperforming loans and the corporate debt overhang will enhance the effectiveness of monetary policy, bolster market confidence, and improve the outlook. Resolving nonperforming loans in euro area banks could deliver 600 billion euro in new lending capacity.

Stress-testing in the US appears to have been more effective than in Europe to date. The manner in which stress tests are carried out is important (Ludwig

2012). The criticism of stress-testing in Europe is that it was 'farcical' because the Irish banking system collapsed four months after passing the stress test in 2011 (Jenkins 2011). Nonetheless, the view that EU stress tests are unsuccessful is incorrect. Although the announcement of the 2009 EU stress test results had a significant negative impact on markets, the 2010 stress results produced a significant positive impact on the valuation of stressed banks (Candelon and Sy 2015). One reason for the more positive US test results is the co-operation between the regulatory authorities. In the US there are only three regulators (the Federal Reserve, the Office of the Comptroller of the Currency and the Federal Deposit Insurance Corporation) involved in stress tests, who worked well together. In Europe, however, co-ordination was less efficient due to the national supervisors working with the EBA (Candelon and Sy 2015).

Despite the positive European Commission report in 2014 on the ESAs, it is evident that there is room for improvement in European supervision at a vertical level. Perhaps the EBA can assist since it has a legally binding mediation role (Article 11 of the Capital Requirements Directive 2013/36/EU). The mediation role aims to facilitate better communication and co-operation between the supervisory authorities. According to the International Monetary Fund (2015), the EBA should carry out more effective tests on the asset quality of loans since the issue of non-performing loans in Europe is a concern. To be fair, the EBA and ECB have been working on this recently. For example, the EBA has carried out its first analysis of asset encumbrance amongst EU banking institutions. It found that there is no significant increase in encumbrance. The EBA will also continue to monitor asset encumbrance in the future (European Banking Authority 2015). The ECB has also contributed on this front by conducting stress and asset-quality tests for nine banks, eight of which were not tested in 2014 (European Central Bank 2015). It is hoped that the ECB and ESAs will continue with robust and rigorous tests.

The Federal Reserve in the US: Superman in a multi-regulatory model?

The fundamental principle structuring the US financial regulatory model is the avoidance of power concentration in a single authority for political and economic reasons (Greenspan 1995). The US financial regulatory model is fragmented and complex for three reasons. First, it combines the four institutional elements of banking, insurance, securities and futures with a functional regulatory approach, with the latter being more prominent (Group of Thirty 2008). Second, it has a dual nature since both federal and state organisations exercise supervisory powers (Group of Thirty 2008). Finally, the securities sector combines regulation and self-regulation. Regulatory authorities were created after the Great Depression in the early 1930s, with new authorities having been added since to meet regulatory needs. The debate about the reduction of banking supervisory authorities created much controversy because this complex, multi-regulatory model has historically served the US well (Lastra 2003; Department of the US Treasury 2008). However, the Dodd–Frank Act 2010 made substantial changes to the US regulatory structure, creating new authorities are changing regulatory oversight. Iglesias-Rodriguez (2014) submits that the US regulatory model is moving towards a twin-peaks model with the creation of two new organisations, the Consumer Financial Protection Bureau, to regulate conduct of business, and the Financial Stability Oversight Council, which is responsible for maintaining financial stability. In fact, the US Treasury's 'Blueprint of a Modernized Financial Regulatory Structure' (Department of the US Treasury 2008) suggested a modified twin-peaks model for the post-global-financial-crisis future. The Treasury believes that an objectives-based regulatory approach is particularly suitable for promoting financial stability, since with the appropriate mandate, there are natural synergies between all the financial institutions.

Iglesias-Rodriguez is right to a certain extent, but the overall impact of the Dodd–Frank Act 2010 is a shift towards financial stability. There is general consensus that macro-prudential regulation was neglected prior the global financial crisis, so this has been the real focus of the reforms under the Dodd–Frank Act 2010. Further, other new agencies and changes in agency oversight have been made which are primarily institution-based. For example, the Office of National Insurance was created within the Treasury, and the Office of Credit Rating Agencies was created within the SEC to tackle issues in the insurance and securities sectors. Regulatory oversight for thrift companies has moved from the Office of Thrift Supervision (now abolished) to the Federal Reserve, Office of the Comptroller of the Currency and Federal Deposit Insurance Corporation. The changes will bring the thrift and bank charters closer together, so that savings-and-loans holding companies will be treated almost the same as bank holding companies. The US regulatory model is therefore still multi-regulatory but with elements of a twin-peaks structure.

Supervision of the banking sector is more fragmented in the US than that of other sectors. The Federal Reserve, the Federal Deposit Insurance Corporation and the Office of the Comptroller of the Currency all share some supervisory responsibilities for various functions and types of banking institution (Iglesias-Rodriguez 2014). The securities sector is supervised by the SEC and the Commodity Futures Trading Commission. The Federal Reserve and the SEC have both been criticised for failing in their supervisory roles (Wallace 2013). The collapse of Lehman Brothers provides a good illustration. The Federal Reserve initially had no supervisory role; the SEC was the regulator responsible for oversight of Lehman Brothers as an investment bank and Lehman Brothers' parent holding company under a voluntary programme called the Consolidated Supervised Entity programme. From March 2008, however, the Federal Reserve increasingly played an important role in macro-prudential financial assistance. The Federal Reserve of New York sent out staff to Goldman Sachs, Lehman Brothers, Merrill Lynch and Morgan Stanley to establish a closer relationship with these investment banks as their lender.

These on-site visits were too late for any supervisory purposes; the SEC continued to be the supervisor of Lehman Brothers (Baxter 2010). Although the SEC and the Federal Reserve communicated and co-operated throughout the process, it was too late to resolve the liquidity issues at Lehman Brothers.

Whalen's view is that the Federal Reserve Bank in the US is too powerful and suffers from a 'superman' syndrome. Whalen (2011) is critical of the Federal Reserve Bank's ability to combine the dual mandates of monetary policy and prudential regulation. He asserts that the Federal Reserve prioritised monetary policy at the expense of prudential regulation and that its attempt to supervise was disastrous. His particular criticism relates to the use of Article 13(3) of the Federal Reserve Act 1913, which, as an emergency support mechanism, allows the Federal Reserve to provide financial assistance. He argues that in lending $85 billion through a credit facility to the American International Group (AIG) during the global financial crisis the Federal Reserve went too far, stretching the original objective of section 13(3) Federal Reserve Act 1913 (Whalen 2011). Meltzer (2010) also argues that section 13(3) 'is now a source of large loans to failing enterprises, an undesirable extension of too-big-to-fail and a misuse of the intent of 13(3)'.

Under normal circumstances, the Federal Reserve only lends to depository institutions. However, it is possible for the Federal Reserve to lend to non-depository institutions by virtue of section 13(3) Federal Reserve Act 1913 under 'unusual and exigent circumstances'. The scale and effect of the global financial crisis would certainly fall into the definition of section 13(3). Equally, the Federal Reserve's measures were extraordinary in terms of extent and creativity. It provided financial assistance to AIG under the Federal Credit Lending Facility, Securities Lending Programme Facility, Residential Mortgage Backed Securities Purchase Security, Multi-sector Collateral Debt Obligation Purchase Facility and the Equity Capital Commitment Facility (Sjostrom 2009). The Federal Reserve justified this pioneering move on grounds of financial stability. Since the AIG incident took place when the financial market was in serious distress, the Federal Reserve was concerned that AIG's size and interconnectedness would seriously undermine the global financial system. It is very difficult to know for definite whether or not the Federal Reserve's rescue of AIG was justified and effective. This is because the government had to make a decision very rapidly without all the information available (Langley 2008). This incident does provide some support for Athanassiou's view that in times of difficulties central banks have more interest in financial supervision due to increased lending and broadening the range of collateral (Athanassiou 2014).

The consolidated/twin-peaks regulatory model in Canada

In comparison to the complicated US financial regulatory architecture, Canada's financial regulatory model is more straightforward, although it cannot be classified neatly into one model, since Canada's financial regulatory structure is a consolidated and twin-peaks hybrid. At federal level, the Office of the Superintendent of Financial Institutions (OSFI) is the key prudential supervisor in banking, insurance and pensions. The Financial Consumer Agency of Canada (FCAC) is responsible for consumer protection. The OSFI also has limited, indirect authority over securities dealers since the provincial governments have direct responsibility over them. This division of prudential regulation from consumer protection resembles the objectives-based approach of the twin-peaks model. However, a large part of the Canadian financial regulatory model is organised by type of financial activity. For example, the OSFI regulates most insurances companies for prudential regulation purposes, although some are regulated by the FCAC. To complicate matters, some provinces delegate this responsibility to the OSFI. The provincial governments regulate the consumer protection aspect of insurance companies. Although there have been attempts to harmonise provincial legislation, each province is unique. In particular, Quebec uses a civil-law system, but most Canadian provinces use a common-law system (Pan 2010). Regulation of insurance at provincial level is therefore complicated, with different legislation for each province.

One particular institution which deserves commendation for regulating mortgage-default-insurance policy is the Canada Mortgage and Housing Corporation (CMHC). Although the US and Canada are geographically close, the latter was not as deeply affected by the global financial crisis as the US, even though the sub-prime-mortgage crisis originated in the US. This is primarily because the CMHC was effective in regulating and enforcing standards. Working closely with the other regulatory agencies, such as the Department of Finance, the Canada Deposit Insurance Corporation, the Bank of Canada, the FCAC and the OSFI, the CMHC ensured that banks had strict lending requirements. Most of the lending took place within the banking sector, with approximately 5 per cent sub-prime lending in Canada compared to more than 20 per cent in the US (Crawford *et al.* 2013). Another positive contribution from the CMHC was the explicit guarantee. It provided 100 per cent coverage of net claims by the lender if the insurance company went insolvent. Mortgages with a loan-to-value ratio of more than 80 per cent had to be insured for the entire sum (Ratnovski and Huang 2009). The structure of the residential-mortgage market is an important aspect of resilience in the Canadian financial system (Kiladze *et al.* 2013). The OSFI regulated around 80 per cent of the lenders which issued mortgages. Further, provincial regulators also regulated these lenders. The combination of the high proportion of mortgages being regulated and the OSFI's principles-based regulatory approach meant that the residential-mortgage market in Canada was much better regulated than that in the US.

Regulation of securities and *caisses populaires* (credit unions) takes place predominantly at the provincial level. The function of securities regulation is the responsibility of the Canada Securities Administrators, which is formed of 13 securities regulators from ten provinces and three territories.

The role of securities regulation is then split at federal and state levels. Although the Canada Securities Administrators are responsible for reviewing applications and co-ordinating initiatives, the provincial and territorial securities regulators deal with complaints and enforcement (Group of Thirty 2008). The Council of Ministers of Securities Regulation has tried to improve co-ordination and access to the securities markets at the provincial level. The solution so far is the 'passport system', which enables market participants to access Canadian capital markets through the principal regulator (the securities regulator in one of the 13 provinces). Approval from the principal regulator will then apply in other participating passport jurisdictions. However, the province of Ontario has chosen not to participate in the passport scheme because the Ontario Securities Commission thinks that the proposal does not facilitate modern financial markets (Ontario Securities Commission 2007). The global financial crisis has sparked a debate about whether Canada should have a national securities regulator in light of the OSFI's weak supervision in the asset-backed commercial paper (ABCP) crisis. The vertical convergence between EU countries and the ESMA might, at first sight, help proponents of a single securities regulator in Canada. Nevertheless, there is little empirical evidence to date that having a single regulator would mean lower capital costs than under the passport system (Thibodeau 2012). Further, the OECD ranked Canada second in a study of securities-market regulation, which begs the question of why Canada should move to a single securities regulator. The answer to this question is largely a matter of political will. The ABCP crisis revealed some cracks in the regulatory system, and Chapter 6 will reveal one of the best kept secrets of the global financial crisis – Canadian banks were not as robust as they were portrayed. Improvements can be made to the Canadian regulatory and supervisory structure.

Conclusion

The Bank of England, ECB and Federal Reserve have become more powerful since the global financial crisis. This is necessary to keep pace with technological advances, globalisation of banking and the increased heterogeneity of market players. The Bank of England, ECB and Federal Reserve had to extend their role as lender of last resort during the global financial crisis. Bagehot's principle is too restrictive and central banks did not have the right tools to deal with excessive leverage. There is general consensus that increased macro-prudential regulatory powers are needed for financial-stability purposes. The issue of whether central banks should have micro-prudential regulatory and supervisory powers is more controversial. Some fear that there is 'central bank diktat' and that central banks are doing too much. Others query whether the skills of managing monetary policy and supervision are the same. All these concerns are valid, and it is very difficult to adopt a uniform policy for all countries. This chapter provided detailed analyses of the UK,

Australia, Germany, EU, US and Canada. What works best for each depends on its history, politics, legal regime and culture. Further, there is little empirical evidence of a correlation between regulatory structure and supervisory effectiveness. The clear trend since the financial crisis is an increase in central banks' roles in prudential supervision. The EBU – and, in particular, the SSM – has contributed to this trend.

In terms of regulatory architecture, the UK and German models are similar, since the latter was inspired by the former. The US regulatory architecture also shares some aspects of the twin-peak' model, although it remains primarily a multi-regulatory model. Supervision in the EU has become more centralised. Effective supervision will rest on clear communication and information flow between the supervisory authorities, flexibility in interpreting the relevant legislation, such as counter-cyclical capital buffers, and proactive intervention. Despite the strong performances of the regulators in Australia and Canada, improvements can be made in relation to their regulatory and supervisory systems.

Bibliography

Adrian, T. and Shin, H. S. (2009) 'Money, Liquidity, and Monetary Policy', *American Economic Review*, 99(2), pp. 600–5.

Andenas, M. and Chiu, I. eds. (2014) *The Rise of Macro-prudential Supervision*, United Kingdom: Routledge.

Athanassiou, P. (2014) 'The Evolving Role of Central Banks in Banking Supervision' in Jung, P. and Schwarze, J., eds., *Finanzmarketregulierung in der Krise*, Germany: Mohr Siebeck.

Australia Prudential Regulatory Authority (2014) *Financial System Inquiry Submission*, Australia.

Australia Prudential Regulatory Authority (2015) *APRA Stakeholder Survey – 2015. Regulated institutions and knowledgeable observers, report of overall findings*, Australia.

Australian Bankers' Association (2011) *A Strong Banking System Fact Sheet*, Australia.

Australian Financial Stability Inquiry (2013) *Financial Stability Inquiry Final Report*, Australia: http://fsi.gov.au/publications/final-report/executive-summary/ [accessed 12 March 2015].

Australian Securities and Investments Commission (2013) *ASIC Stakeholder Survey 2013*, Australia:http://asic.gov.au/about-asic/what-we-do/how-we-operate/stakeholder-liaison/stakeholder-surveys/ [accessed 19 December 2015].

Bagehot, W. (1873) *Lombard Street: A Description of the Money Market*, Wiley Investment Classics (1999 reprint).

Bakir, C. (2003) '"Who Needs a Review of the Financial System? The Case of the Wallis Inquiry"', *Australian Journal of Political Science*, 38(3), pp. 511–34.

Bakir, C. (2009) 'The Governance of Financial Regulatory Reform: The Australian Experience', *Public Administration*, 87(4), pp. 910–23.

Bank for International Settlements (2009) *Roles and Objectives of Modern Central Banks*, Switzerland: Bank for International Settlements.

Bank for International Settlements (2013) *Central Bank Collateral Frameworks and Practices: A Report by a Study Group Established by the Markets Committee*, Basel, Switzerland.

Bank of England and Financial Services Authority (2011) *The Bank of England, Prudential Regulation Authority – Our Approach to Banking Supervision*, London.

Bank of England (2015) *Financial Services (Banking Reform) Act 2013: Memorandum of Understanding between the Bank of England, the Financial Conduct Authority, the Payment Systems Regulator and the Prudential Regulation Authority*, London.

Barth, J., Nolle, D., Phumiwasana, T. and Yago, T. (2002) 'A Cross Country Analysis of the Bank Supervisory Framework and Bank Performance', *Financial Markets, Institutions & Instruments*, 12(2), pp. 67–120.

Basel Committee for Banking Supervision (2010) *Guidance for National Authorities Operating the Countercyclical Capital Buffer*, Switzerland: Basel Committee for Banking Supervision.

Baxter, T. (2010) *Too Big to Fail: Expectations and Impact of Extraordinary Government Intervention and the Role of Systemic Risk in the Financial Crisis* Washington D.C.: Federal Reserve Bank of New York.

BBC (2010) *Q & A: Osborne's Financial Regulation Reforms* [online], available: http://www.bbc.co.uk/news/10343900. [accessed 10 January 2015].

Bernanke, B. S. (2011) 'The Effects of the Great Recession on Central Bank Doctrine and Practice', in *Keynote Address at the Federal Reserve Bank of Boston 56th Economic Conference 'Long Term Effects of the Great Recession,'* Boston, October, pp. 8–19.

Blanchard, O., Dell'Ariccia, G. and Mauro, P. (2010) 'Rethinking Macroeconomic Policy', *IMF Staff Position Note SPN/10/03, 12 February*.

Blinder, A. (2010) 'How Central should the Central Bank Be?', *Journal of Economic Literature*, 48(1), pp. 123–33.

Bonfim, D. and Monteiro, N. (2013) *The Implementation of the Countercyclical Capital Buffer: Rules versus Discretion*.

Borio, C. (2003) 'Towards a Macroprudential Framework for Financial Supervision and Regulation?', *CESifo Economic Studies*, 49(2), pp. 181–215.

Borio, C. (2009) 'Implementing the Macroprudential Approach to Financial Regulation and Supervision', *Banque de France Financial Stability Review No. 13, September*.

Campbell, A. and Lastra, R. (2010) 'The Financial Crisis: Regulatory Failure or Systems Failure?' in MacNeil, I. and O'Brien, J., eds., *The Future of Financial Regulation*, United Kingdom: Hart Publishing.

Candelon, B. and Sy, A. (2015) *How Did Markets React to Stress Tests?*, Washington DC: International Monetary Fund.

Carney, M. (2015) 'The EU, Monetary and Financial Stability, and the Bank of England', *Speech given by Mark Carney, Governor of the Bank of England*.

Chaudhuri, R. (2014) *The Changing Face of American Banking: Deregulation, Reregulation, and the Global Financial System*, United States of America: Palgrave Macmillan.

Cheun, S., Koppen-Mertes, I. and Weller, B. (2009) *The Collateral Frameworks of the Eurosystem, the Federal Reserve and the Bank of England and the Financial Market Turmoil*.

Čihák, M. and Podpiera, R. (2007) 'Experience with Integrated Supervisors: Governance and Quality of Supervision' in Masciandaro, D. and Quintyn, M., eds.,

Designing Financial Supervision Institutions: Independence, Accountability and Governance, Cheltenham, United Kingdom: Edward Elgar, pp. 309–41.

Čihák, M. and Podpiera, R. (2008) 'Integrated Financial Supervision: Which Model?', *The North American Journal of Economics and Finance*, 19(2), pp. 135–52.

Cooper, J. (2006) 'The Integration of Financial Regulatory Authorities – the Australian Experience. Speech to Comissão de Valores Mobiliários', *Securities and Exchange Commission of Brazil 30th Anniversary Conference, Assessing the Present, Conceiving the Future*, pp. 4–5.

Cooper, J. (2010) 'The Regulatory Cycle: From Boom to Bust' in MacNeil, I. and O'Brien, J., eds., *The Future of Financial Regulation*, United Kingdom: Hart Publishing.

Crawford, A., Meh, C. and Zhou, J. (2013) 'The Residential Mortgage Market in Canada: A Primer', *Bank of Canada Financial System Review*, December, pp. 53–64.

Cukierman, A. (2011) 'Reflections on the Crisis and on Its Lessons for Regulatory Reform and for Central Bank Policies', *Journal of Financial Stability*, 7(1), pp. 26–37.

D'Alonsio, T. (2010) *Responding to the Global Financial Crisis: The ASIC Story*, Australia: Australian Securities and Investments Commission.

De Larosiere, J. (2009) *The High Level Group on Financial Supervision in the EU*, Brussels: The European Commission http://ec.europa.eu/internal_market/finances/docs/de_larosiere_report_en.pdf [accessed 20 August 2015].

Department of the US Treasury (2008) *Blueprint for a Modernised Financial Regulatory Structure*, United States of America: Department of the US Treasury.

DeWaal, G. (2015) 'ESMA Says 2016 Goal is Regulation Convergence', *Lexology Online* [online], available: http://www.lexology.com/library/detail.aspx?g=a0acec7f-ef04-4739-94cd-60f7caf4400e&utm_source=Lexology+Daily+Newsfeed&utm_medium=HTML+email+-+Body+-+General+section&utm_campaign=Lexology+subscriber+daily+feed&utm_content=Lexology+Daily+Newsfeed+2015-10-15&utm_term [accessed 27 October 2015].

Eichengreen, B. and Dincer, N. (2011) *Who Should Supervise? The Structure of Bank Supervision and the Performance of the Financial System*. National Bureau of Economic Research.

Engelen, K. (2010) 'Germany's Fight over BaFin', *The Magazine of International Economic Policy*, pp. 54–61.

Engelen, K. (2011) 'Another Merkel Blunder', *The Magazine of International Economic Policy*, Spring, pp. 36–41.

European Banking Authority (2015) *EBA Reports on Asset Encumbrance in EU Banks* [online], available: http://www.eba.europa.eu/-/eba-looks-at-asset-encumbrance-in-eu-banks [accessed 28 October 2015].

European Central Bank (2015) *ECB to Conclude Comprehensive Assessment of Nine Banks in November 2015* [press release], 9 October 2015, available: https://www.bankingsupervision.europa.eu/press/pr/date/2015/html/sr151009.en.html [accessed 10 October 2015].

European Commission (2013) *Legislative Package for Banking Supervision in the Eurozone* [press release], available: http://europa.eu/rapid/press-release_MEMO-13-780_en.htm [accessed 11 November 2015].

European Commission (2014) *Report from the Commission to the European Parliament and the Council on the operation of the European Supervisory Authorities and the European System of Financial Supervision* Brussels: European Commission.

Ferran, E. (2011) 'The Break-up of the Financial Services Authority', *Oxford J Legal Studies*, 31(3), pp. 455–80.

Ferran, E. and Babis, V. (2013) 'The European Single Supervisory Mechanism', *Journal of Corporate Law Studies*, 13(2), pp. 255–85.

Financial Stability Committee (2015) *Recommendation of 30 June 2015 on New Instruments for Regulating Loans for the Construction or Purchase of Residential Real Estate*, AFS/2015/1, Germany: Bundesanstalt für Finanzdienstleistungsaufsicht.

Financial System Inquiry Final Report (1997) *Final Report (S. Wallis, Chair)*, Canberra.

Freixas, X. and Parigi, B. (2014) 'Lender of Last Resort and Bank Closure Policy' in Berger, A., Molyneux, P. and Wilson, J., eds., *The Oxford Handbook of Banking*, United Kingdom: Oxford University Press.

Fujii, M. and Kawai, M. (2009) 'Lessons from Japan's Banking Crisis – 1991 to 2005' in Tilson, M., De Wulf, H., Van der Elst, C. and Steennot, R., eds., *Perspectives in Company Law and Financial Regulation*, United Kingdom: Cambridge University Press.

Galati, G. and Moessner, R. (2010) *Macroprudential Policy-A Literature Review*, The Netherlands: De Nederlandsche Bank.

Gauthier, C., Lehar, A. and Souissi, M. (2010) *Macroprudential Capital Requirements and Systemic Risk* Bank of Canada, mimeo.

Goodhart, C. (2009) 'Liquidity and Money Operations: A Proposal' in Goodhart, C., ed., *The Regulatory Response to the Financial Crisis*, United Kingdom: Edward Elgar.

Goodhart, C. A. (2002) 'The Organizational Structure of Banking Supervision', *Economic Notes*, 31(1), pp. 1–32.

Green, D. (2012) 'The Relationship between Micro Macro-prudential Supervision and Central Banking' in Wymeersch, E., Hopt, K. and Ferrarini, G., eds., *Financial Regulation and Supervision, A Post-crisis Analysis*, United Kingdom: Oxford University Press.

Greenspan, A. (1995) 'Financial Innovations and the Supervision of Financial Institutions', in *31st Annual Conferece on Bank Structure and Competition*, Federal Reserve Bank of Chicago.

Group of Thirty (2008) *The Structure of Financial Supervision: Approaches and Challenges in a Global Marketplace* Washington, DC: The Group of Thirty.

Halligan, L. (2015) 'Currency Wars Threaten Lehman-style Crisis', *The Telegraph* [online], available: http://www.telegraph.co.uk/finance/comment/liamhalligan/11472336/Currency-wars-threaten-Lehman-style-crisis.html [accessed 15 March 2015].

Hartmann, P., de Bandt, O. and Peydró, J. (2015) 'Systemic Risk in Banking after the Great Financial Crisis.' in Berger, A., Molyneux, P. and Wilson, J., eds., *The Oxford Handbook of Banking*, United Kingdom: Oxford University Press.

Hellwig, M. (2014) *Financial Stability, Monetary Policy, Banking Supervision, and Central Banking*, Bonn, Germany: Max Planck Institute for Research on Collective Goods.

Herring, R. and Carmassi, J. (2014) 'Complexity and Systemic Risk: What's Changed Since the Crisis?' in Berger, A., Molyneux, P. and Wilson, J., eds., *The Oxford Handbook of Banking*, United Kingdom: Oxford University Press.

Iglesias-Rodriguez, P. ed. (2014) *Financial Regulation & Supervision in Spain, the UK and the U.S.*, Italy: Wolters Kluwer Law & Business.

Industry Super Australia (2013) *Senate Inquiry into the Performance of ASIC*, Australia.

International Monetary Fund (2015) *Vulnerabilities, Legacies, and Policy Challenges: Risks Rotating to Emerging Markets*, Washington DC: International Monetary Fund.

Jackson, H. (2009) 'Learning from Eddy: A Meditation upon Organisational Reform of Financial Supervision in Europe' in Tisson, M., DeWulf, H., Van der Elst, C. and Steennot, R., eds., *Perspectives in Company Law and Financial Regulation*, United States of America: Cambridge University Press.

Jackson, J. (2013) *Financial Market Supervision: Canada's Perspective*, 7–5700, United States of America.: Congressional Report Service Report for Congress.

Jenkins, P. (2011) 'EU Regulators Outline Stricter Stress Tests', *Financial Times* [online], available: https://next.ft.com/content/d5f9926c-61ca-11e0-88f7-00144feab49a [accessed 20 October 2015].

Jin, J., Kanagaretnama, K. and Lobo, G. (2011) 'Ability of Accounting and Audit Quality Variables to Predict Bank Failure during the Financial Crisis', *Journal of Banking & Finance*, 35(11), pp. 2811–19.

Johnson, C. (2011) 'Exigent and Unusual Circumstances: The Federal Reserve and the U.S. financial crisis' in Alexander, K. and Moloney, N., eds., *Law Reform and Financial Markets*, United Kingdom: Edward Elgar Publishing.

Kaetzler, J. and Ronken, H. (2015) 'The Single Supervisory Mechanism: An Assessment from CMS Germany', *CMS Hasche Sigle* [online], available: http://www.lexology.com/library/detail.aspx?g=24abb705-9078-4993-9fe0-13412f7b9308 [accessed 30 October 2015].

Kiladze, T., Perkins, T., Robertson, G., Nelson, J., Erman, B., Slater, J., Jones, J., Waldie, P. and Keenan, G. (2013) 'The 2008 Financial Crisis: Through the Eyes of Some Major Players', *The Globe and Mail.*

King, M. (2013) 'Challenges for the Future', *International Journal of Central Banking*, pp. 359–65.

Koetter, M., Roszbach, K. and Spagnolo, G. (2014) 'Financial Stability and Central Bank Governance', *International Journal of Central Banking*, 10(4), pp. 31–67.

Kowalik, M. (2011) *Countercyclical Capital Regulation: Should Bank Regulators Use Rules or Discretion?*, United States of America.

Langley, M. (2008) 'Bad Bets and Cash Crunch Pushed Ailing AIG to Brink', *Wall Street Journal* [online], available: http://www.wsj.com/articles/SB122169421247449935 [accessed 25 May 2015].

Lastra, R. (2003) 'The Governance Structure for Financial Regulation and Supervision in Europe', *Columbia Journal of European Law*, 10, pp. 49–68.

Liikanen, E. (2013) *The Economic Crisis and the Evolving Role of Central Banks* [press release], available: [accessed 1 September 2015].

Ludwig, E. (2012) 'Assessment of Dodd–Frank Financial Regulatory Reform: Strengths, Challenges, and Opportunities for a Stronger Regulatory System', *Yale Journal of Regulation*, (1), pp. 181–200.

MacNeil, I. (2010) 'The Trajectory of Regulatory Reform in the UK in the Wake of the Financial Crisis', *European Business Organization Law Review*, 11, pp. 483–526.

Masciandaro, D. ed. (2012) *Determinants of Financial Supervision Regimes*, United Kingdom: Edward Elgar.

Masciandaro, D. and Quintyn, M. (2009) 'Reforming Financial Supervision and the Role of Central Banks: A Review of Global Trends, Causes and Effects (1998-2008)', *Centre for Economic Policy Research, Policy insight No. 30, February 2009.*

Meade, E. (2012) 'The Governance of Central Banks' in Levi-Faur, D., ed., *The Oxford Handbook of Governance*, United Kingdom: Oxford University Press.

Meltzer, A. (2010) 'Testimony, House Committee on Financial Services, 2014; 1–3' [online], available: http://www.house.gov/apps/list/hearing/financialsvcs_dem/meltzer.pdf [accessed 19 August 2015].

Nadauld, T. and Sherlund, S. (2009) *The Role of the Securitization Process in the Expansion of Subprime Credit*, Washington: Board of Governors of the Federal Reserve System.

National Audit Office (2014) *The Financial Conduct Authority and the Prudential Regulation Authority: Regulating Financial Services*, London.

Ontario Securities Commission (2007) *Notice 11–904, Request for Comment regarding the Proposed Passport System*, Ontario, Canada: Ontario Securities Commission.

Pan, E. (2010) 'Structural Reform of Financial Regulation in Canada: A Research Study Prepared for the Expert Panel on Securities Regulation', *Transnational Law and Contemporary Problems*, 19, pp. 796–848.

Peek, J., Rosengren, E. and Tootell, G. (1999) 'Is Bank Supervision Central to Central Banking?', *Quarterly Journal of Economics*, 114, pp. 629–53.

Primikiris, S. (2004) 'Australian and UK Bank Regulators', *Journal of Banking and Financial Services*, 118(3), pp. 16–19.

Ratnovski, L. and Huang, R. (2009) *Why Are Canadian Banks More Resilient?*, Washington, United States of America: International Monetary Fund [online], http://papers.ssrn.com/sol3/papers.cfm?abstract_id=1442254 [accessed 9 December 2015].

Reinhart, C. and Rogoff, R. eds. (2011) *This Time Is Different: Eight Centuries of Financial Folly*, United States of America: Princeton University Press.

Repullo, R. and Saurina Salas, J. (2011) 'The Countercyclical Capital Buffer of Basel III: A Critical Assessment', *CEPR Discussion Paper No. DP8304*.

Riksbank (2015) *About the Riksbank* [online], available: http://www.riksbank.se/en/The-Riksbank/ [accessed 28 September 2015].

Scott, H. (2010) 'The Reduction of Systemic Risk In The United States Financial System', *Harv J L & Pub Pol'y*, 33, pp. 671–734.

Shiratsuka, S. (2011) 'A Macroprudential Perspective in Central Banking', in *Institute for Monetary and Economcis Studies Paper Series*, Japan, Institute for Monetary and Economic Studies Bank of Japan.

Singh, D. (2007) *Banking Regulation of UK and US Financial Markets*, Aldershot: Ashgate.

Sinn, H.-W. (2010) *Casino Capitalism – How the Financial Crisis Came About and What Needs to be Done Now*, Oxford: Oxford University Press.

Sjostrom, W. (2009) 'The AIG Bailout', *Washington and Lee Law Review*, 66(3), pp. 943–94.

Taylor, M. (1995) *Twin Peaks: A Regulatory Structure for the New Century*, London: Centre for the Study of Financial Innovation.

Taylor, M. (2009) 'The Road from "Twin Peaks" – and the Way Back', *Connecticut Insurance Law Journal*, 16(1), pp. 67–88.

Thibodeau, M. (2012) *Proposed Federal Securities Regulator 1: Economic Aspects*, Publication Number. 2012-28-E, Ottawa, Canada: Library of Parliament.

Turner, A. (2009) *The Turner Review: A Regulatory Response to the Global Banking Crisis*, London: Financial Services Authority.

Vletter-van Dort, H. (2012) 'Some Challenges Facing European Central Banks as Supervising Authority', *European Company and Financial Review*, (2), pp. 131–55.

Walker, G. (2010) 'The Global Credit Crisis and Regulatory Reform' in MacNeil, I. and O'Brien, J., eds., *The Future of Financial Regulation*, United Kingdom: Hart Publishing.

Wallace, W. H. (2013) *The American Monetary System: An Insider's View of Financial Institutions, Markets and Monetary Policy*, Springer.

Whalen, C. (2011) 'I am Superman: The Federal Reserve Board and the Neverending Crisis' in Tatom, J., ed., *Financial Market Regulation, Legislation and Implications*, United States of America: Springer.

Wheelock, D. C. and Wilson, P. W. (2000) "Why Do Banks Disappear? The Determinants of U.S. Bank Failures and Acquisitions", *Review of Economics & Statistics*, 82(1), pp. 127–38.

World Bank (2015) *World Development Indicators* [online], available: http://data.worldbank.org/data-catalog/world-development-indicators [accessed 25 August 2015].

Zimmermann, H. (2012) 'No Country for the Market: The Regulation of Finance in Germany after the Crisis', *German Politics*, 21(4), pp. 484–501.

3 UK

Introduction

The UK ranked third in the overall Financial Development Index of the World Economic Forum 2012. However, it was ranked 43rd in financial stability (the financial-stability score is based on currency stability, banking-system stability and risk of a sovereign-debt crisis). The World Economic Forum has recommended improvements in regulation and oversight, including official supervisory power in the UK (World Economic Forum 2012). The regulatory and supervisory framework of the UK financial regulator is thus of importance. Regulation refers to the rules which govern the behaviour of banks. Supervision focuses on the oversight by the regulator to ensure that banks adhere to the rules (Barth *et al.* 2006). In the UK, the Bank of England was responsible for macro-prudential regulation from 1997 till April 2013. Responsibility for micro-prudential regulation was primarily the responsibility of the Financial Services Authority (FSA), but individual organisations are also responsible for implementing the rules. In practice, regulation and supervision are often intertwined. Therefore, although this author tries to separate the two, it is necessary to assess them together at times.

The first part of this chapter aims to analyse the role of the Bank of England and the weaknesses of the tripartite financial regulatory system during the financial crisis of 2007–9. This tripartite system includes the Treasury, the FSA and the Bank of England. The author will also examine the Bank of England's roles and powers under the 'twin peaks' regulatory model. The second part of this chapter focuses on the macro- and micro-prudential regulatory framework in UK banking used in the financial crisis of 2007–9.

The Bank of England and institutional weaknesses during the financial crisis of 2007-9

The tripartite system

The UK Labour government adopted the tripartite system in 1997. The Bank of England had responsibility for monetary and financial stability under the Memorandum of Understanding between the Treasury, FSA and the Bank of

England. Under the Memorandum of Understanding, the Bank of England was meant to reduce systemic risks and advise on the implications of financial-stability developments. The Memorandum was revised in March 2006. Monetary and financial-stability policies are closely linked (Mishkin 2011). Section 11 of the Bank of England Act 1998 defined the Bank of England's objective as 'to maintain price stability and, subject to that objective, to support the government's economic policy, including its objectives for growth and employment'. This objective is similar to the objectives of the German central bank and the ECB (Cobham 2013). From the Bank of England's committee minutes, it appears that the Bank changed its focus as the financial crisis progressed, from, in 2007, 'the main rationale for the Bank's role was financial crisis management' (Bank of England 2007a) to, by 2008, 'its main role was monetary policy, not prudential supervision' (Bank of England 2008a)). The Bank of England's Court of Directors' minutes reveal that the executive management did not want the Bank to be more involved in prudential regulation. This is because the Bank of England did not wish to see any adverse impact on its role as a monetary-policy maker by spending more time on prudential regulation. Further, it believed that the FSA should be the organisation supervising financial institutions (Bank of England 2008a). In 2009, the Bank of England admitted that it focused more on macro-prudential regulation and not enough on micro-prudential regulation (Bank of England 2009). One area for improvement revealed in the crisis is bridging the gap between monetary policy and micro-prudential regulation (Bank of England 2008b).

There are a number of criticisms regarding the Bank of England's monetary policy. The low interest rate between the early 1990s and 2007 coupled with a steady growth rate of 3 per cent during this period gave rise to cheap, easy credit and fuelled a housing boom (Sentance 2011). Property prices soared till the sub-prime mortgage crisis in the US caused a rapid fall in house prices. The Bank of England's Monetary Policy Committee (MPC) followed the 'Greenspan put', whereby the central bank did not react to asset-price growth. Instead, the Bank of England believed that it should be ready to help if there was a fall in asset prices (Mishkin 2011; Cobham 2013). Wadhawani was the only member of the MPC who opposed this view and adopted the 'lean against the wind' policy if there was a fall in asset prices. Cobham (2013) argued that by adopting the 'Greenspan put' the MPC provided an environment of easy growth in asset prices. It also failed to control house-price inflation through interest rates. Relying on the 'Greenspan put' suggests that the Bank of England was rather optimistic about the rise in asset prices and focused too much on the present. There was inadequate forward planning for dealing with risks, and so the Bank of England was primarily a firefighter when the crisis broke out.

The global financial sector became increasingly complex throughout the 1990s with the growth of securitisation. The justification for a tripartite system was that the boundaries between financial institutions have blurred. Banking, insurance and securities overlap. Complex group structures, innovative financial products and processes such as securitisation have led to the phenomenon of 'functional despecialisation' (Taylor 2009). Traditional banks adopted the 'originate to distribute' model in the late 1980s, and boundaries between banks, insurance and securities companies have blurred. Banks and the shadow banking organisations have thus become increasingly interwoven. In theory, a single regulator would be better positioned to monitor modern financial institutions. However, in practice, separating the roles of financial regulation from financial stability created the phenomenon of 'macro-prudential underlap' identified by Lord Turner of the FSA and Paul Tucker of the Bank of England (HM Treasury 2010). Macro-prudential forecast, analysis and reduction were ineffective at the Bank of England as no single organisation was responsible for regulating the financial system in its entirety. The Bank of England lacked the requisite tools to prevent and contain the financial crisis of 2007–9 (Bank of England 2009): Corbo (2010) stated that macro-prudential regulation is itself the best tool to maintain financial stability. Banks should reduce their leverage in boom periods and ensure the robustness of the financial sector in bust periods. Neither the Bank of England nor the FSA adequately focused on systemic risks created by increasing leverage, booming credit supply and asset prices, or the development of shadow banking. This is demonstrated in two examples: Northern Rock and HBOS.

Northern Rock was previously a building society. In 1997, it became a bank when it was listed on the London Stock Exchange. However, Northern Rock combined a traditional reliance on illiquid long-term mortgage assets with a reliance on innovative sources of funding such as securitisation and the wholesale market (Milne and Wood 2009). Mortgages constituted 77 per cent of Northern Rock's assets. Wholesale funding constituted 68 per cent of Northern Rock's liabilities, whilst deposits made up only 27 per cent of its liabilities (Goldsmith-Pinkham and Yorulmazer 2009). At the end of 2006, Northern Rock issued asset-backed securities through its 'granite' securitisation vehicles and obtained 40 per cent of funding (Milne and Wood 2009). Northern Rock was the first UK bank which needed government assistance when the global financial crisis started. The House of Commons Treasury Committee stated that the tripartite system had failed to work well. It was critical of the FSA in both its roles as regulator and supervisor (House of Commons Treasury Committee 2008). As a supervisor, the FSA failed to allocate sufficient resources to monitor Northern Rock's unusual business model. It failed to supervise Northern Rock properly when it adopted an ambitious expansion policy and when its share price fell sharply in late 2007. With regards to human resources, the FSA should not have approved the chairman and CEO of Northern Rock, as they were not qualified bankers. They had significant experience, but running a big bank without suitable qualifications is a hazard (Lui 2012).

The FSA labelled Northern Rock as a 'high impact bank, under close and continuous supervision' (House of Commons Treasury Committee 2008).

However, the FSA only carried out an ARROW (Advanced Risk Responsive Operating Framework) risk assessment every three years. It acknowledged that the interval between assessments was 'inadequate' (House of Commons Treasury Committee 2008). The FSA defended its position by stating that it maintained a close relationship with Northern Rock through 'very regular dialogues... on a full range of supervisory issues' (House of Commons Treasury Committee 2008). Although the main problem at Northern Rock was one of liquidity, the FSA weakened Northern Rock's capital position by approving the Basel II waiver. This meant that Northern Rock was able to increase its dividends and so its balance sheet was weakened. Before the FSA approved the Basel II waiver, FSA reviewed Northern Rock's stress-testing scenarios. The FSA was unhappy with the scenarios but it failed to relay that message to the directors of Northern Rock. It also failed to rectify the scenarios (Lui 2012).

Northern Rock had to ask the Bank of England, as the lender of last resort, for emergency relief. By separating the roles of banking supervision and regulation from the role of lender of last resort, decision-making was slow and inefficient (Lui 2012). The Bank of England was criticised for taking a reactive approach to the Northern Rock episode (Buiter 2008, cited in House of Commons Treasury Committee 2008). In comparison to the Federal Reserve and the ECB, the Bank of England was slow to act, arguing that injecting liquidity would create a risk of moral hazard (House of Commons Treasury Committee 2007). Northern Rock informed the FSA on 13 August 2007 that it was in trouble. The FSA told the Bank of England and the Treasury the next day. Initially, the tripartite authorities wanted a stronger bank to take over Northern Rock. Lloyds TBS Bank was a strong contender but it wanted funding of £30 billion from the Bank of England. The Bank of England refused, so the potential merger failed. The tripartite authorities made a statement that they would provide liquidity support to Northern Rock on 14 September 2007. Discussions on avoiding a retail deposit run took place during the weekend of 15–16 September. On 17 September 2007, the Chancellor guaranteed all Northern Rock's existing deposits. Four days later, the guarantee extended to unsecured wholesale lending (Bank of England 2007b).

The Bank of England was reluctant to provide more liquidity at different maturity dates against weaker collateral (Blei 2008; House of Commons Treasury Committee 2008) when several banks asked the Bank of England for additional liquidity at no penalty rate in August 2007. It refused to engage in liquidity transformation. Wood (2008, cited in House of Commons Treasury Committee 2008) supports the Bank of England's approach. In his view, the ECB and the Federal Reserve were wrong to adopt such a proactive policy, which would lead to problems in the future. The House of Commons Treasury Committee concluded that, whilst it was hard to tell whether the liquidity facility could have saved Northern Rock, the Bank of England should have broadened its range of collateral earlier in the crisis.

One of the tools available to a central bank in managing a crisis is flexibility in lending (Corbo 2010). It can lend money to banks against a broader selection of instruments by relaxing its collateral requirements. By stating that the ECB had acted too hastily and that the Federal Reserve had contradicted its objectives, the Bank of England proclaimed that its lending policy was flexible. It defended its position by arguing that its monetary framework contained reserve targets set by the banks themselves. Since the systemic shocks took place after the respective banks had set their targets, the banks should be responsible for setting their strategies in dealing with liquidity issues (Bank of England 2007a).

According to Breeden and Whisker (2010), the Bank of England introduced new liquidity insurance facilities and broadened its range of collateral to include high-quality private-sector assets such as residential-mortgage-backed securities. However, the Bank of England strongly believed in Bagehot's principle of providing liquidity support against good-quality collateral at a penalty rate (Bagehot 1873). The Bank of England extended liquidity support to avert panic in the market. This extension had to be balanced against the costs of reducing the incentives of banks to be prudent in managing liquidity risks and the risks of it appearing on the Bank of England's balance sheet (Breeden and Whisker 2010). It believed that following such principles reaffirms that the Bank of England is a lender of *last* resort, not lender of *first* resort. The Federal Reserve in the US adopted a similar policy to that of the Bank of England, but the ECB differed. It had already accepted a wide range of collateral from the beginning of the financial crisis (Breeden and Whisker 2010). The Bank of England had been conservative in its approach to being the lender of last resort. It conducted regular stress tests and took into account a number of factors to protect its position such as eligibility of products, valuations of collateral and haircuts.

Adaptability is important during periods of change. The Bank of England was not initially adaptable in managing the financial crisis. It failed to provide emergency support when the Federal Reserve and the ECB offered contingency support to vulnerable banks. To address the strains in the short-term-funding market, the Federal Reserve permitted depositories to borrow for 90 days and to renew the loan as long as they were financially sound. Further, they introduced the Term Auction Facility, whereby set amounts of credit were auctioned every two weeks. This reduced the stigma associated with the discount window (Bernanke 2008). Previously, some banks were concerned that other market players would make adverse assumptions about their financial status if they knew that they were borrowing from the Federal Reserve, but the launch of the Term Auction Facility increased the number of banks borrowing (Bernanke 2008). The ECB started providing liquidity to banks in August 2007 by first pumping €94.8 billion into the money markets. Further liquidity was injected in August and September. The ECB also reduced its overnight interest rates (Hall 2008). The Bank of England finally offered emergency funding at a penalty rate to Northern Rock, which could use mortgages and mortgage-backed securities as collateral. The Bank of England's response has been criticised for being too late and too little.

The Treasury failed in its role set out in clause 4.1 of the Memorandum of Understanding. This is evidenced by its delay in amending the financial-stability stress-testing framework. The Bank of England regularly carried out stress testing of the overall financial system till the financial crisis as part of the Financial Sector Assessment Programme. In its Financial Stability Report of 2005, the Bank of England highlighted that the stress-testing exercise conducted in 2002 confirmed that the Bank was sufficiently sound to withstand externalities (Bank of England 2005). However, there were weaknesses in the 'bottom-up' approach to stress testing. The 'bottom-up' approach has been criticised for being too costly, not flexible enough and only taking into account domestic credit risks (Bank of England 2005). In 2006, following another stress-testing scenario, the Bank of England said it would follow a 'work programme' to address weaknesses. However, although the Treasury started working on these weaknesses, it did not regard these weaknesses as urgent (Black 2012). As a result, the tripartite authorities were not adequately prepared for the Northern Rock run.

The tripartite authorities received mixed feedback in the case of HBOS. HBOS was formed in 2001 when Halifax Plc and the Governor and Company of the Bank of Scotland merged. At the end of 2006, HBOS was the fourth largest UK bank in terms of assets (Milne and Wood 2009). According to the 2007 HBOS Annual Report, HBOS held 20 per cent of the mortgage market and 16 per cent of the savings market (HBOS Plc 2007). Like many other banks, HBOS experienced rapid growth between 2003 and 2008. Debt increased from £112 billion in 2003 to £231 billion in 2007 and total assets increased from £408 billion in 2003 to £667 billion in 2007 (HBOS Plc 2007). HBOS experienced liquidity problems during the financial crisis. Chief Executive Andy Hornby admitted that 'it is clear with the benefit of hindsight that, over many years of reliance on wholesale funding, that left us in a vulnerable position' (House of Commons Treasury Committee 2007). HBOS's share price fell sharply in March 2008 after rumours of short-selling in the bank. FSA carried out a market-rumours investigation. In August 2008, it confirmed that it had not found any evidence that rumours was spread as part of a concerted attempt by individuals to profit by manipulating the HBOS share price. It is commendable that the FSA took action as soon as possible (Lui 2012).

Despite the false allegation of short-selling, HBOS's share price fell a further 18 per cent on 15 September 2008, when Lehman Brothers filed for bankruptcy. Despite reassurance from HBOS Group Communications Director Shane O'Riordain that it had a strong capital base, shareholders were not convinced, and the share price fell a further 22 per cent. Emergency talks took place on 17 September 2008 between HBOS and Lloyds TSB. The Labour government was keen to avoid another Northern Rock scenario. It therefore relied on the argument of public interest, waived European competition law and approved the deal between HBOS and Lloyds TSB; this was despite the initial concerns of the Office of Fair Trading, which stated that the merger might give rise to a 'substantial lessening of competition within a market or markets in the UK for goods or services, including personal current accounts, banking services to small and medium enterprises and mortgage' (Office of Fair Trading 2008; Hasan and Marinc 2013). The Secretary of State for Business and Enterprise was able to intervene in this merger on grounds of the public's interest in 'maintaining the stability of the UK financial system' (section 58D of the Enterprise Act 2002). On 18 September 2008, HBOS and Lloyds TSB announced that the former would be takeover by the latter for £12.2 billion. The House of Commons Treasury Select Committee (2008) believed that the government's action was correct in light of preserving financial stability.

HBOS failed due to a combination of its own weak corporate governance and the FSA's poor regulation (Lui 2012). The FSA first raised its concerns about HBOS back in 2003. They carried out a full ARROW risk of HBOS's retail, corporate, treasury and group functions. Due to limited resources at the FSA, they could carry out only a limited risk review in each division; they then produced a Risk Mitigation Plan for HBOS to follow (Moore 2009a). Moore explained that the FSA would ask HBOS or an external expert to carry out additional work and assessments in the case of any key risks. If the bank carried out the additional work, this would normally be assigned to one of the two Group Risk functions that existed at the bank, either Group Regulatory Risk or Group Financial and Operational Risk (Moore 2009a). The FSA's report contained evidence that 'the risk posed by the HBOS Group to the FSA's four regulatory objectives is higher than it was perceived' (Moore 2009a). In relation to HBOS's retail side at the Halifax, 'there has been evidence that development of the control function in Retail Division has not kept pace with the increasingly sales driven operation' (Moore 2009a).

The FSA's ARROW visit in 2003 identified the key risks. Moore believed that 'the operational staff at the FSA had done a good job on the ARROW visit they had conducted and that they almost certainly had identified the key risks at the bank at that stage in its development' (Moore 2009b). In Moore's view, junior staff at the FSA were not responsible for the demise of HBOS (Moore 2009b). Nevertheless, Moore (2009b) stated that the FSA failed to supervise properly because it adopted a 'light-touch' approach to regulation and supervision. It failed in its statutory duties, which were to maintain market confidence, protect retail customers, fight financial crime and ensure proper consumer education. According to Moore (2009b), the main failure of the FSA was that it failed to act upon the red flags.

The Parliamentary Commission on Banking Standards Report of 2013 shed further light on the failings of the FSA. It asserted that:

> From 2004 until the latter part of 2007 the FSA was not so much the dog that did not bark as a dog barking up the wrong tree.
> (Parliamentary Commission on Banking Standards 2013)

The FSA's regulation of HBOS was 'inadequate'. Although it identified that HBOS's business strategy was too aggressive and risky with weak internal controls, the FSA was too easily reassured. The supervisory style was bottom-heavy in that too much supervision was done at the lower level. The supervisory approach was 'box-ticking' and a great deal of the FSA's actions were 'too little, too late' (Parliamentary Commission on Banking Standards 2013). The FSA thus missed a number of opportunities to prevent HBOS's demise. The FSA did not act as an independent source of guidance to HBOS; instead, it proved to be a hindrance and interference. Initially, the FSA regulated HBOS well (2002–4): it identified a number of serious concerns about control functions at HBOS, including its over-reliance on wholesale funding. Several reviews were carried out consequently and the turning point of the FSA's regulatory approach was the 'skilled persons review' under section 166 of the Financial Services Markets Act (FSMA) 2000 on HBOS's control framework and risk-management processes (Lui 2012). Although the first report made some suggestions for change, the second said that everything was fine. The FSA was more relaxed regulating HBOS after this review and reversed the increase in the capital requirement in December 2004 (Parliamentary Commission on Banking Standards 2013). Further, the FSA's emphasis switched from prudential regulation to conduct of business regulation. It spent a great deal of time implementing Basel II and the FSA's Treating Customers Fairly scheme (Bank of England 2015a). It was only after the Northern Rock episode in March 2008 that the FSA devoted more time to liquidity. The FSA was comfortable for senior management at HBOS to identify and mitigate business and control risks (Parliamentary Commission on Banking Standards 2013' Bank of England 2015a).

The 2004–7 period showed that the FSA adopted the wrong regulatory approach to HBOS. When the FSA gave the Basel II waiver to HBOS, the latter was able to calculate its own risk-weightings. This also distracted supervisors from regulating and supervising liquidity and credit positions. Few members of senior management at FSA supervised HBOS, and, when a stress test took place, challenges would be passed down (Parliamentary Commission on Banking Standards 2013). Senior management at the FSA had little involvement with supervision and was generally inexperienced. Senior managers should have been more probing and sceptical with supervision, especially with the Corporate department of HBOS (Bank of England 2015a). According to an FSA official, the FSA was more interested in the composition of HBOS's wholesale-funding portfolio than in prescribing levels or amounts.

The Bank of England's report into the failure of HBOS was more critical of the FSA's supervisory framework and approach (Bank of England 2015a). Not only did it confirm the above weaknesses of the FSA, it added that the FSA was weak in regulating large systemically important banks due to inadequate resources. Its supervisory approach was reactive; there was inadequate consideration of risks, such as having sufficient capital buffers, since too much reliance was placed on banks' own models and did not focus fully on asset quality and liquidity (Bank of England 2015a).

The case studies of Northern Rock and HBOS have shown that bank bail-outs were political decisions made by the UK government. As such, Blei (2008) submits that the Bank of England should not have been involved in decisions about bank rescues. The failed merger between Northern Rock and Lloyds TSB delayed the rescue of the former bank. The Bank of England did not have micro-prudential regulatory powers over Northern Rock or HBOS: these were given to the FSA. Certainly without the appropriate tools, the Bank of England was not in the best position to 'advise the Chancellor and answer for its advice, on any major problem arising in these [financial and payment] systems' (Brown *et al.* 2006) as stated in the Memorandum of Understanding. Some scholars criticised (Blei 2008; House of Commons Treasury Select Committee 2008) the Bank of England for being reluctant to lend against weaker collateral to banks such as Northern Rock. Although the Bank of England is a lender of last resort and moral hazard should not be encouraged, Mark Carney opined that Bagehot's rule has to be modernised for the twenty-first century with the shadow banking sector increasing in size (Carney 2014). In 2002, the size of the shadow banking sector was worth $26 trillion. In 2011, it reached $67 trillion (Financial Stability Board 2012). The total size of the shadow banking system is around 50 per cent of banking-system assets (Financial Stability Board 2012). It is thus important that the Bank of England can step in and provide liquidity support when necessary, as well as being willing to lend to a 'wider range of collateral and a broader range of counterparties' (Carney 2014). Time is of the essence when it comes to rescuing frail banks. The failed merger with Lloyds TSB delayed the rescue of Northern Rock. However, the government learnt from the experience and the merger between HBOS and Lloyds TSB took place at a faster pace. The government also amended legislation to reflect the public interest in sustaining financial stability.

Although financial stability is crucial during a crisis, it is important that all actions taken by the Bank of England are honest. In November 2014, the Bank of England instigated its own inquiry into whether staff at the Bank of England were aware of, or even took part in, manipulation of money-market auctions in 2007–8. The Bank of England held several money-market auctions to calm liquidity worries before it started injecting liquidity through quantitative easing in March 2009 (Binham and Jenkins 2014). It advised all banks to offer the same amount of collateral so that no bank would need more liquidity. The Bank of England uncovered 50 instances of market manipulation and the Serious Fraud Office (SFO) is now investigating 42 of them (Trotman 2015). This is a blow to the reputation of the Bank of England, which admitted that it did not have a proper procedure for raising the alarm. It has since implemented an 'attestation and escalation policy' to deal with some matters (Trotman 2015). The outcome of the SFO investigation is particularly important after Lord Grabiner's report into the Bank of England's role in the manipulation of the foreign-exchange (forex) scandal. Although he cleared staff at the Bank of England of 'any unlawful or improper behaviour' in the forex scandal, he found that Martin Mallett, the former chief forex dealer, was aware of banks having open discussions about manipulating the forex rate in chat rooms (Binham and Jenkins 2014; Grabiner 2014). Mr Mallett did not report the matter to his superior and Lord Grabiner expressed the view that this was an error of judgement. Mr Mallett has since lost his job, although he was not found guilty of any improper conduct.

Lord Grabiner (2014) recommended that the Bank of England take clear and proper minutes in meetings, especially during the chief dealers' subgroup meetings. Second, staff at the Bank of England should receive training on the voluntary codes of the forex market, such as the Non-Investment Products Code for Principals and Broking Firms in the wholesale markets. Finally, the Bank of England should constantly review its policy and controls on dealing with market intelligence and confidentiality. It should also have a written policy on escalating improper conduct within the hierarchy of the Bank. Information asymmetry is a problem in the financial world due to the opacity and complexity of financial products and processes. When information is available to the regulator, it is therefore important that it follows the right procedure in dealing with it. The new 'attestation and escalation policy' should help restore confidence in the Bank of England. After all, if the regulator cannot set an example to the financial industry, it will not be surprising if the public do not trust the Bank of England or the financial industry.

The Bank of England under the twin-peaks model

With an 'overlap' of financial products and an 'underlap' of macro-prudential regulation, it is little wonder that the balance tipped in favour of financial innovation rather than stability. Against this backdrop, it is necessary to consider whether the UK government can improve financial regulation under the twin-peaks model. Under part 2 of the Financial Services Act 2012, the Financial Policy Committee (FPC) is responsible for macro-prudential regulation. It is a subsidiary of the Bank of England. The FPC comprises bank executives and has macro-prudential tools to regulate financial institutions. Micro-prudential regulation is the responsibility of the new Prudential Regulation Authority (PRA), which deals with prudential and financial regulation (Financial Services Act 2012: section 6). The PRA is a subsidiary of the Bank of England. Its statutory objectives are to promote the safety and soundness of the firms they regulate (Financial Services Act 2012: part 2, section 2B). Its regulatory style has three elements: a judgement-based approach, a forward-looking approach and a focused approach. Andrew Bailey (2013) from the Bank of England submits that this will combine judgement with evidence and analysis – rigorous analysis of the riskiest banks by the PRA Board. The PRA Board is comprised of the Governor of the Bank of England, Deputy Governor for Financial Stability, Chief Executive Officer of the PRA and non-executive members.

The PRA's powers were further widened under part 1 of the Financial Services Reform Act 2013. The PRA can now hold banks to account for the way they separate their retail and investment activities, giving it powers to enforce the full separation of individual banks. Meanwhile, the 'conduct' part of the FSA has been given to the FCA. It is responsible for regulating the business conduct of all financial-services firms, as well as prudential regulation of firms not regulated by the PRA (Bailey 2013). The FCA's objectives are to protect consumers, maintain integrity in the financial sector and promote competition within the industry (Financial Services Act 2012: section 1B(3)). The aim is for the PRA and FCA to work closely together. Due to the twin-peaks model, the FSA Handbook is divided into two: the FCA Handbook and the PRA Handbook. Conduct of business regulation is mentioned in both the FCA and PRA handbooks.

The main advantage of the twin-peaks model is that both macro- and micro-prudential regulation are brought under one institution: the Bank of England. Proponents of the twin-peaks model argued that it is better in times of crises. Bringing together the lender of last resort and the information gatherer as the banking regulator should accelerate the decision-making process (Taylor 2009); and the proximity of the Bank of England and the PRA should assist with preventative measures such as the use of PRA's Threshold Conditions and judgement-based regulatory style. The Threshold Conditions set out the absolute minimum requirements which financial institutions must meet before they can carry out regulated activities (Bank of England 2013). The PRA uses a forward-looking, judgement-based regulatory style, which aims to detect present and potential risks that might affect financial institutions. When macro- and micro-prudential regulation is vested within one umbrella organisation, the PRA can, in theory, react more quickly to market volatility and provide liquidity where necessary. The success of a regulator is measured by its ability to achieve its objectives. Communication and co-operation between the regulatory bodies should be improved under the twin-peaks model, since there are extensive provisions in part 2, section 3 of the Financial Services Act 2012 governing this area. The section sets out the boundaries of each regulatory body and when the PRA can require the FCA to refrain from acting.

BDO and DLA Piper conducted a survey in mid 2012 of 350 executive directors in the financial industry. The survey asked for their concerns and priorities in relation to the twin-peaks model. Seventy-nine per cent of the respondents believe that the twin-peaks model will improve the effectiveness of the UK regulatory system (BDO and DLA Piper 2012). This is positive news, but the respondents are concerned about certain issues once the twin-peaks model has been implemented. The results revealed that the top concerns of respondents are: consumer protection, clarity of objectives and overlaps, existing legislation, and increased costs. This is understandable when changes occur, and the PRA and FCA should therefore ensure that they provide clear and helpful guidance to the regulated organisations during the first 12–24 months of the new regulatory regime. Amongst banks and building societies, 98 per cent of respondents are concerned about increased competition in the industry due to the Vickers' Report on retail ring-fencing. Ninety-six per cent of respondents are worried by the increased focus of the PRA/FCA on a firm's culture (BDO and DLA Piper 2012). Finally, 88 per cent of respondents in the banking industry are concerned by the PRA's use of judgement-based regulation. As seen in Chapter 2, the National Audit Office's Report (2014) found that there is evidence of good co-operation between the PRA and FCA when conflicts arise. Financial institutions have to bear the costs of forming the twin-peaks model, but, hopefully, the improved supervisory style will mean that there is less harm and fewer costs for both them and taxpayers, thus justifying the restructuring in the long-term. With regards to the complexities of the legislation, it is true that there have been some difficultes as to when and what kind of data can be shared between the authorities. Under section 18 of the Memorandum of Understanding between the Bank of England, the FCA, the Payment Systems Regulator and the PRA (Bank of England 2015b), the PRA and FCA have to deal with requests made under the Freedom of Information Act 2000 and Data Protection Act 1998. The combination of uncertainty over the law and market sensitivies meant that the PRA was unsure what kind of data could be shared with the FCA. As a result, the PRA has issued guidance booklets on confidentiality and disclosure. There is evidence that on several occasions, the PRA and FCA have worked well together on information requests (National Audit Office 2014). Good communication flow and co-operation will hopefully improve supervision and regulation in the long-term.

Macro- and micro-prudential regulatory frameworks in the UK 2007–9

Macro-prudential weaknesses

The structure of the tripartite system clearly failed in the UK during the financial crisis of 2007–9. At the macro-prudential level, the Bank of England did not have any power to ask individual banks for information or demand the FSA for such information under the Memorandum of Understanding, despite clauses 8 and 9 dealing with information exchange. Clauses 14–17 of the Memorandum stipulated co-ordination and the keeping of all UK authorities up to date, but the tripartite system failed to achieve these aims. It is arguable that the Bank of England lacked the requisite tools to fulfil its role in achieving financial stability in the Northern Rock and HBOS incidents. The FSA failed to communicate or share information regularly with the Bank of England on Northern Rock before the financial crisis. It would have been helpful if the Bank of England had had information on Northern Rock's risk-taking and maturity transformation prior to the financial crisis.

At the macro-prudential level, the Bank of England felt powerless when faced with nationalising or making a bank insolvent during the financial crisis. UK insolvency law contributed to financial instability: it did not provide a mechanism to resolve a financially distressed bank. The financial crisis of 2007–9 created a spillover effect for banks when the UK government had to nationalise Northern Rock and part of Bradford & Bingley as well as inject £850 million into Royal Bank of Scotland (RBS) and Lloyds Banking Group. With the two former building societies, the UK government faced the choice of insolvency or nationalisation. The Bank Special Provisions Act 2008 was passed on 21 February to facilitate the nationalisation of Northern Rock and part of Bradford & Bingley. The priority of the UK government during the financial crisis was to limit the costs of bank failures within the industry.

The Banking Act 2009, which entered into force on 21 February 2009, replaced the Bank Special Provisions Act 2008 and contains a Special Resolution Regime (SRR) to deal with distressed banks. It has five objectives – promoting and enhancing financial stability in the UK, promoting and enhancing public confidence in the UK, protecting depositors, protecting public funds and not interfering with property rights, which would contravene the European Convention of Human Rights (Banking Act 2009: sections 4(4)–4(8)) – and is divided into two parts: the first deals with pre-insolvency 'stabilisation' and the second with banking insolvency and administration (Ellinger *et al.* 2011). There are three stabilisation mechanisms: first, one can transfer all or part of a bank to a buyer in the private sector; second, one can transfer all or part of a bank to a 'bridge bank' (the Bank of England will set up the bridge bank); finally, a bank can be temporarily nationalised (Banking Act 2009: section 1(3)(c)). The stabilisation mechanisms apply if a bank fails to satisfy the 'threshold conditions' for FSA authorisation regarding capital adequacy and suitability requirements (Banking Act 2009: section 7). The aim is to rescue a bank as soon as there are red flags regarding its financial position. The second part of the Act includes a special banking-insolvency procedure and a bank-administration procedure. The former enables depositors to access their savings guaranteed under the Financial Services Compensation Scheme swiftly. The latter enables the 'good' part of the insolvent bank to carry on with its business activities. This is a new provision which was not possible under the corporate-insolvency regime.

Northern Rock was nationalised in February 2008. The stabilisation mechanism applied because the Treasury wanted to reduce the threat of financial instability (Banking Act 2009: section 9(2)) and it was in the public's interest for the Treasury to exercise the power of stabilisation (Banking Act 2009: section 9(3)). Depositors of Northern Rock were given a 100 per cent guarantee by the Treasury (Singh 2011). Bradford & Bingley was partly nationalised: Santander bought the 'good' part of the bank, comprising savings and the branch network. The 'bad' part of Bradford & Bingley, comprising loans and mortgages, was placed in public ownership.

The positive consequence of this partial nationalisation was that customers of Bradford & Bingley continued to have access to their accounts. However, the problem with partial nationalisation is that the 'bad' debts are in public ownership, creating a financial burden for the state (Singh 2011). The government's interests in Northern Rock and Bradford & Bingley were managed by UK Financial Investments Limited (UKFI) till 2010. UKFI was responsible for managing the Government's entire shareholding and loans in UK Asset Resolution Ltd (UKAR) and its subsidiaries. UKAR was established in November 2010 to combine the activities of Northern Rock (Asset Management) Plc and Bradford & Bingley Plc. UKFI managed the Government's entire shareholding in Northern Rock Plc till its sale to Virgin Money on 1 January 2012. The creation of UKFI and subsequently UKAR had the aim of separating the public interest from the private interest of the relevant banks. Operation at arm's length is important to avoid regulatory capture and conflict of interest.

The nationalisation of Northern Rock and Bradford & Bingley demonstrates that it is impossible to prevent bank failures. The PRA thus rejects a 'zero-failure' regulatory policy. Therefore, with the Special Resolution Regime contained in the Banking Act 2009 (Campbell *et al.* 2009), the PRA's role is to minimise the systemic effect of any bank failure. Further, there are costs attached to clearing up a bank failure. The PRA believes that all firms should have a minimum level of resilience against failure (Bank of England 2013). Early intervention by the PRA should prevent the aggravation of potential problems. Threshold conditions are designed to impose minimum requirements for all firms before they can carry out regulatory activities. The threshold conditions include requirements for the legal status of the organisations, business conduct and effective supervision.

The PRA's supervisory style is based on judgement, risks, being forward-looking and early intervention. The PRA's risk assessment framework and its supervisory responses based on the Proactive Intervention Framework deserve closer analysis. The PRA's forward-looking approach takes into account three factors: the likelihood of firm failure, the impact of firm failure on the stability of the system and the possibility of an orderly resolution. First, the PRA considers the potential impact of firm failure on the overall economy, both whilst the firm is trading and when it fails. External risks and factors surrounding a firm are also taken into account. Since the FPC and the Bank of England are responsible for macro-prudential regulation, their views on external risks will be consulted. Business risks are assessed at the level of the sector or of the firm, as appropriate, taking into account peer analysis (Allen and Overy 2013). A firm's risk profile may be mitigated by factors such as governance measures, internal controls, financial strengths in capital and liquidity and an orderly resolution of the firm.

The PRA aims to intervene early when an organisation is in trouble financially. It forms its own judgement regarding a suitable supervisory response based on the stage an organisation is in. The Proactive Intervention

Framework has five stages. Stage 1 is low risk, and a suitable response would be the usual supervisory risk assessments. As the stages increase, the corresponding supervisory actions increase in intensity. At stage 4, there is an imminent risk to the financial viability of an organisation. The PRA believes that such an organisation is unlikely to meet the threshold conditions. Suitable responses include increasing capital and liquidity levels, as well as an asset disposal. Organisations at stage five will be wound up. One significant difference between the UK and Australian supervisory frameworks is that plans for resolving an organisation are possible as early as stage 1 in the UK. This emphasises the importance of early intervention in the UK supervisory framework.

The PRA realised from the failures of the FSA that staffing is vital to the success of an organisation. Therefore, the PRA has recruited more staff and placed more of them in frontline supervision. Senior staff are supervising high-risk organisations, thus reflecting the principle of minimising the effect of financial failures. Setting policies is one of the PRA's powers within its regulatory framework. It publishes policies in line with its objectives so that senior management at regulated organisations can use them as guidance. As financial safety is the overriding principle of the PRA, regulated organisations are expected to follow the PRA's policy and guidance. In practice, this power of setting policies and the vertical integration of regulators at European level means that it is unlikely the PRA will exercise its powers to set policies very often. A great deal of policy is coded at European level already.

The Northern Rock incident highlighted the need to bridge the lacuna between monetary policy and micro-prudential regulation of financial institutions. There are close ties between asset liquidity and whether the Bank of England accepts such liquidity, so it makes sense for the FSA and the Bank of England to work closely together (Bank of England 2007a). The Bank of England (2009) admitted that it had been poor at monitoring financial institutions. It will supervise banks more and have regular dialogues with them.

Earlier in this chapter we saw that the FSA was passive in its regulatory and supervisory roles. It is now important to examine how the UK legislative framework contributed towards this failure. Part 10 of the FSMA gave the Treasury and the FSA powers to make regulations and guidance. Sections 138–47 provided rule-making powers, and section 156 provided supplementary powers to make rules for specific cases. The FSA's rules and guidance were consolidated in its Handbook of Rules and Guidance. It consisted of several sourcebooks and manuals. Hudson (2009) submits that there were six tiers of regulation in the FSA Handbook: high-level standards, business standards, prudential standards, regulatory processes, redress and specialist sourcebooks.

Under section 2(1) of the FSMA 2000, the FSA had a number of general functions which were subject to regulatory objectives. The functions of the FSA included making rules, preparing and issuing codes, giving general guidance and determining general policy and principles by reference to its functions (FSMA 2000: section 2(4)). Underpinning these functions were the regulatory objectives of market confidence, public awareness (which was later changed by the Financial Services Act 2010 from an objective to a principle, in section 2(3)(h)), consumer protection and the reduction of financial crime (FSMA 2000: section 2(2)). The Financial Services Act 2010 inserted a new regulatory objective of financial stability as section 2(2)(a)(b) FSMA 2000. Finally, in discharging its objectives and functions, the FSA had to pay attention to the principles stated in section 2(3), such as using its resources in the most efficient way, facilitating financial innovation and competition.

The legal structure of the FSMA 2000 was complicated and conflicting. In pursuing a function, the FSA had to consider its objectives and principles as well. The objective of consumer protection conflicted with the principles of the FSA facilitating financial innovation and competition. The use of innovative, securitised products combined with a risky business model and sales culture at Northern Rock and HBOS illustrates that customers were treated as products and not individuals. Bruni and Llewellyn explained that Northern Rock's demise was due to a combination of factors, such as the bank's reliance on securitisation and management of low-probability high-impact risks, the supervisory and regulatory regimes and insolvency-resolution procedure (Bruni and Llewellyn 2009). Northern Rock's mission statement till 2006 was to deliver value for customers and shareholders through excellent products, efficiency and growth. From the bank run and subsequent nationalisation of the bank, it is clear that Northern Rock went too far in favour of financial innovation and range of products at the expense of maintaining checks and balances. Liquidity is the main culprit at Northern Rock. Although Northern Rock was solvent, its assets were mainly illiquid due to its reliance on wholesale funding. HBOS's customers suffered because of its sales culture (Lui 2015). Ellis and Taylor provide an interesting account of the culture at HBOS from Margaret Taylor, an ex-employee of HBOS, who is also a political activist (Ellis and Taylor 2010). Taylor has three reasons why HBOS went wrong. First, the incentive structure had changed from a simple pay package to individualised, performance-driven pay. Secondly, deregulation in the 1980s encouraged retail organisations to expand into banking. This led to a more sales-driven approach and increased emphasis on marketing. Gardener *et al.* (1999) concur with this view. In their paper, they conducted a case study into the evolution of retail banking in the UK. They found that, from the mid 1970s, banks became more market-orientated. Promotion and marketing became more important (Gardener *et al.* 1999). Finally, technological advances replaced human labour (Ellis and Taylor 2010). Paul Moore, Head of Regulatory Risk at HBOS 2002–5, said that HBOS staff were 'being forced to sell things; sell credit; sell mortgages; sell insurance products that were simply not in the best interests of the customer'. The Head of Risk in the division told Paul Moore that 'they [HBOS directors] pay no attention to risk management here at all. The only thing that counts is sales and you know, they are animals around here' (Moore 2009a).

After analysing the weaknesses of the FSA's statutory objectives and functions, it is necessary to examine its rule-making powers and the FSA

Handbook. In particular, this section will focus on the high-level standards, business standards, prudential standards and supervisory rules during the financial crisis of 2007–9. Principle 3 of the Principles for Businesses under high-level standards says that: 'A firm must take reasonable care to organise and control its affairs responsibly and effectively, with adequate risk management systems'. In March 2012, the FSA took enforcement action and censured HBOS's corporate division for 'very serious misconduct' during 2006–8 (Financial Services Authority 2012). This is because the corporate division failed to comply with principle 3 of the FSA's Principles for Businesses. HBOS pursued an aggressive growth strategy even in the period of 2006–8, when the other UK banks scaled back their lending to corporate borrowers. More importantly, the FSA held that HBOS had a culture of focusing on profit at the expense of assessing risks properly. The FSA's censure of HBOS is a public one. It wanted to 'name and shame' the bank and act as a lesson on risk-management failures. Nevertheless, the FSA was criticised for its decision-making process in that it only investigated Peter Cummings, former Head of Corporate Banking, for misconduct.

The Green report (2015) into the FSA's enforcement action in the HBOS episode highlights the narrowness and unreasonableness of the FSA's investigation. It should have conducted a review into Andy Hornby, the former Group Chief Executive Officer of HBOS, as well as the whole bank. The FSA did not monitor the deadline for bringing disciplinary proceedings against Peter Cummings and was too late with others, such as Andy Hornby. The statutory time limit for bringing disciplinary proceedings under section 66 of FSMA 2000 is only two years. Therefore, it was important for the FSA to act swiftly, particularly when it acknowledged that there was 'a quite fundamental problem with the way that the bank had been run as a whole' (Green 2015). Green therefore recommended that the FCA should investigate other members of the senior management at HBOS. However, if one of the senior officers at HBOS is found to have contributed to the downfall of HBOS, only a prohibition proceeding can be pursued. This means that no financial penalty can be imposed. Instead, under section 56 FSMA 2000, a banker can be prohibited from a specific function. Arguably, a prohibition order is more applicable in this context, since it will prevent the wrongdoer from committing the mistake in the future. However, 'credible deterrence' (McDermott 2013) will be more effective if a financial penalty can be coupled with a prohibition order in the right circumstances, such as the ban and fine imposed on Peter Cummings. Finally, Green (2015) states that there were administrative and procedural weaknesses in the decision-making process. For example, there were no records showing the conversations between the Enforcement and Supervisory teams at the FSA as to why HBOS failed.

Learning from the mistakes of the FSA, the FCA has pursued the concept of 'credible deterrence' to date. In 2013, it fined the Lloyds Banking Group £28,038,800 for serious failures in their incentive schemes. Sales advisors at Lloyds were selling products to customers that they did not require or want because advisors were under pressure to hit targets (Financial Conduct Authority 2013). The FCA increased the fine by 10 per cent because the FSA had given several warnings to Lloyds Banking Group in the past of poorly managed incentive schemes. Lloyds also had a previous fine from the FSA for the unsuitable sale of bonds in 2003, which was caused partly by sales targets. It appeared that Lloyds Banking Group had not learnt from its previous mistakes and it was hoped, therefore, that the hefty fine would act as a deterrent. Credit goes to both the FSA and FCA for taking enforcement action against Lloyds for breach of the FSMA's objective of consumer protection and principle 3 of the Principles of Businesses.

The FCA has imposed a number of fines on banks for misconduct in relation to the Libor-, Euribor-, forex-market- and gold-price-fixing scandals. Starting with the Libor scandal, the FCA fined Barclays Plc £60 million in 2012. Another major UK bank, RBS, was fined £87.5 million in February 2013 for breaching section 206 of the FSMA 2000 in the Libor scandal (Financial Services Authority 2013). RBS also breached principle 3 of the FSA's Principles for Business by failing to have adequate risk-management systems and controls in place in relation to its Libor submissions process, as well as committing a number of other breaches. Individual traders colluded with other firms and panels in manipulating the Japanese and Swiss Libor submissions between 2006 and 2010 (Financial Services Authority 2013). At company level, RBS did not have adequate internal controls and processes to monitor risks associated with derivatives trading. Further, RBS attested in 2011 that they had adequate systems in place when they did not. It breached principle 5 of the Principles for Businesses by failing to observe proper standards of market conduct between October 2006 and November 2010, and it manipulated the interest rate by taking the trading positions of its interest rate when making Swiss and Japanese Libor submissions.

In November 2014, the FCA fined five banks for manipulating the forex rate. The guilty included three UK banks: HSBC, RBS and Barclays. Barclays were also fined £60 million for manipulating gold prices in the same year. The manipulation of the forex market took place between 2008 and 2013. It is unfortunate to see such misconduct taking place after the Libor and Euribor scandals and after the financial crisis. In response, the FCA imposed large fines on these banks due to the seriousness of the misconduct. Although the forex market is largely unregulated, soft law applies, whereby relevant codes should be followed. The FCA reprimanded the banks for failing to have robust controls and internal systems to prevent the traders' misbehaviour. A remediation programme has been launched, which includes banks reviewing their internal controls. Senior managers of banks also have responsibility for checking that internal controls and systems are robust enough to meet the risks of manipulation of rates, breaches of client confidentiality and conflicts of interest (Financial Conduct Authority 2014a). This remediation programme is moving in the right direction towards achieving accountability, openness and trust. To date, four former employees in the financial sector have been banned and fined for their involvement in the Libor, gilt and gold fixings (Financial Conduct Authority 2015a). The personal accountability of bank managers was further increased when the Senior Managers Regime and the Certification Regime came into force in March 2016. Under the Senior Managers Regime, the approval process for senior managers is more rigorous because regulators will have to approve their suitability before they join and then on an annual basis (Financial Conduct Authority 2015b). The regime aims to minimise the problem of the lack of experience and knowledge demonstrated by several former directors at HBOS (Bank of England 2015a). With more accountability, the public should be more confident about the financial sector.

Consumer protection is a key objective of prudential regulation. Lord Turner (2009) is of the opinion that the FSA paid too much attention to conduct of business regulation than to prudential regulation during the financial crisis of 2007–9. The FSA spent a great deal of time on the conduct of business initiatives such as the Retail Distribution Review and the Treating Customers Fairly Initiative (MacNeil 2010; Bank of England 2015a) – for example, the FSA's prioritisation of the Treating Customers Fairly Initiative over liquidity at HBOS (Bank of England 2015a). The Retail Distribution Review raises professional standards in the financial advisory industry and provides clearer information to clients about costs and services. The Treating Customers Fairly Initiative protects consumers by highlighting the benefits and risks of the products that they are buying. These are attempts to uphold the principle of acting in the clients' best interests in clause 2.1 of the Conduct of Business Obligations. Although no amount of regulation can fully protect consumers, MacNeil disagrees with Lord Turner and argues that it is right to focus on the conduct of business regulation. This is because increased pressure on banks to raise capital and boost profits may lead to unfair treatment of customers. If such logic applies, customers are always in a vulnerable situation. In the deregulatory, laissez-faire period, banks pursued high-risk aggressive models to maximise profits. The combination of greed, recklessness and the Libor, Euribor and forex scandals left customers very vulnerable. Since the financial crisis, financial stability has been the key aim of the regulator. Banks are under pressure to increase their capital positions, especially after the Brisbane G20 Leaders' summit in November 2014, where the Financial Stability Board proposed ways to end the too-big-to-fail phenomenon. The top 30 banks will have to hold 16–20 per cent of risk-weighted assets or at least twice the Basel III requirement excluding all buffers. Bank also have to hold 6–8 per cent of total assets or at least twice the Basel III leverage capital requirement. Will this lead to inferior treatment of customers? If the top 30 global banks implement such capital ratios then they should be sufficiently sound and robust to withstand any externalities. This should not come at the cost of inferior consumer protection.

The second reason why MacNeil thinks that consumer protection should continue to be important is because, following the implementation of the FSA's Retail Distribution Review, financial advisers have to charge upfront and not by commission (MacNeil 2010). This may deter some customers from seeking investment advice (Collinson 2012). Another concern is that financial advisers will circumvent this ban on commission by selling medical- and life-insurance policies, since they are not caught under the Retail Distribution Review (Collinson 2012). Consumers of financial products need protection because of information asymmetry and moral hazard. Markets alone will not protect consumers and therefore the regulator should pursue the objective of consumer protection. Nevertheless, this pursuance should not come at the cost of poor prudential regulation and supervision.

Micro-prudential regulation

The FSA Handbook also contained prudential standards. The Prudential Standards in the General Prudential Sourcebook set out regulations on the financial robustness of regulated firms. Solvency, liquidity and capital positions are regulated via risk models. The supervision manual in the FSA Handbook set out how the risk models are formed. Under section 1.3 of the supervision manual, the FSA used a 'risk based approach'. The risk models were based on an 'impact and probability' risk assessment. The models considered how each firm's strategy and risks contravened the FSA's core regulatory objectives. The FSA then graded the bank from high risk to low risk. This risk-assessment approach was dependent on assumptions, reactions and the willingness of the FSA to rely upon the regulated bank's provision of information (Hudson 2009). Hudson provides the example of Northern Rock. In this scenario, the FSA admitted that it did not 'stress test' the bank properly. As a result of this omission, it did not reflect the change in Northern Rock's business model and anticipate the increased risk in securitisation and the sub-prime market. Together with a light-touch regulatory approach, the FSA relied too much on Northern Rock providing information, rather than challenging the information given to the FSA. Hudson (2009) argues that the FSA was not proactive enough in supervising Northern Rock. Therefore, the FSA could not accurately predict the risks that Northern Rock would face. The FSA's approach to supervision of banking was 'not fit for purpose' (Hudson 2009). As a result of these failings, the regulatory and supervisory framework, approach and structure have changed. The twin-peaks model has replaced the consolidated model of the FSA: the Bank of England integrates macro- and micro-prudential supervision (Bank of England 2015a).

Since adopting the twin-peaks model', each regulator has had its own handbook. The PRA Handbook has moved away from the FSA Handbook by being more concise. It also contains PRA rules, which are read in line with the PRA's objectives. Together with a judgement-based, forward-looking supervisory method, the PRA and FCA appear to be able to carry out their objectives successfully. This was reflected in the combined joint enforcement action against RBS, National Westminster Bank (NatWest) and Ulster Bank in November 2014 for serious IT failures in 2012. The PRA and FSA worked together and imposed a joint fine of £14 million on the banks (Prudential Regulatory Authority 2014). This is the first fine imposed by the PRA. It investigated RBS, NatWest and Ulster Bank because its inadequate IT system affected the overall financial soundness and safety of the UK banking structure. For several weeks, customers were unable to withdraw cash and some banks were unable to access clearing, which had a negative impact on the efficient operation of the financial system (Prudential Regulatory Authority 2014). The FCA highlighted the importance of widening policy towards IT risk appetite so that banks are resilient when affected by an incident (Financial Conduct Authority 2014b). This successful joint action by the PRA and FCA is most encouraging. The PRA itself has been active in supervision of banks and the design of the new regulatory framework. According to the Bank of England's annual report, the PRA has been closely monitoring the financial ratios of banks (Bank of England 2014). The PRA and the FPC will conduct stress tests of banks every year. Further, the PRA has been designing the new European and international frameworks for solvency and resolution of banks (Bank of England 2014). Of particular notice is the PRA's influence on the Capital Requirements Directive IV, which came into force in January 2014. In November 2014, the PRA discovered that RBS had miscalculated its core Tier 1 capital ratio. RBS reported that it had 6.7 per cent core Tier 1 capital ratio for 2016 when in fact it only had 5.7 per cent. Since the error, RBS has changed its auditors. This incident proves that the PRA has become more proactive and interventionist, which, given RBS's position as the weakest UK bank under the stress test of 123 banks by the European Banking Authority (2014), is what the banking sector requires.

Conclusion

It is evident that Bagehot's rule on central banking needs to keep pace with modern banking. Securitisation and shadow banking have increased opacity and complexity in financial products and processes. The Bank of England lacked the requisite information and tools to perform its roles as lender of last resort and as a crisis manager. It spent too much time on monetary policy and too little on prudential regulation, especially micro-prudential regulation and supervision. Through the examples of Northern Rock and HBOS it has been shown that the tripartite parties failed in their respective roles during the financial crisis of 2007–9.

The twin-peaks model in the UK and the measures taken by both the PRA and FCA to date offer a glimmer of hope of better regulation and supervision. The legislative framework sets out better communication and co-operation between the regulatory bodies. The twin-peaks model and new legislation should provide better regulatory co-ordination and information sharing and avoid potential conflict of interests. It remains to be seen whether the regulatory structure and framework will work in times of crisis. Proximity between the Bank of England and the PRA should assist with preventative measures. As macro- and micro-prudential regulation and supervision are vested under one umbrella organisation, the PRA can, in theory, react quicker to market volatility and provide liquidity where necessary. Macro- and micro-prudential regulation and supervision are closely connected: 'Macro-prudential supervision cannot be meaningful unless it can somehow impact on supervision at the micro-level; whilst micro-prudential supervision cannot effectively safeguard financial stability without adequately taking account of macro-level developments' (De Larosière 2009).

The PRA, FCA, Treasury and Bank of England have entered into a Memorandum of Understanding to co-ordinate their relationships with the European regulators (Financial Services Act 2012: part 2, section 6, clause 3E(3) (a)). The proposed changes to the European regulatory framework suggest a regulatory emphasis on vertical co-operation. Lord Turner and De Larosière both stressed the importance of good regulation on a global scale in their reports (De Larosière 2009; Turner 2009). After all, Mervyn King said that global banks are 'global in life but national in death' (King 2009, cited in Turner 2009). Effective global financial regulation starts at home. Until the UK government has fully learnt and implemented the changes, the question of the structure of the regulator is of secondary importance. The structure only provides the outer shell of an organisation. It requires the necessary tools, equipment, resources, information and co-ordination to perform properly.

The second part of this chapter examined the macro- and micro-prudential frameworks in UK financial regulation. The FSA's regulatory and supervisory powers derived from the FSMA 2000 and FSA Handbook. There were three problems with the pre-crisis legal framework in banking regulation. First, the legal structure of the FSMA 2000 was complicated and conflicted. In pursuing a function, the FSA had to consider its objectives and principles as well. The objective of consumer protection conflicted with the principles of the FSA facilitating financial innovation and competition. Customers of Northern Rock and HBOS suffered in the financial crisis of 2007–9 since the banks pursued high-risk aggressive growth models at the expense of consumer protection. The FSA as a single regulator was unable to decide which principle had priority. Second, the principles-based regulatory approach combined with the supervisory powers under the Regulatory Processes of the FSA Handbook proved to be disastrous. In theory, the risk-based supervisory approach using individual bank's business models and strategies to predict tailored risks sounds admirable. In practice, the use of assumptions, a light-touch regulatory approach and the FSA's over-reliance on the regulated banks' supply of information meant that the risk model failed. The FSA did not have policy-making powers and could not shape the financial system. Third, the FSA's remit was simply too wide. It was a super-regulator, which oversaw banks and licensed deposit-taking institutions and insurance and investments firms. With 'functional despecialisation' of products, the boundaries of financial services blurred and the FSA was overwhelmed by changes in the financial market and technology. Financial innovation gave way to financial stability at a serious cost to the UK financial system. The FSA was a watchdog which failed to detect risks prior to the financial crisis and was too slow to deal with the financial crisis.

Early indications from the enforcement actions in the Libor, Euribor and forex scandals seem to indicate a more proactive stance by the FCA. The imposition of a joint fine by the PRA and FCA against RBS, NatWest and Ulster Bank in November 2014 for IT failures suggests good co-operation between UK regulators. Trust between the authorities is important for achieving an open, co-operative and efficient relationship. The PRA have also been more tough and interventionist, as shown in the discovery of the error in core capital ratio at RBS. Nonetheless, Lord Gardiner's pending reports on whether staff at the Bank of England manipulated money-market auctions during 2007–8 and on the Bank of England's role in the forex scandal suggest that there is still room for improvement.

Bibliography

Allen & Overy (2013) *The Prudential Regulation Authority: An Overview*, London: Allen & Overy..

Bagehot, W. (1873) *Lombard Street: A Description of the Money Market*, Wiley Investment Classics (1999 reprint).

Bailey, A. (2013) *The Prudential Regulation Authority Quarterly Bulletin 2012 Q4*,

Bank of England (2005) *Financial Stability Report*, London: Bank of England.

Bank of England (2007a) *Bank of England Court of Directors' Minutes 2007–2009*, Court Minutes 2007, London: Bank of England.

Bank of England (2007b) *Financial Stability Report*, London: Bank of England.

Bank of England (2008(a)) *Bank of England Court of Directors' Minutes 2007–2009*, 2008B1, London: Bank of England.

Bank of England (2008(b)) *Bank of England Court of Directors' Minutes 2007–2009*, 2008 B2, London: Bank of England.

Bank of England (2009) *Bank of England Court of Directors' Minutes 2007–2009*, London: Bank of England.

Bank of England (2013) *The Prudential Regulation Authority's approach to banking supervision*, London: Bank of England.

Bank of England (2014) *Annual Report and Accounts 2014*, London: Bank of England.

Bank of England (2015a) *The Failure of HBOS plc (HBOS): A Report by the Financial Conduct Authority (FCA) and the Prudential Regulation Authority (PRA)*, London: Bank of England.

Bank of England (2015b) *Financial Services (Banking Reform) Act 2013: Memorandum of Understanding between the Bank of England, the Financial Conduct Authority, the Payment Systems Regulator and the Prudential Regulation Authority*, London: Bank of England.

Barth, J., Caprio, G. and Levine, R. eds. (2006)*Rethinking Bank Regulation: till angels govern*, New York: Cambridge University Press.

BDO and DLA Piper (2012) *The New Twin-peaks Model: A Report on the Financial Services Industry's Views on Upcoming Regulatory Issues*, UK.

Bernanke, B. (2008) 'Liquidity Provision by the Federal Reserve', in *Federal Reserve Bank of Atlanta Financial Markets Conference, Sea Island, Georgia*

Binham, C. and Jenkins, P. (2014) 'Bank of England Opens Probe into Whether Staff Helped Rig Auctions', *Financial Times* 23 November 2014.

Black, J. (2012) 'Managing the Financial Crisis – The Constitutional Dimension', in *LSE Law, Society and Economy Working Papers 12/2010*, London School of Economics, London,

Blei, S. (2008) 'The British Tripartite Financial Supervision System in the Face of the Northern Rock Run', in *Federal Reserve Bank of St Louis Supervisory Policy Analysis Policy Paper*, United States of America,

Breeden, S. and Whisker, R. (2010) *Collateral Risk Management at the Bank of England*, London: Bank of England.

Brown, G., King, M. and McCarthy, C. (2006) *Memorandum of Understanding between the Bank of England, Financial Services Authority, and HM Treasury, 22 March 2006.*

Bruni, F. and Llewellyn, D. eds. (2009) *The Failure Of Northern Rock: A Multi-dimensional Case Study*, Vienna.

Campbell, A., LaBrosse, J. R., Mayes, D. G. and Singh, D. (2009) 'A New Standard for Deposit Insurance and Government Guarantees after the Crisis', *Journal of Financial Regulation and Compliance*, 17(3), pp. 210–39.

Carney, M. (2014) *The Future of Financial Reform – 2014 Monetary Authority of Singapore Lecture*, Bank of England.

Cobham, D. (2013) 'Monetary Policy under the Labour Government 1997-2010: the first 13 years of the MPC', *Oxford Review of Economic Policy*, 29(1), pp. 47–70.

Collinson, P. (2012) 'FSA Ban on Commission-based Selling Sparks "Death of Salesman" Fears', *The Guardian* [online], available: http://www.theguardian.com/business/2012/dec/30/fsa-ban-commission-selling-death [accessed 2 May 2015].

Corbo, V. (2010) 'Financial Stability in a Crisis: What is the Role of the Central Bank? Perspectives on Inflation Targeting, Financial Stability and the Global Crisis', *BIS Papers 51* [online], available: http://www.bis.org/publ/bppdf/bispap51.htm [accessed 7th November 2014].

De Larosière, J. (2009) *The High Level Group of Financial Supervision in the EU, Brussels, 25th February 2009* [online], available: http://ec.europa.eu/internal_market/finances/docs/de_larosiere_report_en.pdf [accessed 10 January 2011].

Ellinger, E., Lomnicka, E. and Hare, C. (2011) *Ellinger's Modern Banking Law*, New York: Oxford University Press.

Ellis, V. and Taylor, M. (2010) 'Banks, Bailouts and Bonuses: A Personal Account of Working in Halifax Bank of Scotland during the Financial Crisis', *Work Employment Society 2010*, 24, pp. 803–13.

European Banking Authority (2014) *Results of 2014 EU wide Stress Test: Aggregate Results*, Germany.

Financial Conduct Authority (2013) *FCA Fines Lloyds Banking Group Firms a Total of £28,038,800 for Serious Sales Incentive Failings* [online], available: http://www.fca.org.uk/news/press-releases/fca-fines-lloyds-banking-group-firms-for-serious-sales-incentive-failings [accessed 12 June 2015].

Financial Conduct Authority (2014a) *FCA Fines Five banks £1.1 billion for FX Failings and Announces Industry-wide Remediation Programme* [press release], available: http://www.fca.org.uk/news/fca-fines-five-banks-for-fx-failings [accessed 19 June 2015].

Financial Conduct Authority (2014b) *FCA Fines RBS, NatWest and Ulster Bank Ltd £42 million for IT Failures* [press release], available: http://www.fca.org.uk/news/fca-fines-rbs-natwest-and-ulster-bank-ltd-42m-for-it-failures [accessed 20 June 2015].

Financial Conduct Authority (2015a) *Benchmark Fines*, London: Financial Conduct Authority.

Financial Conduct Authority (2015b) *FCA Publishes Final Rules to Make Those in the Banking Sector More Accountable* [press release], available: https://www.fca.org.uk/news/fca-publishes-final-rules-to-make-those-in-the-banking-sector-more-accountable [accessed 23 November 2015].

Financial Services Authority (2012) *FSA Publishes Censure against Bank of Scotland plc in Respect of Failings within its Corporate Division between January 2006 and December 2008* [online], available: http://www.fsa.gov.uk/library/communication/pr/2012/024.shtml [accessed 6 June 2015].

Financial Services Authority (2013) *RBS Fined £87.5 million for Significant Failings in Relation to LIBOR* [online], FSA Ref. No: 121882, available: http://www.fsa.gov.uk/library/communication/pr/2013/011.shtml [accessed 8 June 2015].

Financial Stability Board (2012) *Global Shadow Banking Monitoring Report 2012*, London.

Gardener, E., Howcroft, B. and Williams, J. (1999) 'The New Retail Banking Revolution', *The Service Industries Journal*, 19(2), pp. 83–100.

Goldsmith-Pinkham, P. and Yorulmazer, T. (2009) 'Liquidity, Bank Runs and Bailouts: Spillover Effects during the Northern Rock Episode', *Journal of Financial Services Research*, 37(2), pp. 83–98.

Grabiner, A. (2014) *Bank of England Foreign Exchange Market Investigation – A Report by Lord Grabiner QC*, London: http://www.bankofengland.co.uk/Pages/Search.aspx?k=grabiner [accessed 23 November 2014].

Green, A. (2015) *Report into the FSA's Enforcement Actions following the Failure of HBOS*, London: Bank of England.

Hall, M. J. (2008) 'The Sub-prime Crisis, the Credit Squeeze and Northern Rock: The Lessons to be Learned', *Journal of Financial Regulation and Compliance*, 16(1), pp. 19–34.

Hasan, I. and Marinc, M. (2013) 'Should Competition Policy in Banking Be Amended during Crises? Lessons from the EU', *European Journal of Law and Economics*, pp. 1–30.

HBOS Plc (2007) *Annual Report and Accounts 2007*, London: http://www.lloydsbankinggroup.com/media/pdfs/investors/2007/2007_HBOS_R&A.pdf [accessed 7 June 2015].

HM Treasury (2010) *A New Approach to Financial Regulation: Judgment, focus and stability*, Cn 7874, London: HMSO.

House of Commons Treasury Committee (2007) *Banking Crisis: Dealing with the Failure of UK Banks, Seventh Report of 2008-2009*, HC 416, London: HMSO.

House of Commons Treasury Committee (2008) *The Run on the Rock*, Fifth Report of Session 2007–08, Vol. II, HC56-II, Ev253, London: HMSO.

House of Commons Treasury Select Committee (2008) *Treasury Seventh Report, Banking Crisis: Dealing with the Failure of the UK Banks*, London: HMSO.

Hudson, A. (2009) *The Law of Finance*, First ed., Sweet & Maxwell.

Lui, A. (2012) 'Single or twin? The UK Financial Regulatory Landscape after the Financial Crisis of 2007–2009', *Journal of Banking Regulation*, 13(1), pp. 24–35.

Lui, A. (2015) 'Greed, Recklessness and/or Dishonesty? An Investigation into the Culture of Five UK banks between 2004 and 2009', *Journal of Banking Regulation*, 16(2), pp. 106–29.

MacNeil, I. (2010) 'The Trajectory of Regulatory Reform in the UK in the Wake of the Financial Crisis', *European Business Organization Law Review*, 11, pp. 483–526.

McDermott, T. (2013) *Enforcement and Credible Deterrence in the FCA*, London: Financial Conduct Authority.

Milne, A. and Wood, G. (2009) 'Shattered on the Rock? British Financial Stability from 1866 to 2007', *Journal of Banking Regulation*, 10(2), pp. 89–127.

Mishkin, F. (2011) *Monetary Policy Strategy: Lessons from the Crisis*, United States of America: National Bureau of Economic Research.

Moore, P. (2009a) *Memorandum of Further Additional Evidence to the House of Commons Treasury Select Committee relating to the banking crisis.*, UK: s.n.

Moore, P. (2009b) *House of Commons Treasury Select Committee Written Evidence Banking Crisis* [online], Session 2008-2009, available: http://www.publications.parliament.uk/pa/cm200809/cmselect/cmtreasy/144/144w201.htm [accessed 10 October 2012].

National Audit Office (2014) *The Financial Conduct Authority and the Prudential Regulation Authority: Regulating financial services*, London.

Office of Fair Trading (2008) *Anticipated Acquisition by Lloyds TSB plc of HBOS plc Report to the Secretary of State for Business Enterprise and Regulatory Reform, 24 October 2008.*

Parliamentary Commission on Banking Standards (2013) *'An Accident Waiting to Happen': The Failure of HBOS Fourth Report of Session 2012–13*, 1, London: The Stationery Office Limited.

Prudential Regulatory Authority (2014) *Prudential Regulation Authority Fines Royal Bank of Scotland, Natwest Bank and Ulster Bank £14 million for IT Failures* [press release], available: http://www.bankofengland.co.uk/publications/Pages/news/2014/152.aspx [accessed 15 June 2015].

Sentance, A. (2011) *Setting UK Monetary Policy in a Global Context*, European Policy Forum in association with the City of London Corporation, The Guildhall, London

Singh, D. (2011) 'The UK Banking Act 2009, Pre-insolvency and Early Intervention: Policy and Practice', *Journal of Business Law*, 1, pp. 20–42.

Taylor, M. (2009) 'Blurring the Boundaries in Financial Stability.' in Bruni, F. and Llewellyn, D. T., eds., *The Failure of Northern Rock: A Multi-dimensional Case Study.*, Vienna: SUERF – The European Money and Finance Forum.

Trotman, A. (2015) 'SFO Probes "Whether Bank of England Advised Lenders during Auctions"', *The Telegraph* [online], available: http://www.telegraph.co.uk/finance/newsbysector/banksandfinance/11897799/SFO-probes-whether-Bank-of-England-advised-lenders-during-auctions.html [accessed 24 November 2015].

Turner, A. (2009) *The Turner Review: A Regulatory Response to the Global Banking Crisis*, London: Financial Services Authority.

World Economic Forum (2012) *The Financial Development Report 2012* [online], available: http://www.weforum.org/issues/financial-development [accessed 6 April 2015].

4 Australia

Introduction

Luck is what happens when preparation meets opportunity
Seneca the Younger (4BC–65AD)

Crises provide opportunities to learn and change where necessary. Australia was not purely lucky when it emerged relatively unscathed from the financial crisis of 2007–9: it entered the crisis fairly well prepared with a robust regulatory architecture and strong prudential regulatory regime, and it combined past experience, good management skills and opportunity to withstand the challenges. Despite its common-law jurisdiction, Australia's experience of the financial crisis differed from those of the US and the UK. Australia is an economy primarily driven by commodities and natural resources. The strong demand from China for Australia's resources protected the Australian financial sector to a certain extent. Further, the Australian twin-peaks regulatory framework worked well. Australian banks have withstood the financial crisis better than UK banks. Australia did not have any bank runs. Four of the nine AA-rated banks around the world are Australian banks. Australia has also performed well in the Financial Development Index of the World Economic Forum 2012 (World Economic Forum 2012). They are ranked fifth out of 60 countries in the overall index and ninth in banking-system stability.

However, the Australian financial system is not faultless. The World Economic Forum states that the Australia banks had low Tier 1 capital and had high levels of stress. Also, its commercial access to capital is weak. However, financial intermediation is still strong despite the challenging economic conditions (World Economic Forum 2012). The Australian Financial Stability Inquiry (AFSI) 2013 also recommended improving the regulatory objectives of consumer protection, competition in the banking sector and accountability and effectiveness of regulators.

The Reserve Bank of Australia and institutional weaknesses during the financial crisis of 2007–9

The Australian regulatory structure

Simplicity is the key word to describe the structure of the Australian financial regulatory system. At the top of the hierarchy is the Council of Federal Regulators (CFR). It co-ordinates actions between the regulatory authorities when faced with potential threats to the financial system. It also shares information with the other regulatory bodies and advises the government on the strengths and weaknesses of the regulatory arrangements.

Below the CFR are four regulatory bodies. The Reserve Bank of Australia (RBA) has oversight for macro-prudential regulatory matters and pursues the objective of financial stability. The CFR enjoys a close relationship with the RBA since the Governor of the RBA chairs the CFR meetings. This provides co-operation and cohesion between the regulatory bodies. The Australian Prudential Regulatory Authority (APRA) is responsible for micro-prudential regulatory matters, whilst the Australian Securities and Investments Commission (ASIC) is in charge of business matters. The Australian Competition and Consumer Commission (ACCC) is responsible for competition and fair trade. The RBA and APRA have different powers but overlapping and complementary aims in sustaining financial stability. The final regulatory authority is the Treasury, which promotes a competitive and efficient financial market. The APRA and ASIC form the twin-peaks model: they promote the twin aims of prudential regulation and business conduct independently.

Australia adopted the twin-peaks model in 1998 following the Wallis Inquiry of 1997 (Financial System Inquiry Final Report 1997). The Wallis Inquiry was not a consequence of a scandal or crisis. Therefore, it can be argued that the Wallis Inquiry was free from political pressure when reviewing the regulatory structure (Cooper 2006). The G30 Report on the Structure of Financial Supervision of 2008 revealed that both Australia and the Netherlands are amongst the best and most effectively regulated regimes in the world (Group of Thirty 2008). It would appear that the twin-peaks model works very well in Australia. However, the failure of HIH Insurance Limited in 2001 illustrates the failures and weaknesses of the APRA in its early days as a regulator. HIH was the second largest general insurance company in Australia. It collapsed with a debt in the region of AUD\$3.6–5.3 billion (Clark 2007). The Royal Commission into HIH's collapse found that the APRA was reluctant to intervene in HIH when the latter was in trouble. The APRA was formed on 1 July 1998 and it was inexperienced in understanding the extent of HIH's problems (Clark 2007). The fundamental problem was that HIH offered insurance too cheaply without enough capital to absorb any potential losses. This was exacerbated by corporate-governance and management failures, leading to HIH buying troubled insurance business at too high a cost (Wilkins 2011).

Justice Owen of the Royal Commission held that the APRA 'did not cause or contribute to the collapse of HIH' (HIH Royal Commission 2003). However, the APRA 'missed many warning signs, was slow to act, and made misjudgements about some vital matters' (HIH Royal Commission 2003). Justice Owen said that the APRA was weak in a number of areas. First, the APRA did not have staff with the relevant skills or experience; resources were inadequate. Second, there was a lack of information flow upwards to the APRA's board and managers; they were not properly informed on HIH's lack of resources or financial performance. Third, like the FSA in the UK, the APRA adopted a laissez-faire approach to regulation. Although HIH's collapse was ultimately due to corporate-governance failures, this episode reveals that the APRA could have dealt with the problem better (Lui 2012).

To rectify the weaknesses, Justice Owen made three recommendations. First, he recommended that the CEO and executive commissioners should replace the non-executive board of the APRA in order to improve the information flow to the senior level. Second, he called for a restructuring of the APRA. Reorganisation was required to improve accountability. He also urged the creation of a specialist team of staff to supervise insurers. Finally, the APRA was to be more firm and aggressive in its style of prudential regulation and supervision (Lui 2012). The APRA learnt from the experience and in October 2002 it introduced new risk-assessment and supervisory response tools known as the Probability and Impact Rating System (PAIRS) and the Supervisory Oversight and Response System (SOARS). The HIH scenario illustrates that the APRA experienced teething problems in both regulation and supervision. Nevertheless, it has learnt from its experience and made the necessary changes (Lui 2012).

Performances of the RBA and Australian regulators during the global financial crisis

The financial crisis of 2007–9 provided a valuable learning experience for Australian regulators, even though they withstood the crisis better than regulators in other jurisdictions. Whilst the Bank of England was criticised for its decisions in the financial crisis of 2007–9 (House of Commons Treasury Select Committee 2008), the RBA was praised for its decisiveness, particularly when it made several interest-rate cuts which stimulated the economy. Hill (2012) submits that the RBA operates as a third peak in the Australian financial regulatory model. The RBA's mandate derives from a number of statutes, such as the Reserve Bank Act 1959, Payment Systems (Regulation) Act 1998, the Payment Systems and Netting Act 1998 and the Corporations Act 2001. The Reserve Bank Act 1959 sets out the 'charter' of the RBA in relation to monetary policy (Reserve Bank Act: section 10(2)) and payment services (Reserve Bank Act: section 10B(3)).

In October 2008, the RBA reduced the interest rate from 7.25 per cent to 6 per cent. The reduction continued till April 2009 when the rate was

3 per cent (Organisation for Economic Co-operation Development 2012; Cusbert and Rohling 2013). The RBA was able to make independent and objective decisions without undue political influences. RBA Governor Glenn Stevens showed independence, leadership and determination in making these decisions. Yet the RBA's decisiveness in cutting interest rates has been criticised for being too aggressive (Eslake 2009). October 2008 was an important month for the RBA because the Australian economy was in a fragile state. Financial-asset prices dropped dramatically and confidence amongst consumers and businesses was weak (McDonald and Morling 2011). Between November 2008 and early 2009, Australian equity prices dropped more than equity prices in the US (McDonald and Morling 2011); but, in October 2009, the RBA was one of the first central banks to increase interest rates in order to keep inflation in check as the economy started to grow (Australian House of Representatives 2009) as result of the earlier, decisive cuts in interest rates (McDonald and Morling 2011). However, there were some problems associated with the RBA's deftness in its decisions (Wettenhall 2011). For example, the government did not mention at first that the guarantee of bank deposits would involve a fee. The subsequent announcement of a fee was necessary and involved unpopular changes (Wettenhall 2011). Given that time is of the essence in a crisis and decisiveness by the RBA was needed to restore confidence, it is understandable why the RBA made such a mistake.

The RBA played an important role in shaping responses to the financial crisis. It introduced a number of liquidity-support packages during the crisis to maintain financial stability. These included a deposit-insurance scheme, a wholesale-funding scheme, allowing covered bonds, a residential-mortgage-backed-securities initiative and a ban on short-selling (Brown and Davis 2010; Hill 2012). The financial crisis of 2007–9 acted as a catalyst to boost depositor protection. Till the crisis, Australia did not operate a deposit-guarantee scheme. It had however, a depositor-preference scheme. This prioritised the claims of Australian depositors over the claims of other unsecured creditors if a deposit-taking institution failed (Turner 2011). The absence of a deposit-guarantee scheme was due to a very low failure rate of deposit-taking institutions in Australia. Banks such as the state banks of Victoria and South Australia and the Pyramid Building Society failed in the mid 1980s, but depositors did not bear the costs of these failures (Turner 2011). Interconnectedness and the contagion effect of the global financial crisis provided an impetus to enhance the crisis-management powers of the APRA. The Financial Claims Scheme, the Australian deposit-guarantee scheme, was thus introduced shortly after the global financial crisis started. Under the Financial Claims Scheme, Kevin Rudd's government gave the APRA stronger powers to intervene in ailing banks (Hill 2012). Initially, there was no cap to the amount guaranteed to depositors of authorised deposit-taking institutions under the Financial Claims Scheme, but the RBA criticised this decision, warning the APRA that large institutional investors could take advantage of the scheme by injecting large sums of money into Australian banks. This became a reality, and the Treasury, on the advice of the Council of Financial Regulators, replaced the 'no-cap' deposit guarantee with a guarantee scheme of AUD$1 million. In 2012, the Treasury reassessed the Financial Claims Scheme. Following the re-assessment, each depositor is protected up to AUD$250,000 per deposit-taking institution. It is evident that the government made a mistake when it introduced a no-cap guarantee. The RBA was swift in challenging the government's decision when it observed that large institutional investors took advantage of it. The Treasury and the Council of Financial Regulators also worked together to resolve this matter. The Australian regulators demonstrated good communication and co-operation skills.

The second type of explicit guarantee provided by the Australian government was the wholesale-funding guarantee. A unique feature of Australian banks is their heavy reliance on wholesale funding: it constitutes around 35 per cent of the total funding in Australian banks (Stewart *et al.* 2013). As the financial crisis of 2007–9 worsened in late 2008, it became apparent that the Australian government had to step in and inject liquidity into the banking system. The Australian wholesale-funding guarantee was better than the scheme in other jurisdictions, such as the US and UK, for two reasons. First, there was enormous flexibility because there was no set date when the guarantee would come to an end. It was a temporary guarantee to be terminated when market conditions improved (Hill 2012). The fee to access the guarantee was also lower in Australia. The Australian regulatory bodies had to bow to pressure from international banks with branches in Australia. Since they were operating as branches, they could not access the deposit- or wholesale-guarantee scheme. Thus, in October 2008, the Treasurer permitted these branches to access both schemes. Although this can be seen as succumbing to bank lobbying, such explicit guarantee schemes did not have any social costs. The deposit- and wholesale-guarantee schemes were not 'bailout' measures, so the Australian regulators managed to provide financial stability without imposing costs on taxpayers.

Prior to the introduction of a deposit-guarantee scheme, deposit-taking institutions were banned from issuing covered bonds (Turner 2011). The reason for the ban was that depositors would have less protection than covered bondholders, since the latter would have preference over the former. However, the Australian government allowed the issue of covered bonds under the Financial Claims Scheme. This gave Australian deposit-taking institutions more choice regarding funding options. In the build-up to the financial crisis of 2007–9, Australian banks relied predominantly on the wholesale market for funding. Since the financial crisis, however, Australian banks have relied less on wholesale funding and more on deposits. Depositors are further protected by the Banking Amendment (Covered Bonds) Act 2011, which stipulates that the value of the assets in the covered-bond pools should not exceed 8 per cent of the total value of assets in the deposit-taking institution (Turner 2011). The cap protects depositors by ensuring that deposit-taking institutions can pay depositors if there is a bank run.

The RBA was more creative in designing liquidity packages than other central banks (Eslake 2009). This is demonstrated by the way the RBA and the government broadened its range of collateral to include residential-mortgage-backed securities for repurchase agreements (Brown and Davis 2010). They also increased the term of the repurchase agreement to one year. This policy meant that the RBA did not have to introduce quantitative easing into the economy, unlike the central banks in the US and UK. In December 2008, the government and the four major Australian banks (National Australia Bank, Commonwealth Bank of Australia, ANZ Banking Group and Westpac Banking Corporation) created a special purpose vehicle called 'Ozcar' to provide funding for car dealers when GE Money and GMAC Financial Services withdrew funding facilities (Brown and Davis 2010). Hill (2012) submits that by widening the range and term of the collateral, the Australian banking sector became even more concentrated. The smaller non-bank organisations relied heavily on the residential-mortgage-backed-securities market as they could not access the deposit- or wholesale-guarantee scheme. Despite the inclusion of residential-mortgage-backed securities as collateral, second-tier banks and non-bank lenders were overwhelmed by the financial crisis. A number of second-tier banks merged and several non-bank lenders disappeared. Westpac Banking Corporation took over St George Bank and the Commonwealth Bank of Australia took over BankWest (Hill 2012). The big four Australian banks controlled 90 per cent of the mortgage market by 2011. They have become too big to fail and too big to merge. This issue will be discussed later in the chapter.

The final policy response, the ban on short-selling, attracted the most criticism. Short-selling was rumoured to have occurred at ABC Learning and Allco Finance, which later failed (Hill 2012). The attempt to ban short-selling was designed to restore market confidence. The ASIC and the Australian Securities Exchange banned naked short-selling on 22 September 2008 (Beber and Pagano 2010). Two days later, the ban was extended to short-selling. A partial ban on 18 November 2008 lifted the restriction on non-financial securities, and the ban was finally lifted on 25 May 2009 (Beber and Pagano 2010). The Australian ban on short-selling was longer and stricter than those in the US, UK, Canada and Germany in terms of duration and scope. The US and Canada lifted the ban on financial securities on 8 October 2008, whilst the UK lifted its ban on 16 January 2009. The ASIC and the Australian Securities Exchange were criticised for acting too hastily and failing to provide clear guidance on the rules (Hill 2012).

Empirical evidence on the correlation between a ban on short-selling and liquidity is mixed. Boehmer *et al.* (2013) studied the effect of the short-selling ban in the US between 8 September and 8 October 2008. They discovered that the ban had a negative impact on the liquidity of shares subject to the ban. They measured liquidity by spreads and price impact. Kolasinksi *et al.*'s study confirms that a ban on naked short-selling in June 2008 had an adverse effect on liquidity (Kolasinksi *et al.* 2010). Yet older studies into the correlation between short-selling and liquidity produced different results. Jones and Owen (2002) found that a ban on short-selling in 1938 had a positive effect on liquidity. Another study by Charoenrook and Daouk (2009) discovered that restrictions on short-selling produced greater liquidity. It should be noted that they measured liquidity by trade volume and that this has been argued to be a poor indicator of liquidity (Beber and Pagano 2010). Beber and Pagano (2010) investigated the effect of a short-selling ban on liquidity between September 2008 and June 2009 in 30 countries. In their research, liquidity is measured by the bid–ask spread and the Amihud illiquidity ratio. Their results revealed that the short-selling ban in Australia had a serious negative impact on market liquidity and that Australia ranked fourth in deterioration of market liquidity. Canada and the UK fared better than the US and Australia. The ban on short-selling in Australia could thus be construed as an expensive mistake in light of the costs of the liquidity measures.

To summarise, the RBA acted swiftly, decisively and creatively in its policy decisions during the crisis. It was independent and successfully challenged the government's policy on the no-cap deposit-guarantee scheme. The liquidity-support packages were innovative and did not impose social costs on taxpayers in Australia. The RBA also managed interest rates well, both before and during the financial crisis. Australia's economy was strong because of its resilient financial system. The RBA's responses were also effective because of Australia's inherent robust financial system in comparison to the weak financial systems in the UK and the US (McDonald and Morling 2011). Criticisms have, however, been levelled at the ASIC and the Australian Securities Exchange for the duration and scope of the short-selling ban.

Macro- and micro-prudential regulatory frameworks in Australia 2007–9

Despite excellent results, the Australian regulators are not complacent. Although the AFSI did not recommend any changes to the financial architecture of the regulators, it recommended the following improvements to the regulatory system. First, that a new Financial Regulator Assessment Board be established to improve accountability of the financial regulators. Second, due to the high concentration of the banking sector, that the ASIC be given a mandate to consider competition and conduct reviews every three years in relation to competition in the banking sector. Third, that the financial regulators receive funding and appropriate regulatory tools to deliver their mandates properly. Finally, that the process of implementing new financial regulations be improved (Australian Financial Stability Inquiry 2013). The banking sector is constantly changing due to market and technological developments. It is thus encouraging to see that the AFSI is receptive to changes. The second part of this chapter will examine three important areas for improvement in the Australian regulatory framework. The areas are improving accountability and effectiveness of the regulators, consumer protection and more focus on competition (Australian Financial Stability Inquiry 2013).

Improving accountability of the Australian regulators

Chapter 5 of the Wallis Inquiry provides the regulatory principles which guide the Australian prudential supervisory regime. They are: competitive neutrality, cost effectiveness, transparency, flexibility and accountability. Competitive neutrality means that no financial institution in Australia is at an advantage or disadvantage. It has been argued that prudential supervision based on financial products rather than institutions is more effective, efficient and provides a level playing field (Hogan and Sharpe 1990). Cost effectiveness requires minimal state intervention unless there is a reason for it. It also tries to avoid duplicates and overlaps of responsibility amongst the regulators. The principle of transparency covers all communication, promises and duties between the regulators, the regulated and the buyers of financial products and services; and since the financial market evolves with time and technological developments, flexibility is key to the Australian financial regulatory regime. Finally, the principle of accountability demands that Australian regulators be equipped with skilled staff and that regulators are answerable to stakeholders and subject to regular reviews. The five regulatory principles are important in shaping the Australian legislative and regulatory frameworks. The Wallis Inquiry decided that the main purpose of financial regulation is to counteract market failure. Markets become inefficient for four main reasons: anti-competitive behaviour, market misconduct, information asymmetry and systemic instability (Carmichael 2004). Having carefully considered these reasons, the Wallis Inquiry decided that having four separate regulatory agencies is most suitable for Australian banking regulation. Each of these four regulators is responsible for dealing with one source of market failure.

It is clear that, although Australian regulators generally performed well, the RBA and APRA did better than the ASIC and ACCC. The AFSI was therefore keen to see that the government can assess the performances of the RBA, APRA and ASIC in the regulation of the payment function (Australian Financial Stability Inquiry 2013). It called for performance indicators to be made available. Further, a new Financial Regulator Assessment Board (FRAB) will produce an annual report informing the Australian government how the regulators have performed. The main task of the FRAB is to report on how the regulators have balanced the competing challenges in their mandates. For example, the APRA's role in financial stability is set out in the Australian Prudential Regulatory Authority Act 1998. The aims are 'financial safety and efficiency, competition, contestability and competitive neutrality'. Previous legislation, however, is inconsistent with regards to competition and efficiency. The Banking Act 1959 and Superannuation (Industry) Supervision Act 1993 do not mention either aim. Yet the Insurance Act 1973 and Life Insurance Act 1995 state that both aims are regulatory objectives (subject to industry viability). There is no reference to efficiency. The Australian Securities and Investments Commission Act 2001 requires the ASIC to promote commercial certainty, economic development and efficiency whilst reducing business costs. However, the aim of competition is not mentioned in the Australian Securities and Investments Commission Act 2001 or chapter 7 of the Corporations Act 2001. Rather than increasing accountability by calling for performance indicators and producing a report for the FRAB, costs would be better incurred giving a specific competition mandate to the ASIC. The danger with performance indicators is that regulators might choose to target more straightforward cases to aim for a higher success rate. Bird (2011) argues that increasing accountability mechanisms will not increase a regulator's performance in accountability objectives such as efficiency and effectiveness. In fact, such mechanisms will actually 'erode regulator expertise and independence'.

The RBA also has to balance competing regulatory objectives. Its payment mandate is outlined in section 10(B)(3) of the Reserve Bank Act 1959. The RBA is responsible for financial stability, controlling risks in the financial system, promoting competition and efficiency. In the AFSI's Final Report (2013), only the aims of financial stability and controlling risks were mentioned. If financial stability is the chief objective, then producing Financial Stability Reviews is better than other communication channels to achieve this objective (Born *et al.* 2013). Born *et al.* (2013) studied more than 1,000 financial-stability reviews, speeches and interviews of central banks in 37 countries between 1996 and 2009. Their results revealed that financial-stability reviews have a long-lasting effect on market returns and reduce market volatility. Speeches and interviews will have a wider appeal amongst the public, but if stability is to be achieved then more resources should be spent on financial-stability reviews. Further, the RBA has clear accountability duties to Parliament under the Reserve Bank Act 1959 and Public Governance, Performance and Accountability Act 2013. Scrutiny through parliamentary committees is one way of examining whether a regulator achieves its mandate, and such scrutiny is specialised. However, Born *et al.* (2013) believe that it is a weak form of accountability because responses to parliamentary committee reports are political pressure. Yet the UK House of Commons Treasury Select Committee on Banking Standards proved that political pressure can lead to transparency. The publication of the Bank of England Court of Directors' minutes is a clear example of lifting the veil of secrecy from the Bank of England.

The new FRAB mechanism may pose a threat to the independence of the RBA. Under section 13 of the Reserve Bank Act 1959, the RBA and the government have to liaise closely in relation to matters which affect both parties. If the Australian government and the Reserve Bank Board cannot agree, the latter will produce a statement to the government on the matter under section 11 of the Reserve Bank Act 1959. The government will refer it to the Governor-General, who can determine the policy to be adopted by the Reserve Bank. The Reserve Bank Board will then have to accept and implement the decision. It is important to note that section 11 has never been used to date (Reserve Bank of Australia 2014). In light of this, it is arguable whether there is need for a formal mechanism of accountability to the government from the RBA. Unnecessary accountability will only generate more costs and bureaucracy. The independence of the RBA proved to be a positive asset of the Australian regulatory system and it should remain as a strength.

Delivering the regulators' mandates effectively with the right tools

The second area of improvement is that regulators should be well-equipped to cope with the conflicting objectives in their mandates. This is sensible, and the financial crisis has exposed gaps in resources, skills and legislative and regulatory frameworks. Starting with the APRA, its prudential regulatory powers are rather limited in comparison to those of the FSA in the UK. The APRA has three main types of powers: authorisation or licensing powers, supervision and monitoring powers and powers to help financially distressed banks to protect depositors (Cooper 2006). The FSA, on the other hand, had greater powers under sections 138–76 of the Financial Services Markets Act 2000. In particular, the FSA had rule-making and investigative powers, including the ability to make rules regarding price stability, money-laundering and financial promotion (FSMA 2000: sections 144–7). The FSA could ask authorised bodies for information which might be relevant to the financial stability of the UK system and appoint investigators to carry out relevant investigations (FSMA 2000: sections 165–8). The statutory objectives in the FSMA 2000 were also wider. The legal framework in the UK was used to 'set the strategic direction of the regulator, not just to allocate supervisory resources' (Black 2004). In comparison, the Australian legal framework is restricted to allocating supervisory resources and, to a limited degree, formulating a supervisory strategy.

The APRA's powers had to be strengthened during the financial crisis of 2007–9. As banks struggled to cope with the contagion effect of the crisis, the Legislation Amendment (Financial Claims Scheme and Other Measures) Act 2008 (hereafter, the 2008 Act) was passed. This Act gave the APRA stronger powers to intervene in ailing banks, since time is of the essence in a crisis. Section 9.1 of the 2008 Act enables the APRA to collect data for the purpose of prudential regulation or monitoring of banks. The data also facilitates the RBA to make decisions regarding monetary policy. Section 13 of the 2008 Act is a further legislative attempt to enhance the relationship between the APRA and RBA: the APRA can assist the RBA to respond to financial threats and to determine what action should be taken.

Overall, however, the APRA's regulatory approach was successful (Wettenhall 2011). Its proactive, interventionist supervisory style was praised, and it received positive feedback in the APRA Stakeholder Survey 2015. The best scores were given to staff attitude, the single supervisory team for group companies, communication methods, the prudential framework and enforcement of prudential requirements. These high scores confirm that the APRA has addressed the weaknesses of structure, staff, resources and prudential regulation highlighted in the HIH Royal Commission (2003) and the Palmer Report (2002). It is encouraging to see that the APRA framework for prudential supervision is considered effective in achieving its mission. The APRA uses a risk-based, principle-based and outcome-focused style of regulation. Such a combination means that the APRA can allocate resources effectively to high-risks organisations and concentrate on the end results and tailored outcomes rather than the processes used. The unique regulatory style is an affirmation of the APRA's values. The APRA's Framework for Prudential Supervision contains five important values: foresight, accountability, collaboration, integrity and professionalism (Australian Prudential Regulatory Authority 2013). In pursuing these values, the APRA is committed to providing consistent, high-quality supervision in a fair and balanced manner.

After the HIH incident, the APRA also realised that it is important to have skilled staff with the relevant training to deal with prudential supervision, especially of high-risk institutions. The APRA thus adopted a single, integrated risk-based framework, having carefully considered the risk models of the US, Canada and the UK. The US uses a CAMELS risk framework, which stands for Capital, Asset quality, Management, Earnings, Liquidity and Sensitivity to market risk. Each element is given a rating of 1–5, with 1 being the best. The average rating of the six elements is called the composite rating. Banks with an average rating of 5 are of greatest supervisory concern (Coleman 2008). In Canada, the Supervisory Framework assesses the inherent risks of significant activities carried out by banks. Inherent risks can be divided into six types: credit risk, market risk, insurance risk, operational risk, regulatory compliance risk and strategic risk. Each risk is given a level: low, moderate, above average or high. The level of risk will then influence how much control and supervision the supervisor has over a bank (Office of the Superintendent of Financial Institutions 2010). The ARROW II risk framework in the UK is more detailed than the US or Canadian framework in that it divides risks into 52 elements and 10 groups. Each risk is given a level: low, medium-low, medium-high and high. Banks with medium-high and high levels are visited regularly by the supervisor (Petch 2011).

The APRA's risk-based supervisory model consists of PAIRS and SOARS. PAIRS stands for the Probability and Impact Ratings System, and SOARS stands for the Supervisory Oversight and Response System. PAIRS and SOARS were influenced by the Canadian financial regulator, OSFI, and the UK financial regulator, the FSA. Yet the APRA created its own risk-based model, and there are three main differences between the APRA's model and the OSFI's model. First, PAIRS is more radical than the Canadian model because the former goes further and links the concept of 'overall risk of failure' with the APRA's statutory objectives (Black 2004). Secondly, PAIRS produces an overall rating of risks by relying on a formal system of weighted risk assessments (Black 2004). Finally, influenced by the UK risk-based model, the APRA incorporated the requirement of an impact assessment (Black 2004; Laker 2007). It considers the overall economic consequence of a regulated institution's failure.

The APRA's framework for prudential supervision is guided by three principles: flexibility, efficiency and effectiveness. The APRA, as the financial regulator, has to adapt to changes in financial services and technology, so flexibility is important to the survival and reputation of the regulator. Flexibility is often combined with consistency when the APRA decides whether to give its approval to certain activities to be carried out by regulated organisations. The APRA will construe legislation, prudential standards and guidance when conducting a risk assessment of the supervised organisation. The APRA can make structural or prudential approvals. Structural changes can arise through a merger, a sale of business or internal restructuring. Structural changes can affect the staffing and future financial viability of the business. Prudential approvals are given by the APRA to supervised organisations in areas such as capital adequacy and operational risks. Efficiency is one of the key words mentioned in the APRA's mission statement. It fits in with the APRA's regulatory style based on risks, principles and outcomes, because high-risk organisations are given more resources and supervision so that risks are better managed and contained.

The APRA's funding costs for resources are met by the regulated organisations. This is not the case for the ASIC, however. The financial crisis exposed the lack of funding at the ASIC in relation to consumer protection. The AFSI (2013) and Senate Inquiry into ASIC (Industry Super Australia 2013) call for the ASIC to be funded by the banking industry so that there is more stability and resources for the ASIC's increased role. The ASIC has very limited powers to recruit staff since it is subject to the Public Service Act 1999. The ability to attract and recruit highly skilled, quality staff to the ASIC is important. Therefore, a suggestion has been made to remove the ASIC from the scope of the Public Service Act 1999. Regular reviews of human resources will also help identify gaps in skills and talent in the workforce. The AFSI (2013) thus recommended that both the APRA and ASIC conduct six-yearly reviews in this area.

Consumer protection

Financial markets are irrational and unpredictable – market participants can behave like animals and display 'herding' traits (Akerlof and Schiller 2009). Even the most savvy investors will suffer losses in financial investments. In the global financial crisis, many retail and institutional investors suffered financial losses due to exposure to high-risk financial products (Brown and Davis 2010). Since all employed Australians have a superannuation scheme under the Superannuation Guarantee (Administration) Act 1992, many of them witnessed a decrease in the value of their retirement savings (Gallery and Gallery 2010). It has been suggested that the global financial crisis provided an opportunity for investors to rethink whether they are paying enough attention to their investments (Bowerman 2009). To encourage investors to monitor their investments more regularly, the AFSI Final Report (2013) recommended increasing the public's financial literacy skills, aligning the interests of financial organisations and consumers and increasing the financial standards of financial advisors. The challenge in enabling the public to make informed decisions about investment choices is that the ASIC needs to allow investors to discover their own behavioural biases such as over-confidence and taking excessive risks and then produce specific policies to address gaps in financial literacy skills (Gallery and Gallery 2010). Although the ASIC has conducted financial-literacy campaigns over the years, such as Investing between the Flags, it adopts a one-size-fits-all approach and does not take into account behavioural biases.

Corporate governance and financial regulation are inseparable when it comes to aligning the interests of financial organisations and consumers. The principal–agent theory stems from the concern that managers (agents) will pursue their own interests and indulge in perks whilst bearing only a proportion of the costs. Imperfect information (hidden action) and misaligned incentives (hidden information) between principal and agent are the causes of this fear. Financial organisations have wider stakeholders, such as depositors and customers. In Australia, high upfront commission paid to life-insurance advisers created a 'sales' culture within the industry. Ninety-six per cent of the advice given to life-insurance customers was of poor quality due to this perverse incentive (Australian Financial Stability Inquiry 2013). A suggestion has thus been made to amend the law so that upfront commission cannot be greater than ongoing commission (Australian Financial Stability Inquiry 2013). Short-termism in the financial industry has created a culture lacking in ethical values and weak in customer relationships. The current ASIC framework does not allow the regulator to prevent senior bank managers with poor operating habits from managing a new organisation. The Financial Stability Inquiry therefore recommends that poor managers who do not comply with good governance practice be removed by the ASIC.

Lo (2009) argued that the global financial crisis was caused by inexperienced bank officials and directors who 'did not fully understand the risks of the securities in which they were investing'. Although the structure of residential-mortgage-backed securities is not too complex, transactions involving such securities are highly complicated (Gelpern and Levitin 2008). Financial advisers are required under the Corporations Act 2001 to meet certain standards and licences. For example, advisers selling securities, derivatives and superannuation are under the Tier 1 category and thus have a qualification equivalent to a diploma. Financial advisers selling Tier 2 products, such as simple and general banking products, will be subject to less stringent qualifications and standards. Nevertheless, recent ASIC studies (2012) showed that feedback on financial advice given to customers was generally negative. Thirty-nine per cent of the respondents said that the advice given on retirement was 'poor' (Australian Securities and Investments Commission 2012). It therefore seems sensible that qualifications for Tier 1 advisers should be raised. The AFSI's recommendations are that they should have a higher-education degree, competence in a specific field, such as securities, and attend continuous professional-development courses (Australian Financial Stability Inquiry 2013). Such suggestions – and that the ASIC is to create an enhanced, public register of advisers with details of their skills, qualifications and expertise – are to be commended for providing stronger consumer protection. There will be cost implications for such suggestions, but a transition period should provide efficiency.

The two most interesting AFSI recommendations are to oblige financial organisations to design and sell tailored financial products and for the AFSI itself to have temporary product-intervention power. A principle- and risk-based regulatory approach has been recommended in the hope of detecting consumers' behaviourial biases. This is commendable since it should address the behaviourial biases mentioned by Gallery and Gallery (2010). The risk-based approach is in line with the APRA's regulatory philosophy, too. Regulating human behaviour is an extremely difficult task, and no amount of legislation or regulation will provide an absolutely watertight system, due to regulatory arbitrage by perpetrators. A zero-failure regulatory policy is not part of the Australian regulatory philosophy (Black 2006; Cooper 2006). Rather, the rationale of the Australian regulatory regime is to minimise the impact of any potential financial crisis. PAIRS and SOARS have improved the organisational and cultural dimensions of Australian prudential regulation and supervision. From an organisational perspective, PAIRS and SOARS provide a more coherent and unified risk-based model.

Since PAIRS and SOARS have been implemented, the APRA has become more proactive, intervened earlier and increased its on-site visits by 20 per cent (Black 2004; Parliament of Australia Department of Parliamentary Services 2005). The proactive supervisory style has led the APRA to interpret its statutory powers under section 8 of the Australian Prudential Regulatory Authority Act 1998 more widely (in the HIH Royal Commission, the APRA submitted that it felt it could only use its formal legal powers when an organisation is on the verge of financial failure). Finally, the risk-based model of PAIRS and SOARS provides a useful shield against the criticisms of the APRA for rogue trading in National Australia Bank in 2004. This incident led to a loss of around AUD$360 million. The APRA was able to defend its position by explaining that it used a consistent, logical risk-based model to decide which organisations are high-risk and therefore require the allocation of more resources.

A principle- and risk-based approach by the ASIC should be more effective than trying to protect consumers via disclosure. Disclosure can improve transparency but is by no means a panacea for transparency and accountability issues. Disclosure is not effective when consumers' financial literary skills are weak, when there is a lack of engagement from consumers, when products are complex and when interests are misaligned (Australian Financial Stability Inquiry 2013). The Financial Services Reform Act 2001 promotes informed decision-making amongst consumers, so disclosure is essential to achieve this aim. Sellers of financial products must produce public-disclosure statements for consumers under the Corporations Act 2001. This Act does not prescribe what should be included in public-disclosure statements; flexibility, not rigid adherence, was intended. Therefore, the ASIC has issued its own Good Disclosure Principles to assist sellers in drafting public-disclosure statements. The principles include timely disclosure, promoting understanding and having regard to consumers' needs (Gallery and Gallery 2010). Yet many consumers found these principles and guidances too long and complex (Sherry and Tanner 2008).

Another method of protecting consumers is the increase in the ASIC's enforcement powers. Under the Australian Securities and Investments Commission Act 2001, the ASIC has a large range of enforcement powers. Less serious actions are merely persuasive, but serious breaches of the law will lead to punitive sanctions, which include imprisonment, financial penalties and disqualification of directors (Australian Securities and Investments Commission 2015b). The latest six-monthly report from the ASIC highlights its attempt to recover compensation for investors and customers. Examples include a fine of AUD\$5 million against Westpac Banking Corporation to compensate its investors, a AUD\$2.2 million fine against the Commonwealth Bank of Australia and a fine of AUD\$75 million to compensate customers of the Australia and New Zealand Banking Group (Australian Securities and Investments Commission 2015a). Yet the current legislative framework is inadequate because ASIC can only intervene when it is too late, i.e. when a consumer suffers detriment due to a breach in the law. The AFSI's recommendation is that the ASIC should be more proactive and interventionist, like the APRA. The ASIC could then intervene when it believes that there is a risk to consumers after conducting a risk assessment. The power enables the ASIC to amend marketing materials, warn customers and ban products. The power is temporary and lasts for 12 months, but it can be extended if more time is required by financial organisations (Australian Financial Stability Inquiry 2013). The FCA in the UK has similar powers: it could restrict the distribution of contingent convertible instruments between October 2014 and October 2015 (Financial Conduct Authority 2014). The ASIC Stakeholder Survey 2013 (Australian Securities and Investments Commission 2013) also expressed the view that the ASIC should investigate breaches of the law earlier to prevent rather than treat the breach.

Competition law and banking stability

The academic debate on the correlation between competition law and banking stability is inconclusive. Empirical studies supporting the 'competition stability' view reveal that there is a risk of bank failures in more concentrated markets where there is less competition (Boyd and De Nicolo 2005; Boyd *et al.* 2006). Schaeck *et al.* (2006) support this view as their research shows that more competitive banking systems are more stable since they have lower likelihoods of bank failure. On the other hand, scholars supporting the 'competition fragility' view argue that more competition increases financial instability because competition reduces market power, profit margins and the franchise value of banks (Berger *et al.* 2008). As a result of these factors, banks are motivated by perverse incentives to take on more risks to increase their profits (Carletti and Hartmann 2003). It is important to note, however, that even if a bank has a high loan risk and bank exposure, it can reduce its overall risk portfolio by holding more capital or selling some of its loans (Berger *et al.* 2008). Holding more capital is therefore essential for financial stability. Banks argue that increasing capital levels also add to compliance costs. However, Admati *et al.* (2010) submit that bank equity is not expensive. This is because banks which are better capitalised have fewer incentives to take excessive risks and are less affected by distortions created by 'debt overhang'. 'Debt overhang' refers to the condition in which a bank has so much debt that it cannot take on further debt to finance projects even though those projects may be profitable enough to decrease its overall indebtedness. Admati *et al.* (2010) argue, too, that 'better capitalised banks suffer fewer distortions in lending decisions and would perform better'. It has been suggested that to reduce lending costs banks should increase contestability and search for alternative financing models. Contestability involves measures such as making it easier for customers to change accounts, whilst alternative funding models include peer-to-peer lending.

Competition is an essential tenet of Australian financial regulatory philosophy. Deregulation in the 1980s led to four major banks competing in Australia. Successive governments first supported the 'six pillars' policy then the 'four pillars' policy. The six-pillars policy prohibited the four major Australian banks and two largest Australian life-insurance companies from merging with each other. The Wallis Inquiry (Financial System Inquiry Final Report 1997) debated whether the six-pillars policy should be retained. Opinions were diverse. The four major banks asked for the six-pillars policy to be removed. They wanted to grow in size and become more competitive in the global financial market. Other stakeholders were more sceptical. The RBA and the Treasury were worried about the prudential regulatory impact if there were only two banks in Australia (Reserve Bank of Australia 1996). Trade unions and consumer groups were concerned about potential job losses and the social costs if there were mergers leading to redundancies. The Wallis Inquiry (Financial System Inquiry Final Report 1997) was not convinced by the prudential regulatory differences between the failure of a massive bank and a major Australian bank. It therefore recommended the abolition of the six-pillars policy. It also required the ASIC to assess each matter on a case-by-case approach, rather than issuing a complete ban on all mergers (Wu 2008). The Australian government, however, did not adopt the Wallis

Inquiry's recommendation. It was conscious of strong public opposition to mergers between the big four banks. Thus, a modified version of the six-pillars policy was born in 1997: the four-pillars policy. This policy prohibits the four major banks from merging with each other, although a foreign takeover of an Australian bank is permitted. There are around 59 foreign banks operating in Australia. Although only a number of them operate as subsidiaries and can therefore compete in the retail and loan deposit markets, internet-only deposits and aggressive marketing increased competition (Davis 2011).

The four major banks are still advocating for the four-pillars policy to be removed so that they can compete better internationally (Cicutto 2002). In March 2010, the four major Australian banks owned a 73.4 per cent share of the market (Davis 2011). Wu's research into bank competition and financial stability reveals that the four-pillars policy should stay. Wu studied the effect of bank mergers in Australia between 1987 and 2000 and found that mergers between the four banks might lead to a less efficient financial sector. Differences in size, efficiency and style between the acquiring and targeted banks could lead to scale inefficiency. The acquiring banks in Wu's research were bigger, more aggressive and less efficient than the target banks (Wu 2008). Therefore, removing the four-pillars policy might not bring with it the desired results, as advocated by the Australian banking industry. Nevertheless, banking regulation is constantly moving and shaped by technological and international regulatory policies. Constant review of competitiveness at local and international levels is thus required. The AFSI recommended that regulators should conduct three-yearly reviews into the competitiveness of Australian financial system. It also recommended that regulators must be able to demonstrate how they balance competition with the other regulatory objectives. The ASIC currently does not have a mandate to take competition into account. The current legislative framework does not give details as to how the regulators should balance the competing objectives. The AFSI therefore suggested that the ASIC have an explicit mandate to consider competition issues. This mandate will be useful since the long-term effect of the deposit- and wholesale-guarantee schemes and competition law remains to be resolved. As we saw earlier, branches of foreign banks cannot benefit from the deposit- or wholesale-guarantee schemes. Yet their lobbying pressure meant that Australian regulators had to provide these branches with access to the guarantee schemes. It is evident from this incident that, despite the legal framework, political lobbying and the interconnected nature of international banking will have implications for competition in Australian banking.

To counter this, it is important that Australia maintains a robust funding model and supervisory regime. Since the global financial crisis, 'conservatism' has been the key word in the Australian funding model. It relies heavily on deposits, has high capital levels and uses wholesale funding with longer maturity terms (Davis 2011). Deposits are more stable than other sources of funding, such as residential-mortgage-backed securities, which are more expensive. At the micro level, Australian banks have increased deposit funding to reduce liquidity risks. At the macro level, more deposits provide better protection from externalities in the wholesale-funding markets. Capital should act as an absorber to externalities. Indeed, one of the areas of improvement in macro-prudential regulation is a higher capital ratio (World Economic Forum 2012). However, some banking professionals argue that high levels of capital would not have prevented the recent financial crisis (Financial Services Authority 2010). Higher capital retention alone would not be the solution. Better-quality capital is the key to better absorption of shock. Blundell-Wignall and Atkinson (2010) have produced a table which shows that some US and European banks' losses would have absorbed all or most of their capital during the crisis. Their calculation is based on the new leverage ratio (equity less goodwill) under Basel III. Australian banks had 0.2 per cent non-performing loans to total loans in 2004–7, rising to 0.8 per cent in 2008 and 1.1 per cent in 2010. UK banks hovered at 1 per cent in 2002–6, rising to 1.6 per cent in 2009 and 3.3 per cent in 2010 (International Monetary Fund 2010). A better quality of assets is thus important for absorbing losses.

Basel III recommendations include higher and better-quality capital, a counter-cyclical buffer of 0–2.5 per cent, a Tier 1 leverage ratio (ratio of book capital to assets) of minimum 3 per cent and maintenance of minimum liquidity. Tier 1 capital ratio will increase from a minimum 4 per cent to 6 per cent, but the overall capital ratio remains at a minimum of 8 per cent. There is some flexibility for national differences in adoption and implementation by way of a 'comply or explain' provision. Changes will be implemented gradually till 2019. Basel III recommendations are necessary to address the problems encountered by several UK banks during the crisis. Problems, however, exist. Basel III fails to address the problem of regulatory dialectic in the shadow banking sector. Basel III applies only to banks, not the shadow banking sector. Thus, many banks will continue circumventing Basel III rules by relying on securitisation, a way to create apparently risk-free assets out of risky pools. Although the shadow banking sector is only a small part of the Australian financial sector (Davis 2011), Australian regulators have recently increased regulation of shadow banking institutions. The ASIC now grants licences and imposes certain obligations on them. The regulatory coverage of credit products under the National Consumer Credit Code has been expanded to include investor-housing mortgages.

It is evident to Australian regulators that deposit funding is important and is likely to remain so. The introduction of the deposit-guarantee scheme seems to confirm this. However, there are issues with such a scheme. The deposit-guarantee scheme will reduce the risk of a bank run but not of insolvency. It is primarily a method of maintaining confidence and financial stability in an economy. Yet it increases moral hazard, whereby taxpayers usually bear the burden of paying for the mistakes of bankers, and actually weakens the robustness of a banking system. With less incentive to monitor banks and a guarantee that depositors are protected up to AUD$250,000 at each deposit-taking institution, it is no surprise that there are criticisms. First, a deposit-guarantee scheme contravenes the essence of the Wallis Report (Financial System Inquiry Final Report 1997): banks should be allowed to fail. Australian banks are now too big to fail and too big to merge. Wallis advocated for keeping the depositor-preference scheme, arguing that a depositor-guarantee scheme would not offer much greater protection. However, it is clear from the global financial crisis that a deposit-guarantee scheme was necessary due to the contagion effect of systemic risks. Tighter supervision of banks is thus needed. Second, moral hazard leads to banks taking more and even excessive risks. A deposit-guarantee scheme thus has implications for a country's stability and regulatory framework. Countries with weak regulatory frameworks are unable to deal with such perverse incentives (Demirguc-Kunt and Detragiache 2002). Fortunately, Australia has a strong regulatory framework with a robust supervisory regime (Stewart *et al.* 2013). Provided that Australian banks hold high levels of good-quality capital and maintain a conservative funding portfolio, with regulators maintaining a tight control, Australia should be able to deal with issues affecting competition and stability.

Conclusion

'Twin peaks' and 'four pillars' proved to be successful ingredients in the resilience of the Australian financial regulatory system. The twin-peaks regulatory model has been tried and tested in Australia since 1997, after the Wallis Inquiry. The success of a regulator depends on whether it has achieved its regulatory objectives. The author submits that the APRA and ASIC were successful in the financial crisis of 2007–9 in achieving the objectives of prudential regulation and conduct of business. Charles Littrell, Executive General Manager of the APRA, said that the APRA was well-prepared for the financial crisis of 2007–9:

> Australian prudentially regulated entities were generally well capitalised, well managed, and understood the risks they were taking. This was not completely the case for every entity, but was close enough to complete to give confidence that the Australian financial system would survive the global financial crisis in reasonably good shape.
>
> (Littrell 2011)

The APRA and ASIC had their own specialist expertise, but they also shared information and co-operated effectively. The Council of Financial Regulators, RBA and Treasury all worked well as a team. The APRA and ASIC have effective prudential regulatory frameworks, bolstered by mandates which allow them to carry out their functions efficiently. The global financial crisis has now given regulators more powers, especially the ASIC in relation to enforcement and competition, which will further enhance their effectiveness and efficiency. One important element of prudential regulatory success is that it covers a wide range of financial institutions, holding a significant amount of assets. The APRA's principle-based, proactive and interventionist regulatory style worked well and has proved to be a fundamental reason for Australia's sound financial regime.

The APRA monitored Australian banks well in general and, most importantly, it was confident about their financial positions. This confidence is vital to maintaining public confidence and financial stability. Meanwhile, the other branch of the twin-peaks model also proved to be successful, although some improvements have to be made. Tony D'Alonsio, Chairman of the ASIC, explained that the objective of regulating business conduct was achieved for several reasons. First, the Financial Services Reform Act 2001 provided a strong regulatory and licensing framework for financial sales and advice. Market integrity was thus possible under the 2001 Act. Second, Ponzi-type schemes had to be registered and faced more risk-management hurdles before they were offered to consumers. Finally, regulatory oversight for auditors offered important protection (D'Alonsio 2010). Nevertheless, the global financial crisis revealed that more resources are required to deal with the magnitude of complex consumer-protection issues. By producing tailored financial advice, it is hoped that more consumers will engage with the ASIC and be able to make informed financial choices. All working employees are part of the compulsory superannuation scheme in Australia, so the ability to make informed financial decisions is important. Consumer protection is thus high on the agenda from a regulator's perspective. Under the new recommendations from the Financial Stability Inquiry, the ASIC will mirror the APRA's regulatory style, so it should become more proactive and interventionist in regulating conduct of business issues. The ASIC will also have more enforcement powers.

The RBA acted decisively and swiftly during the financial crisis. It cut interest rates despite criticisms from the government, thus demonstrating its independence. It introduced a number of liquidity measures, such as the deposit- and wholesale-guarantee schemes, broadening its range of collateral to include residential-mortgage-backed securities for repurchase agreements and a ban on short-selling. The ban on short-selling was criticised, since it had a negative effect on liquidity. It can be seen as an expensive mistake by the ASIC and the Australian Securities Exchange. Nevertheless, the liquidity support packages were innovative and did not impose social costs on taxpayers in Australia.

The four-pillars policy served Australia well, since no merger between the major four Australian banks is permitted. Although the literature on the correlation between competition and financial stability is inconclusive, a number of authors (Brown and Davis 2010; Davis 2011; Wettenhall 2011) are of the view that the four-pillars policy prevented the banks from taking excessive risks. Yet mergers can still take place between second-tier banks and foreign banks on the one hand and the four major banks on the other. Therefore, the new power given to the ASIC in relation to competition is useful. Regular reviews of the state of competitiveness at local and international levels are required.

Conservatism in the funding models of Australian banks is key to its resilience. Low exposure to the sub-prime market and shadow banking sector means that they did not experience the same consequences as the UK and US banking sectors. Australia's strong reliance on off-shore wholesale funding in comparison to other jurisdictions allowed banks to hedge foreign-currency risk. The maturity profile of many Australian wholesale debts was more than a year, and five years for a long-term wholesale debt (Stewart *et al.* 2013). The RBA plays a role in why Australian banks rely heavily on wholesale funding. Conservatism once again is evident because the RBA treats certificates of deposits and intra-group deposits from off-shore funding as wholesale debt. This is in contrast to the Canadian and US approaches, which treat such instruments as deposit liabilities.

Yet due to the contagion effect of systemic risks in an increasingly globalised world, Australia was affected by the global financial crisis. The most interesting effect is the deposit-guarantee scheme and its impact on competition and financial stability. A deposit-guarantee scheme actually weakens the robustness of a banking system due to moral hazard. Provided that Australian banks hold high levels of good-quality capital and maintain a conservative funding portfolio, with regulators maintaining a tight control, Australia should be able to deal with issues affecting competition and stability. The RBA first produced its Financial Stability Review in 2004, and the increased focus on financial stability should remain high on Australian regulators' agendas.

Bibliography

Admati, A., DeMarzo, P., Hellwig, M. and Pfleiderer, P. (2010) *Fallacies, Irrelevant Facts, and Myths in the Discussion of Capital Regulation: Why Bank Equity is Bot Expensive*, Preprints of the Max Planck Institute for Research on Collective Goods.

Akerlof, G. and Schiller, R. (2009) *Animal Spirits: How Human Psychology Drives the Economy and Why It Matters for Global Capitalism*, Princeton: Princeton University Press.

Australian Financial Stability Inquiry (2013) *Financial Stability Inquiry Final Report*, Australia: http://fsi.gov.au/publications/final-report/executive-summary/ [accessed 12 March 2015].

Australian House of Representatives (2009) *House of Representatives Official Hansard*, 17, Australia: Australian House of Representatives.

Australian Prudential Regulatory Authority (2013) 'Supervision Blueprint' [online], available: http://www.apra.gov.au/AboutAPRA/Publications/Pages/Supervision-Blueprint.aspx [accessed 12 January 2015].

Australian Securities and Investments Commission (2012) *Report 279: Shadow Shopping Study of Retirement Advice*, Sydney.

Australian Securities and Investments Commission (2013) *ASIC Stakeholder Survey 2013*, Australia:http://asic.gov.au/about-asic/what-we-do/how-we-operate/stakeholder-liaison/stakeholder-surveys/ [accessed 19 December 2015].

Australian Securities and Investments Commission (2015a) *ASIC Enforcement Outcomes: January to June 2015*, Australia: Australian Securities and Investments Commission.

Australian Securities and Investments Commission (2015b) *ASIC's Approach to Enforcement – Information Sheet 151*, Australia: Australian Securities and Investments Commission.

Beber, A. and Pagano, M. (2010) 'Short-selling Bans around the World: Evidence from the 2007–2009 Crisis', *Tinbergen Institute Discussion Paper, No 10–106/2/DSF 1*.

Berger, A., Klapper, L. and Turk-Ariss, R. (2008) *Bank Competition and Financial Stability. World Bank, Washington, DC. © World Bank. https://openknowledge.worldbank.org/handle/10986/6794*

Bird, J. (2011) 'Regulating the Regulators: Accountability of Australian Regulators', *Melb. UL Rev.*, 35, 739.

Black, J. (2004) *The Development of Risk Based Regulation in Financial Services: Canada, the UK and Australia, A Research Report*, ESRC Centre for the Analysis of Risk and Regulation: London School of Economics and Political Science.

Black, J. (2006) 'Managing Regulatory Risks and Defining the Parameters of Blame: A Focus on the Australian Prudential Regulation Authority', *Law & Policy*, 28(1), 1–30.

Blundell-Wignall, A. and Atkinson, P. (2010) 'Thinking beyond Basel III: Necessary Solutions for Capital and Liquidity', *OECD Journal: Financial Market Trends*, Vol. 1.

Boehmer, E. and Wu, J. (2013) 'Short-selling and the Price Discovery Process', *Review of Financial Studies*, 26(6), pp. 1363–1400.

Born, B., Ehrmann, M. and Fratzscher, M. (2013) 'Central Bank Communication on Financial Stability', *The Economic Journal*.

Bowerman, R. (2009) *'Anniversary lessons 16 Sep 09', Vanguard Investments* [online], available: http://www.vanguard.com.au/personal_investors/news--commentary/smartinvesting/smart-investing_home.cfm?item=anniversary-lessons [accessed 19 January 2015].

Boyd, J. and De Nicolo, G. (2005) 'The Theory of Bank Risk Taking Revisited', *Journal of Finance*, 60, pp. 1329–43.

Boyd, J., De Nicolo, G. and Jalal, A. (2006) 'Bank Risk Taking and Competition Revisited: New Theory and Evidence', *IMF Working paper, WP/06/297*.

Brown, C. and Davis, K. (2010) 'Australia's Experience in the Global Financial Crisis'', *Lessons from the Financial Crisis: Causes, Consequences, and Our Economic Future, The Robert W. Kolb Series in Finance, John Wiley & Sons, Inc, Hoboken*, 537–44.

Carletti, E. and Hartmann, P. (2003) 'Competition and Financial Stability: What's Special about Banking?, In *Monetary History, Exchange Rates and Financial Markets: Essays in Honour of Charles Goodhart*, Vol. 2, edited by P. Mizen, Cheltenham, UK: Edward Elgar'.

Carmichael, J. (2004) 'Australia's Approach to Regulatory Reform' in Carmichael, J., Fleming, A. and Llewellyn, D., eds., *Aligning Financial Supervisory Structures with Country Needs*, Washington: World Bank.

Charoenrook, A. and Daouk, H. (2009) *A Study of Market-Wide Short-Selling Restrictions*, Internal Report, unpublished.

Cicutto, F. (2002) 'Banking in a Competitive Environment', *Journal of Banking and Financial Services*, 116(2), pp. 4–9.

Clark, T. (2007) *International Corporate Governance, A Comparative Approach*, First ed., Oxford: Routledge.

Coleman, A. (2008) *The Determinants of Supervisory Risk Ratings of Australian Deposit-taking Institutions.*, unpublished thesis University of South Wales.

Cooper, J. (2006) 'The Integration of Financial Regulatory Authorities – the Australian Experience. Speech to Comissão de Valores Mobiliários', *Securities and Exchange Commission of Brazil 30th Anniversary Conference, Assessing the Present, Conceiving the Future*, pp. 4–5.

Cusbert, T. and Rohling, T. (2013) *Currency Demand during the Global Financial Crisis: Evidence from Australia*, Australia.

D'Alonsio, T. (2010) *Responding to the Global Financial Crisis: The ASIC Story*, Australia: Australian Securities and Investments Commission.

Davis, K. (2011) 'The Australian Financial System in the 2000s: Dodging the Bullet', *The Australian Economy in the 2000s. H. Gerard and J. Kearns. Sydney, Reserve Bank of Australia, Sydney*, 301–48.

Demirguc-Kunt, A. and Detragiache, E. (2002) 'Does Deposit Insurance Increase Banking System Stability? An Empirical Investigation', *Journal of Monetary Economics*, 49, pp. 1373–1406.

Eslake, S. (2009) 'The Global Financial Crisis of 2007–2009 – An Australian Perspective', *Economic Papers*, 28 (3), pp. 226–38.

Financial Conduct Authority (2014) *Temporary Product Intervention Rules: Restrictions in Relation to the Retail Distribution of Contingent Convertible Instruments* [press release], available: [accessed 2 February 2015].

Financial Services Authority (2010) *Financial Services Authority, Summary of Feedback to the Turner Review Conference Discussion Paper (DP09/4)* [online], available: http://www.fsa.gov.uk/pubs/discussion/fs10_02.pdf [accessed 15 March 2015].

Financial System Inquiry Final Report (1997) *Final Report (S. Wallis, Chair)*, Canberra.

Gallery, G. and Gallery, N. (2010) 'Rethinking Financial Literacy in the Aftermath of the Global Financial Crisis', *Griffith Law Review*, 19(1), pp. 30–50.

Gelpern, A. and Levitin, A. J. (2008) 'Rewriting Frankenstein Contracts: Workout Prohibitions in Residential Mortgage-backed Securities', *Southern Californian Law Review*, 82, pp. 1077-1152.

Group of Thirty (2008) *The Structure of Financial Supervision: Approaches and Challenges in a Global Marketplace* Washington, DC: The Group of Thirty.

HIH Royal Commission (2003) *The Failure of HIH Insurance, Canberra: Australian Government*, Australia: HIH Royal Commission.

Hill, J. (2012) 'Why Did Australia Fare So Well in the Global Financial Crisis?' in Ferran, E., Moloney, N., Hill, J. and Coffee, J., eds., *The Regulatory Aftermath of the Global Financial Crisis*, Cambridge: Cambridge University Press, pp. 203–300.

Hogan, W. and Sharpe, I. (1990) 'Prudential Supervision of Australian Banks', *The Economic Record*, June, pp. 127–45.

House of Commons Treasury Select Committee (2008) *Treasury Seventh Report, Banking Crisis: Dealing with the Failure of the UK Banks*, London: HMSO.

Industry Super Australia (2013) *Senate Inquiry into the Performance of ASIC*, Australia.

International Monetary Fund (2010) *Global Financial Stability Report* [online], available: www.imf.org. [accessed 12 December 2014].

Jones, C. and Owen, L. (2002) 'Short Sale Constraints and Stock Returns', *Journal of Financial Economics*, 66(2), pp. 207–39.

Kolasinksi, A., Adam, R. and Jacob, T. (2010) *Prohibitions versus Constraints: The 2008 Short Sales Regulations*, Internal Report, unpublished.

Laker, J. (2007) *The Evolution of Risk and Risk Management – A Prudential Regulator's Perspective*, Kirribilli, Australia: Australian Prudential Regulation Authority.

Littrell, C. (2011) 'Responses to the Global Financial Crisis: The Australian Prudential Perspective', in Australian Prudential Regulatory Authority, ed., *APEC Regional Symposium: Enhancing Financial Policy and Regulatory Co-operation – Responses to the Global Financial Crisis, 8 March 2011*, Australia.

Lo, A. (2009) 'Regulatory Reform in the Wake of the Financial Crisis of 2007-2008', *Available at: http://papers.ssrn.com/sol3/papers.cfm?abstract_id=1398207*.

Lui, A. (2012) 'Single or Twin? The UK Financial Regulatory Landscape after the Financial Crisis of 2007-2009', *Journal of Banking Regulation*, 13(1), pp. 24–35.

McDonald, T. and Morling, S. (2011) *Economic Roundup Issue 2 – The Australian Economy and the Global Downturn Part 1: Reasons for Resilience*, Australia: The Australian Treasury.

Office of the Superintendent of Financial Institutions (2010) 'Supervisory Framework' [online], available: http://www.osfi-bsif.gc.ca/eng/fi-if/rai-eri/sp-ps/pages/sff.aspx [accessed 5 March 2015].

Organisation for Economic Co-operation Development (2012) *OECD Economic Surveys-AUSTRALIA*, Australia.

Palmer, J. (2002) *Review of the Role Played by the Australian Prudential Regulatory Authority and the Insurance and Superannuation Commission in the Collapse of HIH Insurancec Group of Companies*, Australia.

Parliament of Australia Department of Parliamentary Services (2005) *Australia's corporate regulators-the ACCC, ASIC and APRA*, Australia.

Petch, T. (2011) *Banking Regulation*, London: Getting the Deal Through.

Reserve Bank of Australia (1996) *Submission to the Financial System Inquiry, Occasional Paper, no. 14.*, Australia.

Reserve Bank of Australia (2014) *Accountability in the Reserve Bank of Australia* [online], available: http://www.rba.gov.au/about-rba/accountability.html [accessed 15 April 2015].

Schaeck, K., Cihak, M. and Wolfe, S. (2006) 'Are More Competitive Banking Systems More Stable?', *Unpublished Working Paper No. 143, International Monetary Fund, Washington, D.C.*

Sherry, N. and Tanner, L. (2008) *Media Release No. 47 'Cutting Red Tape, Protecting Consumers: First Short, Simple Financial Disclosure Statement'* [press release], available: [accessed 3 April 2015].

Stewart, C., Robertson, B. and Heath, A. (2013) *Trends in the Funding and Lending Behaviour of Australian Banks*, Australia.

Turner, G. (2011) 'Depositor Protection in Australia', *Reserve Bank of Australia Bulletin*, pp. 45-55.

Wettenhall, R. (2011) 'Global Financial Crisis: The Australian Experience in International Perspective', *Public Organisation Review*, 11, pp. 77–91.

Wilkins, M. (2011) 'HIH Systemic Risk or Opportunity', *Insurance and Finance*, 8, pp. 1–3.

World Economic Forum (2012) *The Financial Development Report 2012*, [online], available: http://www.weforum.org/issues/financial-development [accessed 6 April 2015].

Wu, S. (2008) 'Bank Mergers and Acquisitions – An Evaluation of the "four pillars" Policy in Australia', *Australian Economic Papers*, 47(2), pp. 141–55.

5 US

Introduction

Financial innovation and stability are difficult to balance. The financial system in the US is the epitome of this difficulty. Ranked first in the Financial Development Index of the World Economic Forum 2012 indexes of non-financial services and financial markets, it is only ranked 38th overall for financial stability (World Economic Forum 2012). The World Economic Forum highlighted this weakness but pointed out that the US improved its ranking for overall banking stability (40th). Statistics from the World Bank also show that in 2009–12, the US had a high ratio of non-performing loans to total gross loans, indicating financial instability. However, this ratio has improved in subsequent years. Undoubtedly, the US suffered financial instability during the financial crisis of 2007–9 since it was at the core of the crisis. Although the American financial regulatory system is complex and fragmented, it is heavily regulated within the banking sector. This chapter studies the roles of shadow banking and securitisation on financial stability as well as important macro-prudential regulatory issues. From a micro-prudential perspective, it is submitted that the Federal Reserve can do more to link monetary policy with micro-prudential regulation. It is also submitted that political influence and lobbying by American politicians have had an impact on the financial regulatory architecture in the US. The pendulum has swung from independent agencies towards more power to politicians in financial regulation after the financial crisis of 2007–9. Whilst banking is always political to the extent that banks are fundamental to a country's economy, countries such as the US and UK, with large financial sectors, will need political will to make changes for the benefit of society at an international level. Jurisdictional competition for financial services means that regulation of the shadow banking sector remains unlikely since co-operation at the international level remains a real difficulty. Other methods of improving financial stability will thus be investigated in this chapter.

The Federal Reserve Board and institutional weaknesses during the financial crisis of 2007-9

The US regulatory structure

Ben Bernanke, Chairman of the Federal Reserve Board between 2006 and 2014, said that 'the Federal Reserve has become much more focused on financial stability' (Bernanke 2013). The Federal Reserve Board is one of four prudential bank regulators in the US financial regulatory system. The other bank regulators are the Office of the Comptroller of the Currency (OCC), Federal Deposit Insurance Corporation (FDIC) and National Credit Union Administration. As prudential regulators, the overriding concept is prudent monitoring and regulating risks of banks (Murphy 2013). Two agencies are in charge of monitoring the information market players provide to customers: the Securities and Exchange Commission (SEC) and the Commodities Futures Trading Commission (CFTC). The US financial regulatory system is complex, and there are regulatory overlaps between the agencies. For example, the bank regulators can regulate the disclosures of their chartered firms, whilst securities and derivatives regulators have some prudential responsibilities. An example is section 731 of the Dodd–Frank Wall Street Reform and Consumer Protection Act 2010 ('Dodd–Frank Act'). It states that the SEC and CFTC can, after consultation with the prudential regulators, set capital requirements for major swap participants. The largely functional-based approach to prudential regulation is illustrated in the example of regulating the derivatives-trading activities of JP Morgan in 2012 (Murphy 2013). Five US regulatory agencies were involved, starting with the OCC regulating at the depository level. The Federal Reserve was responsible for regulating the same activities at company holding level. The SEC regulated the disclosure of information to shareholders, whilst the CFTC regulated the derivatives transactions. Finally, JP Morgan provides insurance services as well, so it was subject to the regulation of the FDIC. Despite these regulatory overlaps, Congress resisted making architectural changes unless there were faults in the system (Wallace 2013). Further, Gadinis (2013) is of the opinion that the independent-agency model in the US provides a high level of independence amongst financial regulatory agencies, which is an indicator of the quality of financial regulation. For example, Congress has the power to approve the SEC's annual budget but is restricted in approving the Federal Reserve's budgetary and audit powers. Yet the financial crisis of 2007–9 proved that there were faults in the financial system.

The Federal Reserve Act 1913 established the Federal Reserve System, the overall central bank of the US. The Act has been amended several times but the law remains broadly similar to the 1913 version. The jurisdiction of the Federal Reserve System was broadened after the Monetary Control Act 1980. Under this Act, the Federal Reserve System became the regulator of all depository financial institutions. The Federal Reserve System consists of the Federal Reserve Board, 12 Federal Reserve banks and the Federal Open Market Committee. The Federal Reserve Board is a central, governmental agency and consists of seven members, who are appointed by the president. They serve a 14-year term (Board of Governors of the Federal Reserve System 2005). In the build up to the financial crisis of 2007–9, the Federal Reserve was criticised for decreasing the interest rate from 1 per cent to 0.25 per cent. This cut created financial imbalances in the global economy, with asset prices rising and credit supply expanding. Together with high leverage ratios and maturity mismatches, the US financial system suffered a tremendous shock when the sub-prime-mortgage crisis struck (Shirakawa 2013).

Performances of the Federal Reserve and US regulators during the global financial crisis

The Federal Reserve and the SEC have both been criticised for failing in their supervisory roles during the global financial crisis (Wallace 2013). Dealing first with the Federal Reserve, its policy actions during the financial crisis can be divided into two groups: conventional and unconventional responses (Cecchetti 2009). Conventional responses include simultaneous cuts in the target federal funds rate and the discount borrowing rate between mid 2007 and mid 2008. By lowering the rates and extending the maturity of discount-window loans, the Federal Reserve provided liquidity to banks to carry out their daily tasks (Bernanke 2013). The discount window is the Federal Reserve's lender-of-last-resort tool. It can also promote financial stability by providing temporary funding to depository institutions experiencing financial difficulties (Board of Governors of the Federal Reserve System 2005). However, firms dealing with securities and derivatives could not benefit from the discount window. Further, the scale of the financial crisis was too vast, and the institutional context of the global financial crisis was different to previous crises. Financial institutions have become more intertwined, complex and interdependent. Although the Federal Reserve stopped the classic bank run by providing liquidity support, the money market experienced a run. As a result of this, the Federal Reserve had to sell commercial paper as quickly as possible. As Bernanke (2013) said: 'it is very important to get in there aggressively' in a financial crisis to stem the systemic risks.

The Federal Reserve had to take unconventional measures to contain the damage inflicted to the US financial system. The measures include reducing the premium on the discount lending rate from 100 to 25 basis points above the federal funds rate; creating the Term Auction Facility, Term Securities Lending Facility (TSLF) and Primary Dealer Credit Facility; and buying further long-term Treasury securities (Cecchetti 2009; Shirakawa 2013). The Federal Reserve had to rely on its emergency powers under section 13(3) Federal Reserve Act 1913 so that it could lend to non-bank institutions.

The Federal Reserve had not used this emergency power since the 1930s (Bernanke 2013). When it realised that banks were still unwilling to borrow from the central bank due to the stigma attached, the Federal Reserve was decisive, creative and aggressive in exercising the emergency power. It created the Term Auction Facility precisely to remove the stigma. The Federal Reserve started lending money in large quantities for 28–35 days. From December 2007, there were bi-monthly auctions where banks could bid for money, stating the interest rate they would pay. Settlement took place two days after the auction. This was advantageous and innovative since the bidders were protected by anonymity. Further, banks were able to use collateral which would otherwise have been of little market value. Although the Federal Reserve increased its balance sheet with the offer of the Term Auction Facility, the overall size of its balance sheet was not affected since it reduced its securities holdings accordingly (Cecchetti 2009). In fact, as the crisis went on, the overall size of the Federal Reserve Bank's balance sheet remained unaltered. It was the composition of the assets which changed. This was important since reducing the size of its balance sheet during a financial crisis could make a financial regulator vulnerable.

Steve Jobs of Apple once said that 'innovation distinguishes between a leader and a follower'. The Federal Reserve certainly led from the front in designing unconventional support mechanisms. In fact, it spent $3.76 trillion on creating money as a form of support package. This is in comparison to $0.32 trillion in the UK and $0.98 trillion in the Eurozone (Alessandri and Haldane 2009). The TSLF is an example of innovative financial support. This facility was introduced to provide liquidity in the securities market. It lends securities to primary dealers overnight with the aim of reducing the number of failed securities transactions (Cecchetti 2009). Lending securities to primary dealers has happened since 1969, so the concept itself is not novel. It is a fundamental method of influencing the supply of balances at the Federal Reserve banks (Board of Governors of the Federal Reserve System 2005). The financial crisis was a catalyst in triggering some changes to the TSLF in that this scheme broadened the range of collateral which the Federal Reserve was willing to accept. This improved the liquidity conditions in financial markets. Flexibility was offered through the TSLF as it did not have an impact on the Federal Reserve's bank reserves or directly affect its policy on setting interest rates (Fleming *et al.* 2009). The TSLF is therefore a good example of the Federal Reserve being able to combine its lender-of-last-resort role and monetary policy role during a crisis.

Invoking Article 13(3) of the Federal Reserve Act in the bailout of Bear Stearns is an example of the Federal Reserve providing emergency liquidity assistance. It also highlights interesting issues regarding the Federal Reserve's independence and regulation of investment banks. Bear Stearns was not a commercial bank and so could not benefit from the conventional liquidity measures offered by the Federal Reserve. By relying on Article 13(3) of the Federal Reserve Act, the board of directors authorised the Federal Reserve

Bank of New York to loan approximately $29 billion to JP Morgan's takeover of Bear Stearns (Cecchetti 2009). JP Morgan injected $1 billion into the bailout. A Primary Dealer Credit Facility (PDCF) was set up on 16 March 2008. This was a backstop lending facility, which is different to the TSLF auction facility and the Term Auction Facility. The PDCF allows primary dealers to borrow funds from the Fed against a broader range of collateral than is eligible for Open Market Operations. Second, the rate on that borrowing is fixed rather than determined through an auction mechanism. Cecchetti (2009) argues that the Federal Reserve was acting as a fiscal agent of the US Treasury because the US Treasury bore the credit risk if there were any losses arising from this PDCF loan facility (Geithner 2008). This is explained by the fact that the Federal Reserve Bank of New York would treat any losses from the PDCF as an expense, which would reduce the net earnings transferred by the Federal Reserve Bank of New York to the US Treasury. The Treasury therefore provided a subsidy in the loan, which is a fiscal not a monetary measure (Cecchetti 2009). Acting as the Treasury's agent does compromise the Federal Reserve's independence as a central bank to a certain extent. However, as we have witnessed from incidents such as the bailouts of Northern Rock, Bradford & Bingley, Royal Bank of Scotland and HBOS in the UK, this phenomenon is inevitable when a financially weak bank is facing collapse. Both the Treasury and the Federal Reserve have a common interest in that they wish to preserve financial stability as quickly as possible. Therefore, some compromise of the Federal Reserve's independence is expected in such circumstances.

The rescue of Bear Stearns is significant because it is the first time a US investment bank was bailed out. Gordon and Muller (2010) criticised the rescue as a case of following the precedent of rescuing Merrill Lynch and Citigroup. They argued that Bear Stearns was not 'too big to fail' or 'too connected to fail': it was simply 'too similar to fail', and politicians took the easy option. This is dubious. Chronologically, Bear Stearns was rescued first, in March 2008, before Merrill Lynch and Citigroup were rescued, in September and November 2008 respectively. Thus, Bear Stearns did not follow precedent: it set the precedent. More importantly, Lehman Brothers collapsed in September 2008. Every decision regarding the fate of a bank involves difficult considerations due to the stakeholder nature of banks and the potential impact on market confidence. The different fates of Bear Stearns and Lehman Brothers deserve closer examination. Bear Stearns' gross profit in 2007 was $5,945 million, whereas Lehman Brothers' gross profit was $19,257 million (Grove and Clouse 2013). In terms of size, Bear Stearns was a third of Lehman Brothers, yet the former was bailed out six months after the demise of the latter. Opinions differ as to why Bear Stearns was rescued whilst Lehman Brothers was wound up. According to Fein (2008) and Baxter (2010), the Federal Reserve rescued Bear Stearns because it had a liquidity issue, whilst Lehman Brothers had a solvency issue. Lehman Brothers had the misfortune of encountering a trio of macro-prudential problems: capital and liquidity inadequacies as well as a weakening of market confidence. Turner (2011), the former SEC Chief Accountant, expressed the view that both banks' heavy reliance on short-term financing and low capital levels was dangerous. Yet being the second bank requiring help was 'fatal' for Lehman Brothers (Turner 2011).

From Baxter's testimony, it is apparent that the US regulators did not allow Lehman Brothers to fail (Baxter 2010). Rather, they failed to save Lehman Brothers. The Federal Reserve, United States Treasury Department and SEC all worked together to try and rescue Lehman Brothers. Initially, the Federal Reserve had no regulatory or supervisory role with regards to Lehman Brothers. The SEC was responsible for regulating Lehman Brothers as an investment bank and Lehman Brothers' parent holding company under a voluntary programme called the Consolidated Supervised Entity programme. From March 2008 onwards, however, the Federal Reserved increasingly played an important role in macro-prudential financial assistance. First, the PDCF mechanism offered to Bear Stearns indirectly helped Lehman Brothers for a while because it calmed down financial markets. Second, the Federal Reserve of New York sent out staff to Goldman Sachs, Lehman Brothers, Merrill Lynch and Morgan Stanley to establish a closer relationship with these investment banks as their lender. These on-site visits were too late for any supervisory role. Rather, the SEC continued to be the supervisor of Lehman Brothers (Baxter 2010). Communication and co-operation between the SEC and the Federal Reserve proved to be fruitful to the extent that the capital position of Lehman Brothers improved after raising capital in June 2008. However, it was too late to improve Lehman Brothers' liquidity problems. In September 2008, the US Treasury, SEC and Federal Reserve spent a weekend deciding the fate of Lehman Brothers. Barclays was a potential buyer but refused to provide a guarantee for Lehman Brothers' trading obligations between signing the agreement and Lehman Brothers closing. A guarantee in the rescue of Bear Stearns meant that the bank was able to operate as a going concern and preserve its value. Barclays' shareholders would have to sanction a guarantee, but time was of the essence. The FSA in the UK would not waive its requirements. Neither would the Federal Reserve. The latter argued that it did not have a legal mandate to issue a guarantee when Lehman Brothers could not offer a credible collateral (Baxter 2010). The collateral provided by Bear Stearns was good, whereas Lehman Brothers failed to provide the same. The Federal Reserve's insistence as the lender of last resort on using reasonable collateral against lending to failing banks saved Bear Stearns. In the case of Bear Stearns, the Federal Reserve provided $29 billion towards a $30 billion loan under the PDCF. JP Morgan's financial support of $1 billion acted as a buffer for the Federal Reserve against any potential losses. Further, the loan was secured against Bear Stearns' good quality assets and the Federal Reserve was fully repaid.

The use of a guarantee partially explains the rescue of Bear Stearns. From a macro-prudential regulatory angle, a guarantee provides a brief period of stability till a deal is completed. It also upholds Bagehot's principle that a central bank should only agree to lend against good collateral. In the US, it was only in October 2008 that the Emergency Economic Stabilization Act (EESA) was passed and there was legal authority to issue a guarantee. Fein (2008) however, argues that the EESA was unnecessary other than for political reasons. Although the EESA legislated in a wide range of areas, the Treasury could have partially provided guaranteed money-market funds under the Gold Reserve Act 1934, which allowed the Treasury to utilise the Economic Stabilisation Fund to fund a guarantee programme. The EESA has not changed this arrangement. Rather, it imposes some restrictions on the Treasury, such as the requirement of reimbursing the fund and not utilising it for future guarantee programmes in the money-market sector (Fein 2008). As we saw earlier, the Federal Reserve Board provided liquidity-support measures to the money-market sector by invoking the emergency section under Article 13(3) of the Federal Reserve Act 1913. It was also able to buy commercial paper from private issuers under the same article. The only new emergency support measure created by the EESA was the Treasury's Capital Purchase Plan. Under this plan, the Treasury was able to use $250 billion to buy shares in the nine largest financial organisations, thus directly injecting capital. The implementation of the EESA was politically necessary for two reasons. First, the Federal Reserve Board is an independent agency accountable to Congress, so it would only be prudent and politically wise to consult Congress. Second, the amount required to assist the banks was in the region of $700 billion. Given this huge figure, obtaining approval from Congress made sense. The result of the EESA is that power has shifted between the independent agencies: that is, the Treasury has been given a great deal more monetary power to rescue financial organisations. Shah (2009) concurs, adding that the 'EESA gives the administration virtually unlimited discretion in spending a vast sum of money'. In times of crises however, history has demonstrated that it is not unusual for emergency powers to be given to the executive (Scheuerman 2000; Shah 2009). An example is the Patriot Act 2001, which was passed with little involvement from Congress after the terrorist attacks of 11 September 2001. The EESA gives the Treasury strategic powers as well. The EESA did not set out the strategic plan for the Troubled Asset Relief Programme (TARP), which meant that the Treasury was able to control the strategic executions of TARP. The EESA provides very wide discretion to the Treasury in dealing with troubled assets. Sections 101(a)(1) and 106 of the EESA enable the Treasury Secretary to enter into any financial transaction in relation to troubled assets at a price he/she determines (Ghosh and Mohamed 2010).

Nevertheless, the EESA imposes restrictions and methods of scrutiny by Congress. First, the wide powers under sections 101 and 106 are subject to the avoidance of potential conflicts of interest and any long-term negative impact (section 103 EESA). Second, the Treasury Secretary has to consider certain factors, such as taxpayers' interests, financial stability, preservation of home ownership, when exercising the authority to sell troubled assets (Ghosh and Mohamed 2010). Third, there is a limited judicial review under sections 119(a)(1) and sections 122 EESA to provide scrutiny. This mechanism will render an action unlawful if the Treasury Secretary's actions are 'arbitrary, capricious and an abuse of discretion' (sections 119(a)(1) and 122 EESA). Yet judicial reviews are lengthy and costly, so a fourth scrutiny mechanism is available. The new Special Inspector General set up under section 121(f) (1) EESA submitted independent reports of all financial transactions under TARP every three months (Cooley *et al.* 2010). Further, Congress set up an independent Oversight Council with the job of reporting monthly on TARP's effectiveness (section 125(b) and 122 EESA). Therefore, it can be seen that the US Congress can limit executive authority through scrutiny measures and provide transparency (Shah 2009).

In practice however, transparency was clouded by the overlap of regulators in regulating TARP. There was little transparency as to how TARP was implemented and how banks used TARP funds (Ghosh and Mohamed 2010). Without reliable and prompt information, it is difficult to revive the secondary mortgage market. Crisis management requires prompt exchange and interpretation of information (Herring and Carmassi 2008). This involves macro- and micro-prudential regulatory agencies working together. The financial crisis of 2007–9 was not the first time when co-operation between US regulatory agencies broke down. In 1999, the OCC and FDIC disagreed over the financial condition of First National Bank of West Virginia. The US Government Accountability Office and a report of the Treasury Inspector General found that effective co-ordination between these two regulators was lacking (US Government Accountability Office 2007). The Federal Reserve Board as the macro-prudential regulator should thus have wider powers over financial oversight (US Treasury 2009). It is unlikely that the Federal Reserve Board can override the decisions of other regulatory agencies. However, giving more regulatory power to the Federal Reserve Board should minimise the potential of micro-prudential regulation at a local level (Ghosh and Mohamed 2010). The Chairman of the Federal Reserve noted that the different supervisory and regulatory regimes for lenders and mortgage brokers have created difficulties for both investors and regulators (US Government Accountability Office 2009b).

Yet minutes from the Bank of England Court of Directors' Committee seem to indicate close co-operation between the Federal Reserve and the FSA in the UK. Between 2008 and 2010, there were frequent referrals and co-operation attempts. Particular examples include the FSA engaging with the New York Federal Reserve and American International Group about deposit insurance and commercial paper (Bank of England 2008, Bank of England 2009). The Federal Reserve also provided support to the ECB by issuing swaps in return for Euros. The ECB was then able to lend US dollars to a number of European banks, which could hold assets in dollars and make loans to support trade in dollars (Bernanke 2013). Further, in October 2008, the Federal Reserve and five other central banks all announced interest cuts on the same day

(Bernanke 2013). This demonstrates that the Federal Reserve co-ordinated and co-operated with other central banks on monetary policy as well.

Consumer protection

In addition to the above monetary-policy and liquidity actions, Geithner (2008) submitted that the Federal Reserve was active in protecting consumers. This is because it worked with various groups in communities across the country to help homeowners identify solutions to avoid foreclosures and their negative effects. This happened too late, though. The Federal Reserve and the other regulators should have cracked down on the explosion of sub-prime mortgages in the first place, although borrowers also played a role. The regulatory structure did not help either. The Federal Reserve had the primary responsibility to protect consumers. However, it was too preoccupied with macro-prudential regulation of banks and the overall economy. Further, the other regulators, such as the OCC and the FDIC, were more concerned with preventing bank failures. Limited supervision of non-bank lending was also a problem (Johnson and Kwak 2010).

Ashcraft and Schuermann (2008) argued that mortgage fraud played a significant role in the sub-prime crisis. Fitch Ratings produced a report in 2007 showing that 45 borrowers defaulted very shortly after origination. Fitch found first-time buyers with questionable income and debts, suspicious items on credit histories and incorrect calculation of debt-to-income ratios. Some lenders were driven by financial rewards and thus became lax with due diligence (Murdoch 2011). Dell'Ariccia *et al.* (2008) found that the decrease in lending standards led to an increase in the demand for sub-prime loans. Additionally, the lax lending standards were more prevalent in areas where lenders securitised large portions of the originated loans. In some instances, borrowers were encouraged to commit mortgage fraud through 'liars' loans', where they did not need to provide evidence of their income or assets. The regulators failed in protecting consumers since 87 per cent of borrowers could not identify the total cost of loans and 51 per cent could not identify the loan amount from the documents. Mortgages are complex financial documents and these figures indicate that there are weaknesses in consumer disclosure and financial literacy. Ashcraft and Schuermann (2008) also stated that credit-rating agencies made mistakes, both honest and dishonest. Honest mistakes included underestimating the collapse of the housing market and the use of limited data. These mistakes are arguably due to financial innovation and complexity of financial products. Dishonest mistakes were made when credit-rating agencies relied too heavily on arrangers, structuring deals to maximise returns for the arrangers.

Some argue that the US government and legislators made mistakes and failed consumers. Wallison (2011) posits that US housing policy led to the creation of 27 million mortgages, of which half were to default in the sub-prime mortgage crisis. Several academics (Bhutta 2008; Demyanyk and van Hemert 2011) argue that bank lending standards fell after the Community

Reinvestment Act 1977 came into force. Much lower deposits amongst lower-income groups and lower underwriting standards in the mortgage industry were common (Demyanyk and van Hemert 2011). The Financial Crisis Inquiry Commission disagreed, stating that US law, especially the Community Reinvestment Act 1977, did not contribute significantly to the sub-prime crisis since many sub-prime lenders were not subject to the Community Reinvestment Act. Their research revealed that loans made by lenders subject to the Community Reinvestment Act were as likely to default as lenders who were not. Research from the US Government Accountability Office (2009a), however, showed that there was a sharp increase in the number of risky loans and that the risk increased with time. Adjustable-rate mortgages grew by 70 per cent in 2004–6, whilst fixed-rate mortgages decreased by 25 per cent during the same period. Further, there was a 600 per cent increase in the dollar volume of sub-prime mortgages, indicating lenders' increased risk appetite.

Feldstein (2010) submits that the Federal Reserve, SEC and other regulators failed to recognise that the triple-A ratings of some bank assets were based on faulty bank models. Yet the regulators did not deal with this and so failed in their supervisory roles (Feldstein 2010). This criticism seems harsh from the perspective of the SEC and other regulators. Timely information is highly valuable and difficult to obtain in the financial industry, since financial products and processes are increasingly complex and opaque. US legislators believe that information available in the market may not be perfect, so the US consumer protection regime is very much based on disclosure (Johnson and Kwak 2010). Since the private market was not providing the SEC with relevant and timely information, it relied on rating agencies (Acharya et al. 2011). The main problem with rating agencies is that they are paid by sellers, which creates a potential conflict of interest because rating agencies are the agents of purchasers. Caprio et al. (2008) suggested that purchasers pay the rating agencies to avoid conflict of interest. There are, however, two difficulties with this solution. First, there is a free-rider problem since potential purchasers might not pay for a rating in hope of another purchaser paying (Tarr 2010). Second, as Calomiris (2009) argues, the omnipresent principal–agent problem in companies will still lead to asset managers buying risky assets. Calomiris (2009) provided an alternative solution whereby rating agencies have to quantitatively assess the percentage of their loans which are likely to default. If the default rate is higher than the percentage then rating agencies have to pay a fine. This solution creates an incentive in the opposite direction: rating agencies may become too risk averse and overestimate risks. Tarr (2010) concurs with Richardson and White's proposal that the seller should apply to the SEC and pay for the rating (Richardson and White 2009). The SEC would appoint the relevant rating officer to provide the ratings, according to the officer's qualifications and experience. The right incentive can be created since good performance is rewarded. It is important that there should not be financial compensation for repeat work since the quality of ratings may be compromised due to pressure for this. Yet the problem of information asymmetry still exists, which does not assist the regulators. Hart and Zingales (2009) argue that the market should inform the regulators through the price of credit default swaps. If the price of a credit default swap rises then the regulator will ask the bank to have more equity since a default is more likely to occur. This increased level of equity remains till the price of the credit default swap decreases. If the bank is unable to raise additional equity, the regulator will intervene and act as a receiver. This seems sensible as risk-taking could potentially be reduced. However, it leads to the question of whether regulators should save large financial institutions. It is argued that regulators can save large financial institutions provided that some gaps in the too-big-to-fail concept are rectified. This will be discussed further later in the chapter.

The structure of the regulatory agencies per se is not the sole contributing factor to the effectiveness of financial regulation. Yet it can ease or hinder regulators' jobs (US Government Accountability Office 2004). In an increasingly globalised and interconnected world of finance, it is important to have an effective regulatory structure in place to deal with macro- and micro-prudential risks. The US regulatory structure has been described as 'dynamic and innovative', which in turn leads to competition between regulators to provide more ingenious ways of regulating and modernising the financial sector (US Government Accountability Office 2004). Given the increased importance of securitisation and the secondary money market, innovation is important in promoting more effective regulation amongst regulatory agencies. The Federal Reserve's responses in the form of reducing the discount-lending rate from 100 to 25 basis points above the federal funds rate, creating the Term Auction Facility, TSLF and PDCF and buying further long-term Treasury securities were creative and helped to reduce financial turmoil during the crisis of 2007–9. Some academics posit that the Federal Reserve acted beyond its role as lender of last resort and became an 'investor of last resort' (Cooley *et al.* 2010). The Federal Reserve invested in certain banks, such as Bear Stearns, but it seems a little extreme to suggest that the Federal Reserve was an 'investor of last resort'. The US regulatory system is also reactive rather than proactive. No one regulatory agency has overall control of the entire financial-services industry, although the Federal Reserve has a substantial share. Congress has decided not to make any structural changes to the overall regulatory system (Wallace 2013), so it is now appropriate to see if the government's responses to the financial crisis will provide adequate resources and tools for the regulatory agencies to carry out their mandates effectively.

Macro- and micro-prudential regulatory frameworks of the US 2007–9

Macro-prudential regulation

The Federal Reserve has the twin mandates of stable prices and maximum employment. Focusing on monetary policy, Carmassi *et al.* (2009) submit that the two main contributing factors to the financial crisis of 2007–9 were lax monetary policy and regulation encouraging excessive leverage. They argue that the Federal Reserve was myopic and concentrated on domestic goals rather than international ones even though the US dollar is the world's reserve currency. This is demonstrated by the combination of low interest rates on long maturities and the reluctance to intervene in foreign-exchange investments by Asian countries. The ultimate aim was to avoid the depreciation of the US dollar (Carmassi *et al.* 2009). These factors were accompanied by regulatory gaps which enabled banks to pursue high leverage ratios. Although US commercial banks generally had an average leverage ratio of 1:10 or 1:12 (Morris and Shin 2008), US investment banks and holding companies are regulated by the SEC and are not subject to the leverage limit under the Basel II Accord (D'Hulster 2009). As such, US investment banks had average leverage ratios of 1:33 (Prasch 2012). A high leverage ratio 'indicates in general a lower capacity to absorb losses and hence greater fragility since it entails that many agents have issued promises to pay a certain nominal amount but do not have the resources to honour these promises' (Hildebrand 2008). Further, the quality of assets held by US banks was poor in general between 2004 and 2006, with a slight improvement in 2007 and marked improvements since 2008 (World Economic Forum 2012). The US had high bank capital-to-asset ratios in 2004–13 and a high Tier 1 capital ratio (World Economic Forum 2012; Brei and Gambacorta 2014). Despite high capital ratios, US banks struggled to cope with the financial crisis due to excessive leverage and poor quality of assets.

Monetary policy and financial stability are linked, and more emphasis should be paid to co-ordinating these two objectives. Adrian and Shin (2009) describe these two objectives as 'inseparable'. Since the financial crisis, the focus on US financial regulation has been on macro-prudential regulation due to systemic risks. The Dodd–Frank Act 2010 stipulates that financial stability is a mandate of the Federal Reserve. King (2013) remarked that macro-prudential policy is one tool in tackling financial-stability risks. The boundary between macro- and micro-prudential policies is grey and the two areas will often share similar interests. There might be a trade-off between the two objectives of monetary and financial stability as they might act in different directions. According to King (2013), having macro-prudential policy as a tool might reduce the extent to which the two objectives are traded off. The Federal Reserve's monetary policy, which was 'accommodating' in the 1990s and 'expansionary' in the 2000s, is an example (Carmassi *et al.* 2009). The Federal Reserve remained passive when demand for credit increased and asset prices were rising. Yet the Federal Reserve was active and frequently intervened to deal with negative bubbles (Carmassi *et al.* 2009). This monetary policy coupled with excessive leverage and excessive maturity transformation contributed to financial instability. Thus, having a macro-prudential policy on regulating leverage ratios and good quality capital, preferably assets of short maturities, could provide more stability in the financial sector.

As a financially powerful country, the US government and regulators were able to bail out parent banks in the US. The group organisational structure allowed banks to channel liquidity throughout its internal system and, overall, spillovers were minimised. However, all this came at a high cost and many US politicians were keen to curb the power of the Federal Reserve (Cooley *et al.* 2010; International Monetary Fund 2014). This is evident in sections 1101–09 of the Dodd–Frank Act, where there are more limitations and accountability measures imposed on the Federal Reserve in areas such as emergency lending, publishing information on the Federal Reserve's website and audits. The Dodd–Frank Act's chief objective is to promote financial stability. It lists four main regulatory objectives, which include 'improving accountability and transparency in the financial system, to end "too big to fail", to protect the American taxpayer by ending bailouts, to protect consumers from abusive financial services practices'. The Dodd–Frank Act is comprehensive and appears to tackle the areas of accountability and transparency well, through reforms to regulate asset-backed securities and the securitisation process. Title VII of the Dodd–Frank Act gives the CFTC and the SEC significant powers to regulate swaps and derivatives. Nevertheless, a number of the provisions require the two regulators to make rules. As a result of this, one will only be able to assess the impact of Title VII in due course. The Dodd–Frank Act requires the financial industry, rather than taxpayers, to absorb the costs of a bank failure. Although this achieves the objective of protecting US taxpayers by ending bailouts, it does not resolve the too-big-to-fail issue. Besides, bailouts may be necessary when a government is the only organisation able to assist weak banks. The rest of this chapter will focus on the too-big-to-fail issue, since it is argued that the Dodd–Frank Act does not adequately deal with this.

Legislative gaps in dealing with too-big-to-fail

This section will look at three issues: first, the impact on society of the size, complexity and interconnectedness of banks and the banking industry; second, how bailouts should be facilitated, since there is evidence that large banks amplify systemic risks; and, finally, the legislative gaps in the Dodd–Frank Act when dealing with the too-big-to-fail principle. Empirical research by Laeven *et al.* (2014) found that large banks create more systemic risks (but are not individually riskier) when they are more complex or engage in market activities through the originate-to-distribute model. However, individual banks' business models matter too. Generally, large banks were found to have fragile business models with lower capital levels and less stable funding. Therefore, macro-prudential regulation of financial ratios such as capital, leverage and liquidity are crucial. To reduce systemic risks, Laeven *et al.* (2014) propose a capital surcharge on large banks to reduce organisational complexity and market-based bank activities. Asking banks to hold higher capital levels has already prompted dissatisfaction from banks, which have argued that such requirements will increase their lending costs. Indeed, HSBC and Deutsche Bank have been planning to become simpler, smaller banks due to the requirements of more capital (Smith 2015). HSBC is subject to over 500 regulators (Doward 2015), yet queries have been raised as to why non-executive directors at HSBC, such as Rona Fairhead, were not aware of the bank's alleged tax-avoidance scandal in Switzerland. Lee Hale, Global Head of Sanctions at HSBC, said that due to the bank's size and scale, 'it is a cast-iron certain[ty] … at some point in the future we're going to have some big breach, some regulatory breach' (Davies and Ball 2015). The sheer size and complexity of HSBC makes it difficult to manage.

Admati *et al.* (2012) do not think that the size of individual banks is the real problem; rather, it is the size of the entire banking industry. They gave the example of the government bailout of the US savings-and-loan industry in 1989. No single bank proved a threat but it was the entire sector which produced cost externalities. Small banks with high leverage can still affect each other due to the interconnected nature of their investments. However, Bush *et al.* (2014) do not believe that the size of a banking industry is a robust indicator of banking crises. When factors such as credit booms and leverage ratios are taken into account, regression analysis has shown that there is no clear evidence that a large banking sector is more likely to enter into a financial crisis (Bush *et al.* 2014). Neither are larger banking sectors associated with lower growth after a crisis. However, there is evidence from the global financial crisis that countries with larger banking sectors will incur more direct fiscal costs when they fail (Bush *et al.* 2014). Therefore, the introduction of 'bail-in' mechanisms so that banks pay for the social costs of bank failures should provide a more resilient banking sector. Bailouts are, nevertheless, still required in some circumstances, as the government may be the only organisation which can help.

Although the US financial sector is big and international, it is ranked behind the UK in both areas. Amongst the banks of the countries studied in this book, those in the US had the highest ratios of capital to assets and non-performing loans to total gross loans in the period prior to the global financial crisis (World Bank 2015). The US banking sector was in theory, therefore, fairly resilient in terms of macro-prudential statistics. This leads to the question why the US banking sector was vulnerable in the global financial crisis. It is submitted that US banks are too complex and opaque to manage. Complexity is due to banks' size and the activities in they are involved. Opacity is due to the use of securitisation and the shadow banking sector. The securitisation of sub-prime mortgages is an excellent example of this. Complex products such as collateralised debt obligations and collateralised debt obligations squared made it difficult for investors to understand the risks involved. With limited information available due to the opaque nature of securitisation, many investors turned to credit-rating agencies to assess the risks. Some investors lost confidence in securitisation because 16 per cent of securitised products with triple-A ratings defaulted, when they should only have had a 0.1 per cent default rate (European Commission 2015).

US banks managed to grow because of their access to regulators and the influence they exerted over them. Wall Street yields significant power: it was an 'oligarchy', where the ideology of 'unfettered innovation and unregulated financial markets' permeated the US regulatory system (Johnson and Kwak 2010). Two examples will be provided here. In April 2004, the SEC allowed the five large US investment banks to use their own bank models to calculate the amount of net capital required. Second, the SEC allowed the same banks to increase their leverage ratios between 2003 and 2007. In return for this increase in leverage ratios, the SEC had the power to monitor the banks through the Consolidated Supervised Entity programme. However, it did not exercise this power. This can be seen in the case of Bear Stearns, where the SEC simply ignored the red flags (Johnson and Kwak 2010). To combat lobbying, therefore, it is crucial to have specific legislation dealing with identified weaknesses. More importantly, proactive supervision is necessary. The regulatory structure and approach will impact on the effectiveness of supervision.

The current legislation and architecture of US financial regulators do not adequately deal with the too-big-to-fail phenomenon. Dealing first with the legislation, the Dodd–Frank Act restricts the ability of the Federal Reserve to lend to non-banks in an emergency under section 13(3) of the Dodd–Frank Act. Under the Dodd–Frank Act, the Federal Reserve can only lend to 'participants in any programme or facility with broad-based facility' (Cooley *et al.* 2010). It seems nonsensical to differentiate between banks and non-banks in an emergency. Cooley *et al.* (2010) posit that non-banks will simply convert into banks to access emergency lending from the Federal Reserve. Goldman Sachs and Morgan Stanley did that in 2008 when Lehman Brothers collapsed. This implicit guarantee will not resolve the too-big-to-fail issue.

Further, section 204 of the Dodd–Frank Act *allows* 'failing companies' which pose a significant risk to the financial system to fail. Congress particularly wanted to reduce the moral hazard of the too-big-to-fail doctrine and shift the burden of costs from taxpayers to the financial industry (Wallace 2013). The word 'allows' simply permits financially fragile companies to fail. It does not eradicate the too-big-to-fail concept. The combined effect of section 13(3) and section 204 of the Dodd–Frank Act is that shadow banks may convert into banks in a financial crisis. Since the size of the US shadow banking sector outgrew the regular banking sector (Pozsar *et al.* 2010), it is likely that Congress will intervene in an emergency to rescue such banks rather than let them fail.

Market forces can determine the size of banks. Financial organisations grow by mergers and acquisitions. Growth depends on competition law and regulatory and economic conditions. Regulators can control such growth. Between 1980 and 1994, there were 6,347 mergers, of which the Federal Reserve approved 4,507, the OCC approved 972 and the FDIC approved

868 (Rhoades 1996). Karmel (2011) argues that this was the regulators' fault for permitting these mergers, which led to the growth of banking giants. As a result, the top six US banks have total assets in excess of 63 per cent of US GDP. This is a huge increase from 17 per cent of GDP in 1997 (Johnson and Kwak 2010). Chapter 4 of this book has seen that the literature on competition and financial instability is inconclusive. It would therefore be hasty to suggest concentration or consolidation of US banks, even though the high concentration of the banking sectors in Australia, Canada and Germany provided a degree of resilience. Competition can be healthy but intense competition can lead to financial instability. Big banks can reduce risks by 'enhanced asset diversification' (Caprio *et al.* 2014), but risks can increase due to the too-big-to-fail doctrine. In times of crisis, financial stability will often prevail over competition law to safeguard public interest. This is demonstrated by the merger between Lloyds Banking Group and HBOS in the UK as well as Westpac and St George in Australia. The relevant regulators relaxed competition-law procedures to preserve financial stability. This is understandable due to the impact of externalities on the economy in a crisis. The Dodd–Frank Act does not deal with competition law directly. Further, the Dodd–Frank Act relies on the assumption that healthy banks will acquire weaker ones. When systemic risks can spread very quickly in a globalised network, there is a possibility that the government is the only organisation left which can bail out frail banks. The ban on government bailouts in the Dodd–Frank Act does not seem realistic (Conti-Brown 2011). The question we should consider, therefore, is how bailouts should be facilitated.

Admati *et al.* (2012) suggest an interesting method of dealing with the too-big-to-fail concept. They proposed the model of Liability Holding Companies (LHC), where shareholders have increased liability without removing the limited-liability concept of publicly traded security. It works by having LHCs hold all the equity of the systematically important financial institution, which does not enjoy limited liability. LHCs will hold additional assets 'in escrow' to ensure that they can meet increased liabilities. They submit that their model will reduce agency costs and government subsidies. This is because LHCs are funded entirely by equity and cannot take on debt, which reduces the possibility of a bailout (Admati *et al.* 2012). Conti-Brown (2011) goes further with his elective-shareholder-liability model. He suggests that shareholders, especially shareholders who are also directors and officers of a company, should have the control to take two actions. First, they should be able to change the capital structure of the company and reduce the level of leverage by raising the level of capital. Second, the shareholders should bear the costs of the bailout. The second strand of Conti-Brown's suggestion internalises social costs and is a good idea. However, the first strand is problematic. Unless the shareholders are officers of the company or are very knowledgeable in finance, they are unlikely or unrealistic to implement his suggestion. Although shareholder engagement is important in improving corporate governance, it has to work in conjunction with other initiatives, such as better risk management, regulation and enforcement (Lui 2015). Besides, with regular stress tests and micro-prudential information provided to regulators, regulators are better positioned to monitor banks' financial ratios.

One solution to reduce the complexity and interconnectedness of banks is to rely more on the traditional originate-to-hold model. Caprio *et al.*'s research (2014) revealed that countries with the originate-to-hold model rather than the originate-to-distribute model had a lower probability of crisis in 2008. It is important to remember that the various factors affecting the fragility of a country's economy are different. However, focusing on the financial crisis of 2007–9, Greenwood and Scharfstein (2013) explain that the shadow banking sector increased financial instability in three ways. First, it issued short-term claims and instruments which do not enjoy the benefit of explicit government guarantees. Ricks (2012) asserts that almost all the US government's financial support in the financial crisis was targeted at stabilising the market for short-term instruments. Second, shadow banking increased the length of the intermediation chain, which increases information asymmetry. Finally, shadow banking increased household leverage, although it also made household credit cheaper.

It can be argued that the above proposal is unrealistic since shadow banking is part of modern banking. It also produces some benefit in that it increases liquidity and the efficiency of the financial market (Cochrane 2013). In 2007, the US financial industry constituted 7.9 per cent of US GDP. Since 2007, however, the size of the financial industry has decreased as the shadow banking sector has shrunk considerably. An example is the size of outstanding asset-backed commercial paper. In 2001, the amount was $600 billion. Six years later, it had increased to $1.2 trillion. In 2013, the figure was $300 billion (Cochrane 2013). With time and the nature of business cycles, this figure may increase. Regulators will have to be prepared to regulate the US financial system so that is more resilient and easier to manage. One way of achieving this is for originators to retain a certain percentage of the securitised product. Evidence from the global financial crisis has revealed that the default rate of the worst securitised products in the EU is 0.1 per cent, compared to 16 per cent in the US. This is because EU originators usually keep a large part of the securitised product. The rationale of retaining a portion of the securitised product is that it incentivises originators to monitor the quality of the product (Buiter 2007; Pozen 2009). Pozen (2009) suggested that all originators should retain at least 5 per cent of the risk of loss for any loans they originate and sell into the secondary market. This has been adopted by the European Commission's framework for simple and transparent securitisation in 2015.

Other authors, such as Keller (2008) and Fender and Mitchell (2009), are less enthusiastic about retention of equity tranches. Keller (2008) said that, although it is not a requirement to retain an equity tranche, managers often buy or hold a portion of the equity tranche as part of the financial remuneration. There is still little evidence whether retention of tranches has a positive effect on the performance of collateralised-debt-obligations management. Only the market and future events can judge this. Retention of a tranche of the securitised product alone is unlikely to provide a panacea. However, given the comparison between the default rates of EU and US securitised products, mentioned earlier, it is worth adopting this proposal. The other recommendations in the European Commission's framework for simple and transparent securitisation are also sensible. In particular, measures such as homogenous packaging of loans so that there is no mixing of assets and no securitisation of securitisations should make the US financial system simpler (European Commission 2015). Other recommendations to improve transparency, such as a clear outline of the rights and obligations of the parties in securitisation and ongoing publication details of packaged loans, should also be adopted (European Commission 2015).

Structural gaps in US regulation dealing with too-big-to-fail

The US regulatory style is largely functional but it has some institutional elements. The functional approach to regulation and the focus on regulatory competition make it difficult for the various US regulators to co-ordinate and co-operate. The institutional approach to regulation is reflected in various sections of the Dodd–Frank Act, where a distinction is made between emergency lending by the Federal Reserve to banks and to non-banks. If the Federal Reserve wants to lend to non-banks, it needs approval from the Treasury. This combination of institutional and functional approaches to financial regulation is confusing and unlikely to achieve the demands of global banking. Further, till regulatory agencies are adequately funded, they are unlikely to perform well. Prasch (2012) submits that the US regulatory agencies were chronically underfunded due to 'regulatory capture'. Bankers and politicians share interests in banking, and underfunding the regulatory agencies meant there were fewer staff to conduct research and identify potential problems. As a result of this, the Financial Stability Oversight Council (FSOC) was established. It consists of members from all the federal financial regulatory agencies, who will identify and respond to systemic risks in the financial sector (Dodd–Frank Act: sections 111–76). The FSOC is supported by the Office of Financial Research. The FSOC will try to co-ordinate information sharing between the regulatory agencies, which is vital in a fragmented and complicated regulatory structure. The Federal Reserve has the power to regulate and set prudential standards for non-bank financial institutions if the FSOC requests. This is an attempt to regulate the regulatory lacuna where no agency had authority to regulate non-bank institutions (Wallace 2013). The Federal Reserve also has the power to recommend higher standards of liquidity and credit for bank holding companies and non-bank institutions.

Yet the Federal Reserve lacks powers to provide funding for solvent financial institutions affected by externalities (Acharya *et al.* 2011). This limitation may potentially lead to the winding up of large bank holding companies through the newly created Orderly Liquidation Authority (OLA). The OLA replaces the US bankruptcy process for large, complex banks. Acharya *et al.* (2011) posit that the OLA is unlikely to promote financial stability. Instead, since there are uncertainties with the procedures, the novelty and untested nature of the OLA and its impact on creditors' rights will contribute to financial instability. Yet the Dodd–Frank Act does provide the Federal Reserve and FDIC with the flexibility to design resolution procedures. To put an end to taxpayer bailouts of banks, Acharya *et al.* (2011) suggest that prudential regulators need to design resolution mechanisms for both systematically important and smaller financial institutions. Further, there should be appropriate mechanisms to deal with defaults by short-term creditors. These are both solid and sound suggestions which should be implemented to fulfil the aim of financial stability set out in the Dodd–Frank Act. For successful implementation, adequate resources should be given to regulators, in particular the newly formed FSOC, Office of Financial Research and the Systemic Risk Council, which regulates non-bank financial institutions. Early and timely information is the key to effective design of prudential supervision and crisis prevention. Financial crises will reoccur, albeit in different forms. Effective crisis resolution also requires timely exchange of information and co-operation between regulators. Friendly competition between regulators is harmless since it should create an incentive for better regulation and supervision. However, regulators should be working together as partners, not as rivals. This is particularly important given the combination of functional and institutional approaches to regulation in the US and its fragmented structure.

Deposit-guarantee schemes

A weak regulatory framework, including factors such as government deposit schemes, prudential regulation and capital requirements, also contributes to financial instability (Duke and Cejnar 2013). Academics have studied the relationship between deposit-guarantee schemes and financial stability. Gropp and Vesala (2004) found lower bank risk in the EU since the adoption of deposit guarantees. Karels and McCaltchey (1999) discovered similar stabilisation effects in the US when deposit guarantees were offered to credit unions. Yet deposit-guarantee schemes create moral hazard since banks have the assurance that the government will bail them out should they become financially fragile. Several academics (Barth *et al.* 2004; Demirguc-Kunt and Huizinga 2004; Duke and Cejnar 2013) submit that long-term use of deposit-guarantee schemes may actually threaten financial stability since it promotes risk-taking behaviour.

A recent paper by Anginer *et al.* (2014) studied the relationship between deposit-guarantee schemes and financial stability in 96 countries in 2004–6. They found that generous implicit government support in the form of deposit-guarantee schemes increased bank risk and financial instability in several countries in the years leading up to the financial crisis of 2007–9. During the crisis, however, deposit guarantees provided greater financial stability, and bank risk was lower, as confidence amongst depositors is vital to a financial system. On balance, Anginer *et al.* (2014) call for better bank supervision rather than relying on deposit-guarantee schemes. This is because the overall destabilisation effect of deposit-guarantee schemes in good times is greater than the stabilisation effect during financial crises. Boyle *et al.*'s (2015) research uses conjoint analysis, whereby they asked respondents from countries with explicit deposit-insurance schemes and those without to assess hypothetical deposit accounts (the accounts are insured to different degrees). Their results revealed that deposit-insurance schemes are only partially successful. This is because countries without explicit deposit insurance had a higher risk of bank withdrawals. Deposit insurance schemes which are more generous are also more effective, but the disadvantage is that they have more long-term systemic risks (Boyle *et al.* 2015). A limitation of Boyle *et al.*'s research is that it is based on hypothetical scenarios. If actual depositors are involved and incentives are different, the outcome may be different. Nonetheless, policymakers should be cautious of the impact of deposit-insurance schemes, especially their long-term systemic risk. Deposit-insurance schemes can provide confidence in the financial system (Breydo 2015) but greater confidence amongst depositors can be built via better banking regulation and supervision.

Micro-prudential regulation

The relationship between central-bank monetary policy and prudential regulation, especially micro-prudential regulation, is close. These days, currency prices are driven more by central-bank actions than economic factors, such as GDP growth and cross-border trading. The price of the Euro fell after the ECB launched its quantitative-easing programme in March 2015; and the Federal Reserve is likely to increase its interest rate and rely less on its quantitative-easing programme. From a regulatory angle, these indicators are interesting. When interest rates are low, banks will generally try to invest in non-traditional financial activities for higher yields (Barth *et al.* 2009). The Federal Reserve and regulators failed in the financial crisis of 2007–9 since they permitted a lax monetary policy, excessive leverage, maturity transformation and insufficient capital (Carmassi *et al.* 2009). By raising interest rates in March 2015, the Federal Reserve seemed to adopt the 'lean against the wind' policy to control credit and asset prices by trying to control the flow of credit, asset prices and leverage. This also increases US competitiveness and limits the value of its debts owed to countries such as China (Halligan 2015). The Eurozone is trying to depreciate the value of the Euro and thus increase its competitiveness. Depreciating the Euro during a long period of negative rates will only prolong a period of loose monetary policy. A potential currency war may arise and the loose monetary policy may cause the stock market to be more vulnerable to crashes. The Federal Reserve will have to ensure that the same mistakes of the financial crisis are not made again.

Regular stress tests will identify the micro-prudential weaknesses of each bank. The second round of the US Comprehensive Capital Analysis and Review (stress tests) took place in March 2015 and provided mixed results. Out of the biggest 31 banks operating in the US, 29 passed the Comprehensive Capital Analysis and Review. However, deep-seated problems remain with Bank of America, especially with its internal controls. Further, US banks have suffered a drop in profit after raising their equity-capital ratio (the ratio of high-quality capital to risk-weighted assets) from 5.5 per cent in 2009 to 12.5 per cent in the final quarter of 2014 (*The Economist* 2015). The average return on equity of the 31 banks is now approximately 8 per cent, much lower than before the financial crisis of 2007–9 (*The Economist* 2015). Shareholder activists will thus keep an eye on share performance and the Federal Reserve might come under pressure to relax capital requirements. The Federal Reserve will have to ensure that each bank's capital and leverage ratios are healthy and able to withstand externalities. Although the Federal Reserve and shareholders have different views on what constitutes good performance in a bank, the current sanction for failing to fulfil the stress tests is a change of management, as seen in Citigroup in 2014. A change of management at board level may align the interests of the regulator and shareholders since this would remove weak, non-performing directors. Shareholder activism could thus be a way to alert stakeholders, including the regulator, of potential weaknesses in a bank. Yet shareholder activism is difficult to achieve in countries such as the US with dispersed share ownership. Hill (2010) explains that, traditionally, the US corporate-law system focused on protection of shareholders, whilst the UK and European systems increased shareholder protection. In the UK, shareholders enjoy more statutory rights than in the US. For example, shareholders with a 5 per cent stake in the UK can compel a general meeting to be called in order to debate and vote on a valid resolution proposed by the relevant shareholder(s) (Companies Act 2006: section 292). The preamble to the US Sarbanes–Oxley Act 2002 confirms the reluctance to empower shareholders: 'an Act [t]o protect investors by improving the accuracy and reliability of corporate disclosures made pursuant to the securities laws, and for other purposes'. The Sarbanes–Oxley Act 2002 does not provide any greater opportunities for shareholder activism.

Other methods of improving information flow to the regulator are thus required. On-site supervisory visits by regulators give a solid picture of a bank's financial condition but they are costly for the supervisor and the supervised bank (Krainer and Lopez 2004) It appears that there is some consensus on using financial-market information for supervisory purposes. US supervisors have used market information 'informally' since the 1990s (Hamalainen *et al.* 2012). The combination of debt- and equity-based indicators have proved to be useful for supervisors in identifying 'problem' banks (Gropp *et al.* 2006). Hamalainen *et al.* (2012) conducted research into the use of four financial instruments to signal problems at Northern Rock in the UK: credit-default-swap spreads, subordinated debt spreads, implied volatility from options prices and equity measures of bank risk. They concluded that equity-market information provided the timeliest and clearest signal of bank conditions. Their results also showed that credit default swaps and subordinated debt were useful but structural problems hindered the signalling effect of these products. Due to market structure, it is difficult to obtain clear signals from subordinated debt. With credit default swaps, the market is not sufficiently deep in small banks. For the UK regulator, equity-market information provided early signals of concern, whilst subordinated debt and credit default swaps were only useful to the regulator once it started to communicate with Northern Rock.

Market prices which are 'informationally efficient' can be a complement to effective financial regulation (Gilson and Kraakman 2014). Gilson and Kraakman (2014) believe that the Federal Reserve did not have more information than the market about derivatives and mortgage-backed securities. Therefore, they submit that more informed market prices could have enabled the Federal Reserve to design better and quicker intervention. Market efficiency is relative in that it identifies weaknesses and frictions which reduce price efficiency. Gilson and Kraakman believe that the stress tests and Dodd–Frank attempts to improve transparency should lead to relative 'informationally efficient' market information. Mishkin (2010) said that: 'The stress tests were a key factor that helped increase the amount of information in the marketplace, thereby reducing asymmetric information and adverse selection and moral hazard problems'. Through regular and robust stress tests, the Federal Reserve should closely monitor the capital and leverage ratios of individual banks and tailor suitable interventions where appropriate. Equity-market information should provide early warning signals to the Federal Reserve. To fully utilise the signals which credit default swaps and subordinated debt can provide, the Federal Reserve should also engage and communicate regularly with banks.

Conclusion

The first part of this chapter examined the Federal Reserve's responses during the financial crisis of 2007–9 and the institutional weaknesses in the US regulatory agencies. In the build-up to the financial crisis, the Federal Reserve were criticised for keeping interest rates low, thus allowing leverage ratios to build up. The Federal Reserve and the SEC were also criticised for their supervisory failures. As the impact of the crisis deepened, the Federal Reserve responded in two ways: with conventional and unconventional mechanisms. Conventional mechanisms included cuts in the target federal funds rate and the discount-borrowing rate from mid 2007 to mid 2008. It also extended the maturity of discount-window loans. However, the financial market has grown in complexity since the 1980s (financial innovation has led to the use of innovative financial products and processes such as securitisation) and the Federal Reserve also had to limit the damage caused by the money market, securities and derivatives by reducing the premium on the discount-lending rate from 100 to 20 basis points above the federal funds rate, creating the Term Auction Facility, TSLF and PDCF and using emergency powers under section 13(3) of the Federal Reserve Act 1913 to lend to non-banks. The Federal Reserve tried to protect consumers during the financial crisis by identifying solutions to avoid foreclosures and their negative effects. Nevertheless, along with lenders, borrowers and other regulators, the Federal Reserve was criticised for contributing to the explosion of sub-prime mortgages. Regulation and supervision were too weak to tackle mortgage fraud, lax borrowing standards and the perverse incentives imposed on lenders.

US financial architecture is inherently complex and fragmented. One pervasive issue is the problem of regulatory overlap. An example of regulatory overlap is the implementation of TARP during the financial crisis; and the lack of transparency was primarily due to regulatory overlap. There are, however, examples of regulators working together, such as on-site visits to Goldman Sachs, Lehman Brothers, Merrill Lynch and Morgan Stanley. These visits were useful to the extent that Lehman Brothers improved its capital position, but it was too late. The Federal Reserve did, however, try to co-operate with other international regulators and central banks in the UK and Europe on monetary and regulatory policies.

The second part of this chapter examined the macro- and micro-prudential regulatory frameworks in the US under the Dodd–Frank Act. It has been demonstrated in this chapter that the Federal Reserve's monetary policy and regulatory and supervisory functions are complementary and should not be separated. The chapter also focused on the issue of too-big-to-fail in the US. This is a tricky issue, particularly since the US has a large number of systematically important financial institutions. Although the Dodd–Frank Act states that it will eliminate the too-big-to-fail problem and require the financial industry to bear the costs of bank failures, there are still legislative and structural gaps. From a legislative perspective, the dichotomy between the Federal Reserve's ability to lend to banks in an emergency and its inability to lend to non-banks seems nonsensical. Non-banks created financial instability during the financial crisis, and providing liquidity is a way of limiting systemic risks. Sub-prime mortgages illustrate the twin problems of complex and opaque securitised products. There should be US legislation introducing measures similar to the EU framework for simple, transparent and standardised securitisation to reduce complexity and opacity in the financial sector. Recent empirical research on deposit-insurance schemes shows that, at best, they provide short-term financial stability during a financial crisis. However, they involve long-term systemic risks. Better preventative measures such as more effective regulation and supervision may be preferred to deposit-insurance schemes. One important aspect of macro-prudential regulation is to ensure compliance and implementation of healthy capital, liquidity and leverage ratios. The important point with capital is that it has to be of good quality to absorb losses, thus asset quality is crucial.

Stress tests are a good way of informing regulators of potential weaknesses in micro-prudential regulation and supervision. On-site visits are expensive for both regulators and banks, so market information (about both equity and credit default swaps) is useful to regulators in providing 'informationally efficient' information. Shareholder activism is also useful for raising potential problems in a financial institution. Yet the nature of the Sarbanes–Oxley Act and the dispersed ownership structure of share ownership in the US are not conducive to greater shareholder activism.

The key ingredients to remedy structural defects in a regulatory system are adequate resources, close co-operation and communication of timely information. US politicians need to ensure that regulatory agencies are well staffed and have sufficient resources to carry out their jobs. The combination of functional and institutional regulatory approaches in the Dodd–Frank Act is unhelpful, but this can be overcome by the regulatory agencies working in harmony and not as rivals. The balance of financial stability and financial innovation is difficult to achieve, particularly in the US, where financial innovation plays a big part. To achieve financial stability, the above legislative and structural weaknesses have to be addressed.

Bibliography

Acharya, V., Cooley, T., Richardson, M., Sylla, R. and Walter, I. (2011) 'The Dodd–Frank Wall Street Reform and Consumer Protection Act: Accomplishments and Limitations', *Journal of Applied Corporate Finance*, 23(1), pp. 43–56.

Admati, A., Conti-Brown, P. and Pleiderer, P. (2012) 'Liability Holding Companies', *UCLA Law Review*, 59(4), pp. 852–913.

Adrian, T. and Shin, H. S. (2009) 'Money, Liquidity, and Monetary Policy', *American Economic Review*, 99(2), pp. 600–5.

Alessandri, P. and Haldane, A. G. (2009) *Banking on the State*, London: Bank of England.

Anginer, D., Demirguc-Kunt, A. and Zhu, M. (2014) 'How Does Deposit Insurance Affect Bank Risk? Evidence from the Recent Crisis', *Journal of Banking & Finance*, 48, pp. 312–21.

Ashcraft, A. and Schuermann, T. (2008) 'The Seven Deadly Frictions of Subprime Mortgage Credit Securitisation', *The Investment Professional*, Fall, pp. 1–11.

Bank of England (2008) *Bank of England Court of Directors' Minutes 2007–2009*, B2, London: Bank of England.

Bank of England (2009) *Bank of England Court of Directors' Minutes 2007–2009*, London: Bank of England.

Barth, J., Caprio, G. and Levine, R. (2004) 'Bank Regulation and Supervision: What Works Best?', *Journal of Financial Intermediation*, 13(2), pp. 205–48.

Barth, J., Li, T., Lu, W., Phumiwasana, T. and Yago, G. (2009) *The Rise and Fall of the US Mortgage Markets*, John Wiley and Sons, Hoboken, NJ

Baxter, T. (2010) *Too Big to Fail: Expectations and Impact of Extraordinary Government Intervention and the Role of Systemic Risk in the Financial Crisis* Washington D.C.: Federal Reserve Bank of New York.

Bernanke, B. S. (2013) *The Federal Reserve and the Financial Crisis*, Princeton University Press.

Bhutta, N. (2008) '"Giving Credit Where Credit is Due?" The Community Reinvestment Act and Mortgage Lending in Lower income Neighborhoods', Finance and Economics Discussion Series, Federal Reserve Board, Washington, DC [online], available: www.federalreserve.gov/pubs/feds/2008/200861/200861abs.html'.

Board of Governors of the Federal Reserve System (2005) *The Federal System Purposes and Functions*, Washington DC.

Boyle, G., Stover, R., Tiwana, A. and Zhylyevskyy, O. (2015) 'The Impact of Deposit Insurance on Depositor Behavior During a Crisis: A Conjoint Analysis Approach', *Journal of Financial Intermediation*, 24(4), pp. 590–601.

Brei, M. and Gambacorta, l. (2014) *BIS Working Papers No 471. The Leverage Ratio over the Cycle*.

Breydo, L. (2015) 'Structural Foundations of Financial Stability: What Canada Can Teach America about Building a Better Regulatory System', *University of Pennsylvania Journal of Business Law*, 17(3), pp. 973–1082.

Buiter, W. (2007) 'Lessons from the 2007 Financial Crisis', *Social Science Research Network (SSRN) Working Paper No. 1140525*.

Bush, O., Knott, S. and Peacock, C. (2014) *Why is the UK Banking Sector So Big and Is That a Problem?*, 54, United Kingdom: Bank of England.

Calomiris, C. (2009) 'A Recipe for Ratings Reform', *The Economists Voice*, 6(11), Article 5.

Caprio, G., D'Aprice, V., Ferri, G. and Puopolo, G. (2014) 'Macro-financial Determinants of the Great Financial Crisis: Implications for Financial Regulation', *Journal of Banking & Finance*, 44, pp. 114–29.

Caprio, G., Demirguc-Kunt, A. and Kane, E. (2008) *The 2007 Meltdown in Structured Securitisation: Searching for Lessons, Not Scapegoats*.

Carmassi, J., Gros, D. and Micossi, S. (2009) 'The Global Financial Crisis: Causes and Cures', *Journal of Common Market Studies*, 47(5), pp. 977–96.

Cecchetti, S. (2009) 'Crisis and Responses: The Federal Reserve in the Early Stages of the Financial Crisis', *The Journal of Economic Perspectives*, 23(1), pp. 51–76.

Cochrane, J. (2013) 'Finance: Function Matters, Not Size', *Journal of Economic Perspectives*, 27(2), pp. 29–50.

Conti-Brown, P. (2011) *Elective Shareholder Liability*, Internal Report, unpublished.

Cooley, T., Schoenholtz, K., Smith, G., Sylla, R. and Wachtel, P. (2010) 'The Power of Central Banks and the Future of the Federal Reserve System' in Acharya, V. V., Cooley, T., Richardson, M. and Walter, I., eds., *Regulating Wall Street: The Dodd-Frank Act and the New Architecture of Global Finance* Wiley.

D'Hulster, K. (2009) *The Leverage Ratio– A New Binding Limit on Banks*, Washington D.C.

Davies, H. and Ball, J. (2015) 'HSBC Is "Cast-iron Certain" to Breach Banking Rules Again, Executive Admits', *The Guardian* [online], available: http://www.theguardian.com/business/2015/apr/02/hsbc-cast-iron-certain-breach-rules-executive [accessed 15 January 2016].

Dell'Ariccia, G., Igan, D. and Laeven, L. (2008) *Credit Booms and Lending Standards: Evidence from the Subprime Mortgage Market* New York: International Monetary Fund.

Demirguc-Kunt, A. and Huizinga, H. (2004) 'Market Discipline and Deposit Insurance', *Journal of Monetary Economics*, 51(2), pp. 375–99.

Demyanyk, Y. and van Hemert, O. (2011) 'Understanding the Subprime Mortgage Crisis', *Rev. Financ. Stud.*, 24(6), pp. 1848–80.

Doward, J. (2015) 'HSBC: Five Questions for a Bank That Grew Too Big to Control', *The Guardian*, 17 February 2015.

Duke, A. and Cejnar, L. (2013) 'Competition and the Banking Sector: Friend or Foe?', *Law & Financial Markets Review*, 7(3), pp. 152–8.

The Economist (2015) 'Stress Testing America's Banks – Looking Peaky' [online], available: http://www.economist.com/news/business-and-finance/21646276-c-day [accessed 15 March 2015].

European Commission (2015) *European Commission Fact Sheet-A European framework for Simple and Transparent Securitisation*, Brussels: European Commission.

Fein, M. (2008) *The Emergency Economic Stabilization Act of 2008: Was It Necessary?* (November 1, 2008). Available at SSRN: http://ssrn.com/abstract=1647094, Internal Report, unpublished.

Feldstein, M. (2010) 'What Powers for the Federal Reserve?', *Journal of Economic Literature*, 48, pp. 1343–62.

Fender, I. and Mitchell, J. (2009). 'The Future of Securitisation: How to Align Incentives?' *BIS Quarterly Review*, September, pp. 27–43.

Fleming, M., Hrung, W. and Keane, F. (2009) 'The Term Securities Lending Facility: Origin, Design, and Effects', *Federal Reserve Bank of New York Current Issues in Economics and Finance*, 15(2).

Gadinis, S. (2013) 'From Independence to Politics in Financial Regulation', *California Law Review*, 101, pp. 327–406.

Geithner, T. (2008) 'Testimony before the US Senate Committee on Banking, Housing and Urban Affairs, Washington D.C.', *Turmoil in U.S. Credit Markets: Examining the Recent Actions of Federal Financial Regulators*.

Ghosh, S. and Mohamed, S. (2010) 'The Troubled Asset Relief Program (TARP) and Its Limitations: An Analysis', *International Journal of Law and Management,*, 52(2), pp. 124–43.

Gilson, R. and Kraakman, R. (2014) 'Market Efficiency after the Financial Crisis: It's Still a Matter of Informational Costs', *Virginia Law Review*, 100(2), pp. 313–76.

Gordon, J. and Muller, C. (2010) *Avoiding Eight-alarm Fires in the Political Economy of Systemic Risk Management*, Internal Report, unpublished.

Greenwood, R. and Scharfstein, D. (2013) 'The Growth of Modern Finance', *Journal of Economic Perspectives*, 27(2), pp. 3–28.

Gropp, R. and Vesala, J. (2004) 'Deposit Insurance, Moral Hazard and Market Monitoring'. European Central Bank Working Paper No. 302.

Gropp, R., Vesala, J. and Vulpes, G. (2006) 'Equity and Bond Market Signals as Leading Indicators of Bank Fragility', *Journal of Money, Credit and Banking*, 38, pp. 399–428.

Grove, H. and Clouse, M. (2013) 'A Financial Risk and Fraud Model Comparison of Bear Stearns and Lehman Brothers: Was the Right or Wrong Firm Bailed Out?', *Corporate Ownership and Control, Special Issue: Financial Distress: Corporate Governance and Financial Reporting Issues*, 11(87).

Halligan, L. (2015) 'Currency Wars Threaten Lehman-style Crisis', *The Telegraph* [online], available: http://www.telegraph.co.uk/finance/comment/liamhalligan/11472336/Currency-wars-threaten-Lehman-style-crisis.html [accessed 15 March 2015].

Hamalainen, P., Pop, A., Hall, M. and Howcroft, B. (2012) 'Did the Market Signal Impending Problems at Northern Rock? An Analysis of Four Financial Instruments', *European Financial Management*, 18(1), pp. 68–87.

Hart, O. and Zingales, L. (2009) 'To Regulate Finance, Try the Market', *The New Foreign Policy.com*[online], available: http://experts.foreignpolicy.com/posts/2009/03/30/to_regulate_finance_try_the_market [accessed 3 March 2015].

Herring, R. and Carmassi, J. (2008) 'The Structure of Cross-Sector Financial Supervision', *Financial Markets, Institutions & Instruments*, 17(1), pp. 51–76.

Hildebrand, P. (2008) *Speech by Mr Philipp M Hildebrand, Vice-Chairman of the Governing Board of the Swiss National Bank, at the Financial Markets Group Lecture, 15 December 2008.*, London: London School of Economics.

Hill, J. (2010) 'Then and Now: Professor Berle and the Unpredictable Shareholder', *Seattle University Law Review*, 33(4), pp.1005–23.

International Monetary Fund (2014) *Cross-border Bank Resolution: Recent Developments*, Washington D.C.

Johnson, S. and Kwak, J. (2010) *13 Bankers: The Wall Street Takeover and the Next Financial Meltdown*, Toronto: Pantheon Books.

Karels, G. and McClatchey, C. (1999) 'Deposit Insurance and Risk-taking Behavior in the Credit Union Industry', *Journal of Banking and Finance*, 23(1), pp. 105–34.

Karmel, R. (2011) 'An Orderly Liquidation Authority Is Not the Solution to Too-big-to fail', *Brooklyn Journal of Corporate Finance and Commercial Law*, 6, pp. 1–46.

Keller, J. (2008) 'Agency Problems in Structured Finance—A Case Study of European CLOs', available: SSRN 1258982.

King, M. (2013) 'Challenges for the Future', *International Journal of Central Banking*, pp. 359–65.

Krainer, J. and Lopez, J. (2004) 'Incorporating Equity Market Information into Supervisory Monitoring Models', *Journal of Money, Credit and Banking*, 36(6), pp. 1043–67.

Laeven, L., Ratnovski, L. and Tong, H. (2014) *Bank Size and Systemic Risk*, SDN/14/04, Washington DC: International Monetary Fund.

Lui, A. (2015) 'Cross-border Share Voting and Improving Voting Chain Deficiencies in the 21st century', *International Journal of Corporate Governance*, 6(1), pp. 70–85.

Mishkin, F. (2010) 'Over the Cliff: From the Subprime to the Global Financial Crisis', *Journal of Economic Perspectives*, 25(49), pp. 49–62.

Morris, S. and Shin, H. (2008) 'Financial Regulation in a System Context', *Brookings Papers on Economic Activity*, 2, pp. 229–61.

Murdoch, C. (2011) 'The Dodd–Frank Wall Street Reform and Consumer Protection Act: What Caused the Financial Crisis and Will Dodd–Frank Succeed in Preventing Future Crises?', *S.M.U.L. Review*, 64, pp. 1243–30.

Murphy, E. (2013) *Who Regulates Whom and How? An Overview of U.S. Financial Regulatory Policy for Banking and Securities Markets*, 7–5700, United States.

Pozen, R. (2009) 'How to Restore Confidence in Loan Securitisation', *Financial Times* [online], available: http://www.ft.com/cms/s/0/f45e6dbc-e8af-11de-9c1f-00144feab49a.html#axzz2SzwE82lm [accessed 15 December 2009].

Pozsar, Z., Adrian, T., Ashcraft, A. and Boesky, H. (2010) 'Shadow Banking', *Federal Reserve Bank of New York Staff Report*, 458, pp. 1–38.

Prasch, R. (2012) 'The Dodd–Frank Act: Financial Reform or Business as Usual?', *Journal of Economic Issues*, XLV1(2), pp. 549–55.

Rhoades, S. (1996) *Bank Mergers and Industrywide Structure, 1980–1994*, United States of America: Board of Governors of the Federal Reserve System.

Richardson, M. and White, L. (2009) 'Fixing the Rating Agencies: Is Regulation the Answer', *Voxeu* [online], available: www.voxeu.org/index.php?q=node/2958 [accessed 13 July 2015].

Ricks, M. (2012) 'Reforming the Short-Term Funding Markets,', *Harvard John M. Oline Discussion Paper, No. 713.*

Scheuerman, W. (2000) 'Exception and Emergency Powers: The Economic State of Emergency', *Cardozo Law Review,* 21, pp. 1869–84.

Shah, A. (2009) 'Emergency Economic Stabilization Act of 2008', *Harvard Journal of Legislation,* 46, pp. 569–84.

Shirakawa, M. (2013) 'Central Banking: Before, during and after the Crisis', *International Journal of Central Banking,* (January), pp. 373–87.

Smith, G. (2015) 'Deutsche, HSBC Say Goodbye to Being Too-big-to-manage', *Fortune Magazine* [online], available: http://fortune.com/2015/04/27/deutsche-hsbc-say-goodbye-to-being-too-big-to-manage/ [accessed 11 January 2016].

Tarr, D. (2010) 'The Political, Regulatory, and Market Failures That Caused the US Financial Crisis', *Journal of Financial Economic Policy,* 2(2), pp. 163–86.

Turner, L. (2011) 'Does Wall Street Really Run the World?' Town Hall Discussion, School of Accountancy, Daniels College of Business, University of Denver, September 15, 2011.

US Government Accountability Office (2004) *Financial Regulation: Industry Changes Prompt Need to Reconsider U.S. Regulatory Structure,* GAO-05-61, United States of America.

US Government Accountability Office (2007) *Financial Regulation Industry Changes Prompt Need to Reconsider U.S. Regulatory Structure,* Report to the Chairman, Committee on Banking, Housing, and Urban Affairs, U.S. Senate.

US Government Accountability Office (2009a) *Characteristics and Performance of Nonprime Mortgages,* United States of America.

US Government Accountability Office (2009b) *Financial Regulation: A Framework for Crafting and Assessing Proposals to Modernize the Outdated U.S. Financial Regulatory System,* United States of America.

US Treasury (2009) 'Treasury, Federal Reserve and the FDIC Provide Assistance to Bank of America', 16 January [online], available: www.treas.gov/press/releases/hp1356.htm.

Wallace, W. H. (2013) *The American Monetary System: An Insider's View of Financial Institutions, Markets and Monetary Policy,* Springer.

Wallison, P. (2011) *Financial Crisis Inquiry Commission: The Financial Crisis Inquiry Report 444,* United States of America.

World Bank (2015) *World Development Indicators* [online], available: http://data.worldbank.org/data-catalog/world-development-indicators [accessed 25 August 2015].

World Economic Forum (2012) *The Financial Development Report 2012* [online], available: http://www.weforum.org/issues/financial-development [accessed 6 April 2015].

6 Canada

Introduction

In an increasingly complex world of finance, simplicity and conservatism worked well in Canada. Canada is evidence that stronger financial regulation can lead to financially stable and successful outcomes through entire economic cycles of boom and bust (Porter 2010). No Canadian bank experienced a bank run nor was any government bailout required. Moreover, banks continued to lend money when, across the border, US banks were unable to do so due to a liquidity freeze. Although the US and Canada share a border and have close bilateral relationships in trade, the differences between the US and Canadian financial regulatory structure and their experiences during the financial crisis of 2007–9 are stark. There was relatively little damage done to the Canadian financial system for a plethora of reasons, including the economic history of the Canadian financial structure and framework, good compliance with the Basel III Accord, an extensive branching network which gives financial stability, a conservative funding model with short-term debts, a relatively simple financial regulatory structure, strong prudential regulation and supervision by one prudential regulator, regular updating of financial legislation, a well-designed system of deposit insurance, crisis management of failed banks and less interconnection amongst banks than in the US because of the originate-to-hold model (Anand 2010; Jackson 2013). Most importantly, Canadian investment dealers were regulated by the same rules as commercial banks, and the law regulating the Canadian mortgage market was strict, thus reducing the exposure of Canadian banks to the problems associated with sub-prime mortgages (Mohsni and Otchere 2014). All these reasons did not happen overnight. A steady history of sound and prudent regulation and supervision by the Office of the Superintendent of Financial Institutions (OSFI) coupled with sound, long-term monetary and fiscal policies have had a positive impact on the Canadian financial system.

Has Canada's framework achieved an effective balance of financial stability and innovation? Canada's performance in the Financial Development Index of the World Economic Forum 2012 was mixed. Overall, it ranked sixth for the third consecutive year. Its strengths were in institutional and financial environment, ranking sixth and ninth respectively (World Economic Forum 2012). Although Canada's banking system is stable (ranked fifth), the overall ranking for financial stability is low due to a weak score for currency stability (ranked 46th). The unstable Canadian dollar led to a decrease in the net-international-investment-to-GDP indicator. Other weaknesses included a decrease in the size (ranked 19th) and efficiency (ranked 16th) of Canadian banking financial services. Canada can also improve its access to commercial capital (ranked 12th) (World Economic Forum 2012). In light of these rankings, it is argued that there are certainly areas for improvement in the Canadian financial structure. It is understandable that there is a trade-off between financial stability and innovation. Although some academics argue that financial innovation leads to greater economic efficiency (Merton 1995; Merton and Bodie 1995), an effective balance of financial stability and innovation in Canada has yet to be found. This chapter will focus particularly on two macro-prudential issues: first, whether Canada needs a single national securities regulator and, second, whether the tight oligopoly of Canadian banks intensifies the 'too big to fail' problem and the concentration of the banking sector. The federal government tried to establish a federal regulator responsible for implementing a single statue on Canadian securities. In December 2011, however, the Supreme Court of Canada held that the legislation was unconstitutional. Since this decision, scholars have debated whether a single securities regulator is desirable, especially after the 2012 budget recommended it. The best kept secret of the global financial crisis will also be revealed.

The Bank of Canada and institutional weaknesses during the financial crisis of 2007-9

The Canadian regulatory structure

As it is in the US, financial supervision is split at provincial and federal levels in Canada. Thirteen securities regulators at the provincial level supervise securities dealers, mutual funds, credit unions and provincially incorporated trusts (Jackson 2013). At the federal level the Parliament of Canada sits at the apex of the financial structure. The Minister of Finance reports directly to Parliament and heads of the Department of Finance. There are four independent government agencies responsible for supervising all banks, federally incorporated insurance companies, trust and loan companies, co-operative credit associations and federal pension plans (Jackson 2013). The four agencies are the Office of the Superintendent of Financial Institutions (OSFI), Bank of Canada, Canada Deposit Insurance Corporation (CDIC) and Department of Finance. These four agencies regulate systemic risks in the Canadian financial system. The OSFI is the integrated financial regulator of Canada. After the collapse of two small banks in Canada (Northland Bank of Canada and Canadian Commercial Bank), the Estey Commission (1986) proposed that the OSFI should have a stronger mandate and increased independence (Choudhri and Schembri 2013). The Bank of Canada was established in 1934 and its main function is to 'to promote the economic and financial welfare of Canada' (Bank of Canada Act 1985). The fact that Canada did not have a central bank till 1934 is interesting since free banking in the 1920s meant that private commercial banks controlled monetary and credit policies, although the Ministry of Finance provided access to a lending window (Choudhri and Schembri 2013). Canada had very little macro- or micro-prudential regulation and supervision in the 1920s, but this changed after the Great Depression when the Canadian regulatory framework was bolstered. Canada learnt from the Great Depression and entered the global financial crisis of 2007–9 with a stronger and more robust regulatory framework.

As the central bank, the Bank of Canada is responsible for setting the country's monetary policy, promoting safe and sound financial systems, designing Canada's bank notes and managing public debt and foreign reserves. Parliament created the CDIC in 1967 to protect customers by insuring deposits in banks, trust and loan companies. The FCAC is responsible for consumer protection and promoting responsible financial conduct. The Estey Commission (1986) also introduced better macro- and micro-prudential supervision between agencies, establishing the Financial Institutions Supervisory Committee, Senior Advisory Committee and Heads of Agencies (Choudhri and Schembri 2013).

Prior to the financial crisis of 2007–9, the Bank of Canada pursued a conservative macro-economic policy, which reduced the government's debt relative to GDP, and a relatively tight monetary policy, which focused on price stability (Jackson 2013). The IMF believes that these tools increased Canada's resilience in weathering the financial crisis. The government's debt in 2004 was 72.5 per cent, which was then reduced to 66.5 per cent in 2008 (Statistics Portal 2015). Introduced in 1991, the inflation target in Canada is 2 per cent and this is reviewed every five years. Statistics reveal that both the headline and core-consumer-price-index inflation rates between 2003 and 2007 were not far off the 2 per cent target, and the general-financial-conditions index shows that the overall financial conditions were exceptionally accommodative (International Monetary Fund 2015). These measures protected Canada to a certain extent, but it was by no means immune to the spillover effect of systemic risks in the global financial system.

Performances of the Bank of Canada and Canadian regulators during the global financial crisis

The financial crisis of 2007–9 has demonstrated that a conservative funding model and culture did not fully protect Canadian banks. At a macro-prudential level, Canadian banks were more resilient than banks in other jurisdictions. Canada's experience in the financial crisis is an interesting comparison to the experiences of the US and UK. It demonstrates how the Canadian central bank, government and regulators exerted better control over housing policy and financial stability. According to Gordon Nixon, the Chief Executive Officer of Royal Bank of Canada,

> Everybody wants to take credit for why Canada managed through – the government, the regulators, the central bank, the banks, bank management – and frankly everyone deserves some credit... But, in my judgment, the single most relevant and most important differentiator for Canada was *the structure of our residential mortgage market.*
>
> (Kiladze *et al.* 2013)

The global financial crisis started as a sub-prime mortgage crisis in the US. In Canada, sub-prime mortgages accounted for around only 5 per cent of mortgages, which significantly reduced exposure to the toxic nature of the mortgages. Securitisation is not widespread in Canada. In fact, around only a third of mortgages are securitised because securities law dictates that mortgages held by banks with a loan-to-value ratio of 80 per cent need to be insured (Jackson 2013). Finally, the term of mortgages is short, around 5–10 years because pre-payment penalties reduce the demand for long-term mortgages. The relationship of debt and asset bubbles was better understood and controlled in Canada than in other jurisdictions, such as the US and UK. But with banks being required to hold more capital, how can they ensure that they have sufficient liquidity and flexibility to deal with another crisis? Jim Leech of the Ontario Teachers' Pension Plan said:

> The biggest thing you've got to concern yourself about in an institution like ours is liquidity... So although we had, by all of our formulas, lots of liquidity, I remember the fatal discussions of why don't we just double the liquidity requirement for the sake of it.
>
> (Kiladze *et al.* 2013)

The financial crisis affected Canada in two stages. The first stage, in 2007, was the asset-backed-commercial-paper (ABCP) problem. ABCP is a short-term debt of less than a year. It is different to commercial paper since ABCP is backed by assets. It is a type of collateralised debt obligation. In July 2007, the ABCP market froze because investors began to worry about the quality of their securities, particularly the values of the longer-term assets backing the ABCP, when the sub-prime mortgage crisis hit the US. In Canada, these investors included both retail and institutional investors, such as the Caisse de dépôt et placement du Québec, which had around CAD$13.2 billion of third-party ABCP (Anand 2010). When the sponsors (non-bank financial companies) requested funding under their liquidity facilities and were denied, the issuers were unable to refinance the maturing ABCP. There was a drought in the ABCP market. Knight (2012) praises the government for imposing a moratorium on repayments of ABCP borrowings till the problems in the market were resolved, but Anand (2010) criticises the failure of the regulators to work together to thaw the ABCP market. This was demonstrated by the contrasting reactions from regulators, where some of the provincial securities regulators initially refused to accept responsibility.

A report from the Investment Industry Regulatory Organisation of Canada in 2008 revealed that dealers were partly to blame for the ABCP incident. Some dealers in Canada paid little attention to the underlying assets of the ABCP instruments. This was negligence on the part of the dealers because three US rating agencies refused to rate the ABCP instruments due to their liquidity provisions (Brzezinski 2009). Yet this warning was ignored by some Canadian dealers. In 2009, the Hockin Report (2009) found that the OSFI was also to blame for the ABCP turmoil. Systemic risks are no longer confined to banks. Rather, they are prevalent in the capital markets, and the Hockin Report (2009) criticised the OSFI for failing to supervise firms which created non-bank ABCP. This meant that these firms were not subject to Canadian capital guidelines (Brzezinski 2009). In the second part of this chapter, the question of whether Canada needs a single national securities regulator will be discussed in depth. The second stage of the financial crisis of 2007–9 manifested in early 2008 in the form of a drought in the short-term money market in the US. This is the period when Bear Stearns and AIG were rescued by the US government. Fortunately, since Canadian banks had conservative funding models, with heavy reliance on deposit funding, fewer securitised assets and sound loan books, this drought in the short-term money market had a minimal impact on the Canadian financial system (Knight 2012).

Minimal yet clever intervention by the Bank of Canada and the government was a positive point of the Canadian financial framework (Blakely 2008). Between 2008 and 2009, the Bank of Canada did not inject any capital into the economy, in contrast to the US's Capital Purchase Programme within the Troubled Asset Programme, which allowed financial institutions to apply for non-voting, preferred shares. The Bank of Canada did inject liquidity into the economy, however. This was achieved by increasing the size of the term purchase and resale agreements (TPRA) and by extending the range of acceptable collateral under the Standing Liquidity Facility (Longworth 2009; Baron 2012). The Bank of Canada has been praised for being 'aggressive yet flexible' (Porter 2010). The TPRA is a good example of this since the Bank of Canada added three elements to its usual lending arrangements: the range of counterparties, eligible securities, which included ABCP and certain US Treasury securities, and the size of the funds, from CAD$4 billion in the spring of 2008 to CAD$37 billion in December 2008 (Longworth 2009). These are extraordinary lending measures but are justifiable in terms of their scale and speed due to the magnitude of the potential damage of the global financial crisis.

Even more impressive is the staggered approach of the TPRA, since it later introduced more generous lending facilities to the money markets and then private-sector securities in response to the problems emanating from secondary financial markets. The private-sector-securities TPRA facility allowed dealers access to funding because they were unable to obtain funding under the regular TPRA mechanism. Close monitoring by the Bank of Canada also demonstrated its initiative and readiness for future troubles. It set up an additional liquidity-support mechanism in the form of a US$30 billion swap line. Swap lines are advantageous for two reasons: first, they ensure a smooth flow of liquidity at the international level; second, they allow Canadian financial institutions to borrow in a foreign currency (Longworth 2009). Most Canadian banks have branches or subsidiaries in the US and can use the Federal Reserve's discount window. Therefore, this swap line might not be used at all. In fact, it has not been used to date. However, it is an example of the forward-thinking, bold and innovative approach to providing financial stability in Canada.

The extension of the Canada Mortgage Housing Corporation (CMHC) programme to purchase government-insured mortgages also provided much needed liquidity in the financial market. The CMHC sells mortgage insurance. In Canada, mortgages with a loan-to-value ratio of more than 80 per cent need to be insured 100 per cent to reduce risk. The government expanded the CMHC programme and released liquidity into the market when the securitisation market dried up. This was achieved by the launch of a CAD$125 million programme whereby the Department of Finance bought CMHC bonds from Canadian banks. Selling these bonds was not a sign of bank distress, so it was not intrusive (Blakely 2008). The CMHC scheme is a demonstration of the government's innovation and judgement. Jim Leech of the Ontario Teachers' Pension Plan described the CHMC programme as very 'smart' since 'it really didn't increase the government's risk, it just slammed liquidity into the system, which was badly needed' (Kiladze *et al.* 2013). Finally, whilst the US Federal Deposit Insurance Corporation increased deposit insurance from US$100,000 to US$250,000 per depositor, the Canada Deposit Insurance Corporation provided deposit insurance of CAD$100,000 per depositor (Baron 2012).

The Canadian government also improved access to capital and provided additional finance under the Extraordinary Financing Framework of 2009. The government bought $50 billion of insured mortgage pools in the first half of 2009–10 under the Insured Mortgage Purchase Programme. This provided long-term, stable funding to lenders. Second, the government allocated up to $12 billion to a new Canadian Secured Credit Facility to buy term backed by loans and leases on vehicles and equipment. Third, in order to enable Canadian deposit-taking financial institutions access to the global credit market, the Canadian Lenders Assurance Facility was set up. Fourth, the creation of the Canadian Lenders Assurance Facility and the Canadian Life Insurers Assurance Facility provided insurance on wholesale borrowing of deposit-taking institutions regulated at the federal level. All these government measures made substantial contributions to improving access to funding for financial institutions (Government of Canada 2009). The Bank of

Canada was, overall, proactive in maintaining financial stability during the global financial crisis through a number of extraordinary liquidity and capital injections.

Working closely with the Bank of Canada, the OSFI was commended for its regulatory and supervisory style (Blakely 2008; Porter 2010). In particular, Julie Dickinson, the former Head of the OSFI, was very effective in supervising Canadian banks. In contrast to the US emphasis on telling banks to comply with regulations, Julie Dickson focused on the *principles and outcomes* of regulation, rather than the *act* of compliance. Chief executive officers of banks were told that 'they are the Chief Risk Officers' (Porter 2010; Baron 2012). This permeated banks such as TD Bank, where there is good corporate governance and a strong risk-management culture. Effective corporate governance is achieved through the realisation that regulation is part and parcel of good business practice. This is consolidated in section 4(4) of the Office of the Superintendent of Financial Institutions Act 1987, which posits that, although the OSFI will regulate financial institutions at the federal level, ultimate responsibility lies with the board of directors if an institution collapses. Further, financial institutions may fail. The aim of prudential regulation is not to prevent financial disasters since this is impossible in a market economy. Therefore, 'zero failure' regulatory policy is not part of the Canadian regulatory philosophy (Office of the Superintendent of Financial Institutions 2014). The realisation of a bank closure set out in legislation provides 'spine' to supervisors because a bank failure will indicate that the OSFI is at fault (Dickson 2010).

Regulating human behaviour is an extremely difficult task and, because of regulatory arbitrage, no amount of legislation or regulation will provide an absolutely watertight system. Rather, the rationale of the Canadian regulatory regime is to minimise the impact of any potential financial crisis. If corporate governance is seen as a 'tick box' compliance chore, then it is unlikely to be effective. The close relationship between the OSFI and the top six Canadian banks demonstrates that good corporate governance within banks can provide the first level of micro-prudential regulatory defence against externalities. The regulator then provides a second level of defence in the form of macro-prudential regulation and supervision. This collaborative style of regulation and supervision enables the OSFI to obtain useful information from banks regarding financial ratios and risk management. Woods, Chief Risk Officer at CIBC, remarked that

> The quality of the dialogue between regulators and financial institutions has improved significantly… If regulation requires more information on micro matters, that will do no good. But if it is having senior, experienced people discuss the big issues or realistic worst case stress scenarios-that's good regulation and that will continue.

The message from the industry is that regulation and supervision should be more holistic, realistic and use a partnership style. The OSFI managed to demonstrate this style through the Supervisory Framework. The Supervisory Framework provides principles and concepts for supervising federally regulated financial institutions. It assesses the inherent risks of significant activities carried out by banks in Canada. Inherent risks can be divided into six different types: credit risk, market risk, insurance risk, operational risk, regulatory compliance risk and strategic risk. Each risk is given a level: low, moderate, above average or high. The level of risk will then influence how much control and supervision the supervisor has over a bank (Office of the Superintendent of Financial Institutions 2010). Its supervisory principles of forward-looking, early intervention (principle 2) and assessment of whole institution (principle 7) worked particularly well for Canada. The principles-based supervisory style of the OSFI is thus important to the regulatory success of the OSFI.

The OSFI has two particular strengths: wide discretionary powers to issue and clarify guidance to financial institutions and broad enforcement powers (Baron 2012; Jackson 2013). Baron (2012) opines that Canada was praised for its strong regulatory and prudential framework because the OSFI made the rules on risk-based capital adequacy and stress-testing very clear to banks. For example, in 2007–8, the OSFI set up the Emerging Risk Committee to identify early signs of serious risks and problems across all industry sectors for federally regulated financial institutions (Office of the Superintendent of Financial Institutions 2009). The Emerging Risk Committee proved to be effective and its operations were enhanced in 2009 by being made responsible for checking market risks as well. Communication between the banks and the financial industry was good. This is demonstrated by risk-management seminars between 2008 and 2009, at which the life-insurance sector was included for the first time. At the international level, the OSFI continued with the practice of organising meetings for bank executives from Canadian banks and supervisors from the several jurisdictions they dealt with (Office of the Superintendent of Financial Institutions 2009).

The OSFI pursued the maxim of 'prevention is better than cure' in intervening progressively with problematic financial institutions. The four-stage approach ranges from an early warning in stage 1 to a decision that a financial institution is not viable in stage 4. At the end of March 2014, 35 financial institutions received a warning. Most of the 'staged' institutions were categorised as stage 1, apart from a few (Office of the Superintendent of Financial Institutions 2014). At the end of March 2013 and 2012, there were 43 and 38 'staged' financial institutions respectively (Office of the Superintendent of Financial Institutions 2012, 2013). Again, most of them received a stage 1 warning. This seems to indicate that the OSFI intervened early and kept a tight supervisory control over financial institutions.

Another Canadian financial regulatory agency which maintained a tight grip over supervision is the FCAC. The FCAC is responsible for consumer protection. Porter (2010) posits that the FCAC promoted market-conduct issues well, in particular that of the complex language used by financial institutions about financial products. In the Commissioner's Decision #104 of

2008 (Financial Consumer Agency Commission 2008), the FCAC fined a bank CAD$50,000 for breaching subsection 12(5) of the Cost of Borrowing (Banks) Regulations. A customer received promotional cash-advance offers at a low interest rate when his credit-card statements stipulated a higher interest rate. This particular bank failed to rectify the disclosed failure for several years and so the FCAC penalised it. The FCAC does offer banks a chance to amend their mistakes before it takes action. This is demonstrated by the Commissioner's Decision #102, when it realised that a bank did not stipulate when the annual fee of a credit card would apply (Financial Consumer Agency Commission 2008). The FCAC issued a Notice of Violation pursuant to subsection 22(2) of the Financial Consumer Agency of Canada Act 2001. The bank concerned immediately changed its terms and conditions. When the FCAC was satisfied with the revised terms, it did not impose a fine of CAD$5,000 (Financial Consumer Agency of Canada 2008; Porter 2010). An FCAC survey of 2006 showed that 87 per cent of Canadian consumers were satisfied with the amount of information regarding financial products (Financial Consumer Agency Commission 2006). Nevertheless, 66 per cent of those consumers acknowledged that the language used was not entirely comprehensible and that they were not clear about their rights. Older consumers felt particularly powerless in the financial market, but younger and more educated consumers disagreed. They understood the products and were able to choose wisely in a competitive market. Yet the trustworthiness of banks was thrown into question because around 45 per cent of consumers did not feel that financial institutions told them everything they needed to know about a product before buying it (Financial Consumer Agency Commission 2006). As a result of these weaknesses, the FCAC attempted to raise financial awareness. In 2014, the FCAC launched its Canadian Financial Literacy Database at its national conference, at which businesses taught consumers the skills required to make financial decisions. The FCAC has embraced modern technology. Consumer and stakeholder engagement on the FCAC's Facebook and Twitter accounts is more active than ever.

'Put simply, Canada's success is a function of having a regulatory system suited for a modern financial sector' (Breydo 2015). Canadian regulators worked well together during the financial crisis of 2007–9. Nevertheless, the ABCP crisis in the early stage of the financial crisis proved to be a challenge for regulators, especially the OSFI. It was criticised for not regulating and supervising the non-banks that created ABCP. Apart from this, the OSFI was commended and praised for its strict yet effective regulatory approach. The Bank of Canada was also commended for its innovative, flexible and decisive policy measures. It supported Canadian banks through extraordinary capital and liquidity measures. The FCAC was also effective in promoting market conduct and protecting consumers. In her final OSFI annual report, Julie Dickinson remarked that Canada weathered the financial turmoil well because there was 'strong cooperation and communication with our federal partners, such as the Bank of Canada, the Department of Finance, Canada

Deposit Insurance Corporation and the Financial Consumer Agency of Canada' (Office of the Superintendent of Financial Institutions 2014).

Macro- and micro-prudential regulatory frameworks of Canada 2007–9

Dickson (2010) argues that the real strengths of the OSFI are a clear strategy, formed out of legislation, and a strong focus on supervision. The mandate set out in the Office of the Superintendent of Financial Institutions Act 1987 specifically requires the OSFI to supervise and advise federally regulated institutions, to control and manages risk and to monitor the financial system. Specifically, the supervisory role is set out in some detail, requiring the OSFI to 'determine whether financial institutions and private pension plans are in sound financial condition and meeting minimum plan funding requirements respectively, and are complying with their governing law and supervisory requirements' (Office of the Superintendent of Financial Institutions Act 1987). From these objectives, the OSFI pursued two strategic outcomes: balancing the twin objectives of protecting depositors' interests and ensuring the financial system is effective by taking reasonable risks. The Basel Committee on Banking Supervision believes that the financial safety and soundness of the banking system is the primary aim of financial supervision (Office of the Comptroller of the Currency 2013). When there are other objectives, they have to be subordinate to this. The Basel Committee on Banking Supervision's call for a safe and sound banking system is certainly in line with the Canadian mandate.

The securities regulators' principal objective is to protect investors (Securities Act (Ontario): section 1.1). This does not work in parallel with the other regulators' – the Bank of Canada, OSFI, CDIC and Department of Finance – principal objective of reduction of systemic risks (Anand 2010). The ABCP crisis discussed earlier in this chapter demonstrated that the OSFI and the provincial securities regulators lacked a co-ordinated response. In 2009, the Hockin Report (2009) found that the OSFI was also to blame for the ABCP turmoil. Systemic risks are no longer confined to banks. Rather, they are prevalent in capital markets, and the Hockin Report criticised the OSFI for failing to supervise firms which created non-bank ABCP. The second part of this chapter will focus on two macro-prudential issues: the importance of having a unified, national securities regulator and, second, whether the tight oligopoly of Canadian banks intensifies the too-big-to-fail problem.

A single, national securities regulator and securities legislation for Canada

Canada is the only developed country without a national securities regulator (Hockin 2009). This is an interesting fact but by no means a reason for change per se. The current 'passport system' enables market participants to access

Canadian capital markets through the principal regulator (the securities regulator in one of the 13 provinces). Approval from the principal regulator will then be applicable to other participating passport jurisdictions. This mutually recognisable system facilitates free trade between the US and the other G7 countries (Thibodeau 2012a). It is also in line with the EU, which relies on the passport system and not a unified, national securities commission (Thibodeau 2012a). Arguments for removing the passport system for securities regulation and creating a single, national securities regulator include the need to facilitate innovation and the competitiveness of the Canadian capital markets (Hockin 2009). Further, Ontario has refused to participate in the passport system. Although the proposal for a single, national securities regulator may improve administrative issues and efficiency, the Ontario Securities Commission (OSC) felt that the proposal does not facilitate modern financial markets (Ontario Securities Commission 2007). According to the World Economic Forum (2012), Canada needs to improve its access to commercial capital, so it appears that there is a genuine need to make improvements in this area.

From a legal perspective, the OSC had no obligation to join the passport system since it did not sign the Provincial/Territorial Memorandum of Understanding Regarding Securities Regulation. The OSC prefers to have a unified, national securities regulator, consistent with the interpretation and application of securities law. Hockin (2009) argued that a single, national securities regulator will reduce costs and improve the decision-making process. In particular, he criticised the fragmented nature of the existing financial architecture and highlighted the weaknesses of the structure in dealing with two incidents during the financial crisis of 2007–9. First, in September 2008, Canadian regulators were slower than their US and UK counterparts to restrict short-selling. Further, the response from the 13 Canadian provincial regulators was inconsistent. The second example is the failure of the OSCI in dealing with the ABCP crisis. Supervision at the OSCI regarding non-bank firms issuing ABCP was weak and the provincial regulators denied responsibility (Anand 2010).

It was submitted in the Hockin Report (2009) that a national securities regulator would reflect the unique nature of Canada's capital markets. The size of most Canadian public companies is small. Large, public companies listed in Canada are often cross-listed on other stock exchanges, particularly in the US. Out of the 13 provinces in Canada, market capitalisation is concentrated in four provinces and in different sectors: Ontario is the hub of financial services, Alberta has a strong oil and gas sector, British Columbia has a vibrant mining industry and Quebec has active transportation and forestry industries. Some stakeholders consulted for the Hockin Report (2009) suggested that securities regulation should target particular industries or company size. Hockin rejected this suggestion, stating that this would increase the costs and complexity of regulation as well as reducing transparency. The report therefore proposed a proportionate and risk-based regulatory style for securities to enable the regulator to concentrate on the greatest risks to the economy. In particular, the report mentioned the FSA in the UK and the merits of a single regulator. The Hockin Report (2009) therefore recommended the establishment of the Canadian Securities Commission in a single piece of securities legislation.

The Hockin Report (2009) is the detailed product of a consultation procedure. However, with the benefit of research and hindsight, any suggestion that Canada should look towards the FSA as a template for a single regulator should be treated with care. Lessons can be learnt from the failure of the FSA and legislative weaknesses in the UK. The Northern Rock and HBOS incidents make it clear that the FSA was weak in a number of respects. The FSA's remit was too wide: it was responsible for regulating banks, deposit-taking institutions and insurance companies. With the development of complex products, increased use of securitisation and merging of financial services, the tripartite system increasingly found it difficult to delineate its component institutions' scope and responsibility. Overall, the FSA's passive, non-interventionist and laissez-faire regulatory approach led to criticisms that its measures were too little too late. The tripartite system created a 'macro-prudential underlap'. It would have been helpful if the Bank of England had had information on Northern Rock's risk-taking and maturity transformation prior to the financial crisis, but the FSA failed to communicate or share information often enough. Prior to the global financial crisis, mitigating systemic risks was not one of the FSA's regulatory objectives (Anand 2010). Financial stability was inserted as a regulatory objective under section 2(2)(a)(b) FSMA 2000. Regulating systemic risks requires good communication and the co-operation of all regulators, not just the securities regulators (Anand 2010), but communication with stakeholders will not necessarily reduce regulatory problems (Ford 2010). This was seen in the Northern Rock episode in the UK. The FSA Consumer and Practitioner Panel consulted practitioners and consumers in line with section 8 of the Financial Services and Markets Act 2000 (FSMA 2000), but the participatory process did not prevent Northern Rock's liquidity problem. The Canadian Securities Commission needs to have healthy scepticism about the industry (Ford 2010).

The global financial crisis highlighted two communication and co-operation weaknesses in Canada. First, communication between provincial and national regulators was ad hoc and less co-ordinated than communication between federal regulators. This is because regulators of provincial deposit-taking institutions and provincially incorporated financial institutions are not represented on the Federal Institutions Supervisory Committee. The Federal Institutions Supervisory Committee facilitates the exchange of information between federal regulators. Thus, there were some information gaps regarding securities and the interconnectedness of financial markets (International Monetary Fund 2014). Canada has a strong culture of co-operation because it has a habit of rotating senior civil servants between government agencies. This allows the fusion of different institutional cultures (International Monetary Fund 2014). However, co-operation on monitoring systemic risks was a weakness in Canada since there was not a single agency with a mandate to monitor systemic risks before the global financial crisis. The establishment of the Systemic Risk Committee by members of the Canadian Securities Administrators in October 2009 was therefore the right step towards managing systemic risks in the securities markets.

Opponents of a single securities regulator argue that evidence of significant cost savings is dubious (Carpentier and Suret 2009). There is also little empirical evidence that having a single regulator would decrease the cost of capital under the passport system (Thibodeau 2012a). Further, the OECD ranked Canada second in a study of securities-market regulation, which begs the question of why Canada should move to a single securities regulator. To date, there are five provinces which support a single federal regulator: Saskatchewan, New Brunswick, British Columbia, Prince Edward Island and Ontario (Yedlin 2015). It is important to note, however, that this took nine years from 2006, when the conservative government proposed a single national regulator. Moreover, Quebec has repeated its refusal to join the single, national regulator, since its Finance Minister argues that it would lead to job losses (Argitis 2014). Alberta is an energy giant, so it appears that the securities regulation of Alberta by a single regulator is unsuitable. Yet Alberta's energy activities constitute approximately 29 per cent of Canada's capital markets (Yedlin 2015). It would take political will, time and co-operation to implement a single, national regulator.

The Hockin Report also recommended a single piece of securities legislation. The proposed Canadian Securities Act's primary principles of securities regulation would be

> to provide protection to investors from unfair, improper or fraudulent practices; foster fair, efficient and competitive capital markets in which the public has confidence; and to contribute, as part of the Canadian financial regulatory framework, to the integrity and stability of the financial system.
>
> (Canadian Securities Act: section 16)

Section 17 of the Canadian Securities Act sets out guidance as to how the principles can be achieved. It pays close attention to timely information, the financial stability of markets and co-operation and co-ordination with Canadian and foreign regulators. Although the Canadian Securities Act has similar objectives to the FSMA 2000, the primary means set out in section 17 reflect what most scholars believe are the key elements of successful regulation. Naturally, these elements have to be put into practice, and the real test of a financial crisis would reveal whether the Canadian Securities Act is drafted well.

There are, however, two main hurdles for the Canadian Securities Act to clear. First, the constitutional position of a single federal regulator was held to be invalid by the Supreme Court of Canada in May 2010 as it was not within the legislative authority of Parliament under section 91(2) Constitution Act

1967 to regulate trade and commerce as a general branch of federal power (Thibodeau 2012b). The Supreme Court explained that the Canadian Securities Act's main aims of investor protection and market fairness have always been a matter of provincial concern. As a country, Canada has not produced sufficient evidence of a change in the securities market to support securities regulation at a federal level. The Supreme Court acknowledged that securities regulation has a federal dimension but that this alone was insufficient to justify Parliament's attempt to regulate the whole securities system. As the Supreme Court cannot rule on political matters, it did not decide what the appropriate regulatory system should be.

Another area of concern with the proposed Canadian Securities Act is that its requirement for all issuers to produce disclosure information in both English and French will impose additional costs. As only 37 per cent of Canadian companies listed on the Toronto Stock Exchange in 2010 publish an annual report in French, and 60 per cent of companies produce a French Management Information Circular, the requirement of bilingualism seems onerous (Lortie 2010). However, the Canadian government can argue that it has to promote equality of status through bilingualism. Timely and reliable information has to be disclosed to investors. If investors demand that disclosure documents should be in both languages then the costs can be justified. Empirical research amongst investors should be conducted so that a cost–benefit analysis can be carried out.

Oligopoly in the Canadian financial sector

The World Economic Forum has highlighted the efficiency of Canadian financial services (currently, Canada is ranked 16th in the World Economic Forum index (World Economic Forum 2012)). Canada has a very concentrated financial sector. The top six Canadian banks (Royal Bank Financial Group, Bank of Montreal, Canadian Imperial Bank of Commerce (CIBC), TD Bank Financial Group, Bank of Nova Scotia and National Bank) constitute approximately 90 per cent of the financial sector in Canada (Allen and Engert 2007). Linked to this is the research of Berger *et al.* (2000), which showed that mergers and acquisitions amongst large, international financial institutions will be of benefit in the long-term only if they substantially increase efficiency. From the empirical evidence and legislation studied in this section we conclude that Canadian banks are relatively efficient producers of financial services. There is little evidence of monopoly or oligopoly (Allen and Engert 2007). The Canadian banking sector was oligopolistic in the period of 1907–29 since each Canadian bank formed a larger proportion of the banking sector (Bordo *et al.* 2015). Yet oligopoly did not lead to higher costs or limited banking services during this period (Bordo *et al.* 2015). In fact, Bordo *et al.*'s study revealed that Canadian banks had similar rates of equity to US banks during this period, although the former had a larger portion of loans. An interesting fact from a financial-stability perspective is that, although there were bank failures, banks runs did not take place in Canada. Instead, when Sovereign Bank collapsed in January 1908, solidarity manifested itself as 12 members of the Canadian Bankers Association agreed to guarantee all the liabilities of Sovereign Bank and shared its assets amongst the 12 banks.

To evaluate whether Canadian banks are efficient, one must consider the factor of competition. According to Allen and Engert (2007), a more competitive environment should lead to more efficient outcomes if other factors are equal. A brief summary of the development of competition in the Canadian financial sector will thus be helpful. From 1920–80, the Canadian banking landscape was segmented by four pillars: chartered banks, trust and loan companies, insurance companies and securities dealers (Brean *et al.* 2011). The functional approach to regulation prevailed since the philosophy was that specialisation would make institutions more robust and less likely to fail (Brean *et al.* 2011). Similar to the UK's financial regulatory structure and style, the issue in Canada was whether functional specialisation served the financial sector well in light of the blurring of the boundaries of banks, insurance and securities. In Canada, 'quasi banks' started to compete with the main chartered banks in the 1950s. They were attractive to customers because they were situated in convenient locations, had a customer-focused approach and were not subject to a 6 per cent cap on loan rates. As a result of the latter, quasi banks were able to offer higher deposit rates and lower borrowing costs (Brean *et al.* 2011). The institutional regulatory style and the four pillars crumbled with the advent of the Bank Acts 1967 and 1980, which enabled regular revisions of financial legislation (Allen and Engert 2007). The Bank Acts 1967 and 1980 provided more flexibility and efficiency, whereby financial institutions could develop new products and services in a competitive environment (Brean *et al.* 2011).

Competition increased in the Canadian financial sector due to the lowering of entry barriers under the Bank Act 1980 and the North American Free Trade Agreement 1999 (Allen and Engert 2007). Under the Bank Act 1980, banks in Canada could establish subsidiaries in financial-services markets. This meant that banks could compete with trust companies in the mortgage-lending sector. The Bank Act 1987 enabled Canadian banks to own securities dealers, too. As a result, four of the five major banks all began dealing in securities after buying securities dealers. With the shift to functional despecialisation, the OSFI moved towards an institutional approach to regulation. It took responsibility for regulating insurance institutions and federally incorporated trust companies, pension funds and banks. Foreign banks also benefited from the Bank Act 1980 as they could also set up subsidiaries in Canada with the ability to offer a full range of banking services (Allen and Engert 2007). In 1987, the overlap between traditional banks and quasi banks became even clearer when legislative amendments enabled financial intermediaries to carry out brokerage activities. In 1999, foreign banks could also set up branches in Canada, rather than just subsidiaries. Nevertheless, foreign-bank branches were only allowed to carry out wholesale banking activities (Allen and Engert

2007). Despite the liberalisation of the financial industry, Canadian banks were protected from foreign competition under the Competition Act 1985 and Investment Canada Act 1985. Investors cannot own more than 20 per cent voting shares or 30 per cent non-voting shares of the bigger banks without direct approval from the federal Minister of Finance. Foreign acquisition of Canadian banks is therefore very difficult (Seccareccia 2013).

A number of empirical studies have been carried out in relation to the concentration, competition and contestability of banks. Bikker and Haaf (2002) studied 23 European banks and their results agree with the traditional view that concentration inhibits competition. On the other hand, Claessens and Laeven's (2004) research produced different results. Their sample of 4,000 banks in 50 countries between 1994 and 2001 revealed that concentration did not inhibit competition. In particular, they referred to the concept of 'contestability', which is the ability of companies to enter a market and compete with rivals. A market is contestable if it does not have prohibitive entry barriers (Allen and Engert 2007). Further research into the contestability of banks has been carried out by scholars such as Rosse and Panzar (1977), Panzar and Rosse (1982) and Allen and Liu (2007). These studies focus on a bank's contestability in three forms of market structure. At one end of the scale is monopoly or oligopoly and at the other is perfect competition. Monopolistic competition sits in the middle of the scale and is the dominant market structure in market economies (Allen and Liu 2007). Under this market structure, there are several banks in the financial sector but they differentiate themselves from each other through their brands and services. From a competition-law angle, monopolistic competition does not generally pose a problem because contestability is good. Banks can enter and exit the market if they wish. We have seen that foreign banks can establish subsidiaries and branches in Canada although there are restrictions on the range of services which foreign bank branches can provide. Further, foreign ownership of Canadian banks is limited.

Allen and Liu's study (2007) of 10 domestic and 15 foreign banks in Canada between 2000 and 2006 supports Claessens and Laeven's (2004) study. Together, these two pieces of research show that Canada had a monopolistic competitive market between 1994 and 2006. Allen and Liu's research revealed that Canadian banks are relatively efficient producers of financial services. Their research is different from previous studies since they used quarterly bank-level balance-sheet and income-statement variables. Despite structural changes in Canada, a monopolistic competitive model in the Canadian industry was sustained. The conservative nature of Canadian banks and the OSFI's strict regulatory style are unlikely to lead to bigger, more complex Canadian banks dealing with innovative products alongside US or UK banks (Bordo *et al.* 2015). With a less fragmented structure than the US, and regional branches, Canadian banks feel less pressurised to compete in size or engage in offshore activities (Jackson 2013; Seccareccia 2013). In light of the global effort for more financial stability, perhaps more efficiency in the Canadian financial market is not an immediate priority. Oligopoly of the Canadian financial sector does not seem to lead to more growth within Canada due to the restrictions in Canadian legislation. It also seems unlikely that Canadian banks are pressurised to engage in offshore activities, although Canadian banks may look towards cross-border growth if they wish to increase in size and compete internationally. If this is the case, then the issues of the interconnectedness and size of Canadian banks need to be analysed.

The size and interconnectedness of Canadian banks

Some academics posit that Canadian banks may become too big to fail because the financial sector is highly concentrated (Knight 2012; Mohsni and Otchere 2015). If Canadian banks continue to merge and grow in size, systemic risks may increase. In 2000, the Canadian financial system consti-tuted approximately 5 per cent of Canada's GDP (Roy 2005), In 2014, the figure was 9.8 per cent (Canadian Bankers' Association 2014). It is important to remember, though, that Canadian banks are not large by global standards. The top six Canadian banks are D-SIBs and not G-SIBs (Financial Stability Board 2015). Empirical results to date on the results of mergers are incon-clusive, but industry players would still prefer to consolidate and grow in size. The Canadian government has been, understandably, less keen.

In 1998, the Canadian Competition Bureau blocked the potential merg-ers of Royal Bank of Canada with Bank of Montreal and that of Toronto-Dominion Bank with CIBC after issuing its analysis of the proposed mergers. In its view, the two mergers would produce abnormal returns, especially for Royal Bank of Canada, Bank of Montreal and Toronto-Dominion Bank, with statistically significant declines ranging between –5.5 per cent and –7.5 per cent (Bessler and Murtagh 2002). With reference to Canadian banks, Aintablian and Roberts (2005) found that between 1998 and 2001 take-overs of foreign banks (especially in the areas of retail banking and wealth management) produced positive results. However, it would be too simplistic to establish a correlation between high concentration and financial stabil-ity. Competition can be healthy but intense competition can lead to finan-cial instability. Big banks can reduce risks by 'enhanced asset diversification' (Caprio *et al.* 2014) but risks can increase due to the too-big-to-fail doctrine. Although the size of Canadian banks is a potential threat to its economy, complexity is not as big a problem since reliance on securitisation and other innovative financial products is low compared to US or UK banks. Since the Canadian Competition Bureau discouraged the growth of Canadian banks through mergers within Canada, Focarelli and Pozzolo (2001) argued that Canadian banks have grown as much as they could have domestically. It is likely that any further growth will be through cross-border activities. This means that Canadian banks will be more interconnected, and systemic risks are more likely to take place. To reduce the problem of interconnectedness, there needs to be a simpler and more transparent securitisation framework in place. In light of Canada's close proximity to the US, the recommendations set out in Chapter 5 should also apply to Canada. Further, Canada needs a robust resolution framework to deal with distressed banks, including cross-border resolution of Canadian banks.

Improved insolvency framework for Canadian banking

Since banking is 'global in life but national in death' (Turner 2009), a suitable insolvency framework is required to minimise externalities. Whilst branches have the advantage of easy transfer of funds, subsidiaries have the limited-liability principle and are less expensive to wind up in financial insolvency. Therefore, there must be effective and co-operative international insolvency regimes (Lui 2012). In Canada, bank insolvencies are rare. Since 1985, there have only been three bank insolvencies: Northland Bank, Canadian Commercial Bank (both in 1985) and Bank of Credit and Commercial National in 1991 (Ben-Ishai 2009). Canadian banking supervision is particularly strong, thanks to an effective and robust OSFI and regulatory changes made by the Estey Report (Estey Commission 1986). These factors suggest that emphasis is paid particularly to the *ex ante* position of bank supervision and regulation, rather than dealing with the *ex post* position of liquidating distressed banks. Nonetheless, it will be argued that Canadian insolvency law needs to adapt to potential bank insolvencies. The existing legislative framework is archaic (Telfer and Welling 2008) and needs to deal with distressed banks swiftly. Depositors should be protected adequately.

In Canada, the federal bankruptcy legislation does not apply to banks. The liquidation of insolvent banks is regulated in the Winding-up and Restructuring Act of 1985 (WURA). The federal Bank Act SC (1991) provides the Superintendent with significant powers to take control of a bank with a view toward its restructuring. The Canada Deposit Insurance Corporation (CDIC) has the power to acquire the assets, shares or debt of a bank and act as a receiver. There are a number of weaknesses with the WURA. First, it only deals with liquidation of financial institutions 'under the control, or its assets are under the control, of the Superintendent and [be] the subject of an application for a winding-up order under section 10.1' (WURA: section (6)(1)(c)). Liquidation is the last resort for financially distressed companies. With distressed banks, liquidation is too late. Pre-stabilisation is important so that depositors are protected and public confidence and financial stability maintained. Mechanisms such as provisions allowing the private purchase of distressed banks, temporary nationalisation of weak banks and the formation of bridge banks might potentially stabilise the economy. To this end, the UK Banking Act 2009 could be of use to Canada, since its objectives are aligned to protect depositors and enhance financial stability.

Second, the WURA is a time-consuming process since its proceedings are mainly court driven. Proceedings have taken ten years to resolve complex bank liquidations (Ben-Ishai 2009). Clearly, this is not ideal since time is of the essence with bank failures to minimise externalities. Government authorities need powers to rescue banks immediately to avoid widespread panic. A special resolution procedure for banks might help, whereby depositors can access their savings swiftly under a guaranteed compensation scheme. A bank-administration procedure will enable the 'good' part of the insolvent bank to carry on with its business activities. Third, the WURA provides little guidance on the role of stakeholders, apart from the Court and the liquidator. Provisions detailing the administrator's roles and responsibilities are required in light of the importance of a new bank-administration procedure. Finally, there is uncertainty in relation to the distribution of a bank's assets under the WURA since the Court has wide discretion with regards to the timing and process of claims. Further, the status of employees and the CDIC needs to be strengthened in the distribution of assets. Employees are given less protection under section 72 of the WURA than under the Wage Earners Protection Programme Act (SC 2005). This is a particular issue for Canada since banks are major employers, providing jobs to over 250,000 Canadians (Government of Canada 2003). The CIDC is currently not given priority status in a bank insolvency. However, loans made by the CDIC have a higher priority than unsecured shareholders and creditors. This is unsatisfactory since depositors are vulnerable without priority status or a compensation scheme through which they can access their savings speedily. The IMF suggested a depositor-preference scheme, which would have the benefits of boosting depositor confidence and reducing claims from unsecured creditors, since the depositor-preference scheme clearly favours depositors. Canada is currently considering such a scheme. In particular, it needs to think about the effect of imposing costs on unsecured creditors, namely increasing their loss exposure (International Monetary Fund 2014). Canada has issued a consultation document on a bail-in mechanism for its D-SIBs. If Canada does adopt the bail-in mechanism, creditors will have to bear the cost of rescuing a D-SIB.

In relation to the cross-border resolution of banks, the CDIC has made good progress in some aspects. First, it has signed two cross-border Memoranda of Understandings with the Instituto para la Protección al Ahorro Bancario from Mexico, in 2012, and with the Federal Deposit Insurance Corporation from the US, in 2013, to improve cross-border cooperation (International Monetary Fund 2014). Second, the OSFI and CDIC have been closely involved with policy debates and planning bank resolutions internationally. Since 2013, they have been working closely with UK and US regulators on these matters. Canada has 29 foreign bank branches and 24 foreign bank subsidiaries in 2016 (Office of the Superintendent of Financial Institutions 2016). Compared to 150 foreign bank branches and 100 foreign bank subsidiaries in the UK, Canada is less international. Systemic risks across borders are less likely to happen. Foreign branches of Canadian banks cannot take retail deposits of less than CAD $150,000. The CDIC has resolution powers to deal with foreign subsidiaries of banks but not foreign branches (International Monetary Fund 2014). This is the same under the EU Second

Banking Directive 1989, where the home-country regulator has primary responsibility for prudential regulation of branches. When Icelandic banks such as Glitnir, Landsbanki and Kaupthing ran into financial trouble during the global financial crisis, the Icelandic government did not have enough financial resources to compensate UK depositors. The UK government had to step in and provide compensation to UK depositors even though the FSA had only secondary responsibility for regulating and supervising the branches of the Icelandic banks. Although Canada did not experience a similar problem, it might wish to consider increasing the home-country regulator's supervisory powers regarding foreign branches if the number of foreign branches continues to increase. To conclude, Canada has not experienced many bank liquidations recently mainly due to an efficient, effective and robust supervisory regime. However, since bank failures have a widespread systemic effect on the economy, it is prudent to have an effective legislative framework to deal with bank insolvencies.

The best kept secret of the global financial crisis

One of the best kept secrets of the global financial crisis is that Canadian banks received around US$122 billion between end of 2008 and mid 2010 without public disclosure (MacDonald 2012; Mohsni and Otchere 2015). The financial support was from the Bank of Canada, Canadian federal government, Canada Mortgage and Housing Corporation and US Federal Reserve. The US Federal Reserve and Bank of Canada offered short-term collateralised loans which peaked at CAD$33 billion and CAD$41 billion respectively (MacDonald 2012). Yet, by July 2010, Canadian banks had repaid all the loans. Further, three Canadian banks remained profitable during the rescue period, with a total profit of $27 billion between them. Only Royal Bank of Canada and CIBC reported losses for one quarter.

The academic literature on the relationship between government financial assistance and bank risk-taking remains inconclusive. In Germany, Gropp *et al.*'s study (2014) showed that the removal of government guarantees made banks less risky since they cut their credit risks and loan sizes. In the US, two recent pieces of research provided contrary results. Duchin and Sosyura (2014) revealed that banks assisted by the Capital Purchase Programme took more risks, approving riskier loans and investing in riskier securities. Black and Hazelwood (2013) found that large US banks which benefited from TARP increased the risk of loan originations but that small banks did not. Black and Hazelwood explain this difference by the fact that large bailed-out banks felt obliged to lend since they were owned by the US government after receiving financial assistance.

In Canada, Mohsni and Otchere (2015) studied the effect of non-disclosure of government assistance and risk-taking in major Canadian banks. Their results can be summarised in four points. First, banks which benefited from the liquidity injection took fewer risks. This reduction of risk-taking increased financial stability in Canada. Second, banks which received liquidity support invested in more traditional interest-income-generating activities, away from non-interest-income-related activities. This suggests higher risk-taking beyond a certain threshold. Third, banks which received financial assistance experienced a reduction in risk after the support period. Finally, the authors found that the reduction of risk-taking in banks was due to more investment in traditional interest-generating activities. MacDonald (2012) criticises the non-disclosure of the government financial assistance and the lack of transparency. In his view, a healthy financial sector should be transparent and accountable. The study by Mohsni and Otchere (2015) revealed that the reduction in risk in the period after the liquidity injection proved that their non-disclosure hypothesis is correct, namely that banks receiving liquidity support were more conservative and took fewer risks. Therefore, in a tightly regulated, conservative and highly concentrated banking environment such as Canada, non-disclosure of government financial assistance led to banks taking fewer risks. Yet there was a shift to more investment in traditional, interest-generating activities. This suggests that the government may have provided too much liquidity to banks which had good levels of capital (Mohsni and Otchere 2015). It would be desirable for more research to be conducted into the relationship between non-disclosure of government support and bank risk-taking. In the meantime, the Canadian legal system needs to have a sound and robust insolvency framework for banks in case the government decides not to rescue a distressed bank.

MacDonald's study (2012) into the secretive government assistance to banks from Canada and the US is interesting from a micro-prudential perspective as well. Three Canadian banks (CIBC, Scotiabank and Bank of Montreal) encountered serious financial difficulties during the global financial crisis. In fact, CIBC was the most vulnerable because it was the only bank which held large amounts of derivative securities tied to US sub-prime mortgages (Gueyie 2013). It sold CAD$2.9 billion of stock in early 2008 to support its balance sheet. CIBC also sold its US investment-banking division to Oppenheimer Holdings and entered into an agreement with Cerberus to reduce its exposure to US residential assets (Gueyie 2013). CIBC's financial situation was so poor that it was actually cheaper to buy all the shares of CIBC than provide it with financial assistance (MacDonald 2012). CIBC relied heavily on the CMHC mortgage-purchase programme and Bank of Canada programmes. Before the CMHC scheme started, CIBC was selling around CAD$375 million worth of new mortgages per quarter. Once it started to use the CMHC scheme, CIBC sold CAD3 billion of mortgages in the final quarter of 2008 and CAD$6 billion in the first quarter of 2009. A remarkable fact about CIBC is that, although it is the smallest of the five Canadian banks, the financial support it received relative to its size was similar to Royal Bank of Canada. CIBC was permitted to have a support ratio of 80 per cent or higher for approximately eight months and a support ratio of 100 per cent or higher for approximately three months (MacDonald 2012). This level of government support demonstrates the extraordinary length the Canadian government was prepared to bail out the banks. Nevertheless, every crisis is different, and whether a bank will be bailed out is a political decision, as seen from the financial crisis of 2007–9. Prudent, robust and effective financial supervisory, regulatory and stabilisation frameworks are required.

As the biggest Canadian bank, and with more assets than Morgan Stanley (Breydo 2015), Royal Bank of Canada borrowed less than the other Canadian banks relative to its size. However, at its peak, Royal Bank of Canada borrowed CAD$25 billion, which is the third highest level of support after Toronto-Dominion Bank and Scotiabank. Toronto-Dominion Bank was the heaviest user of the CMHC programme since it sold CAD$22 billion worth of mortgages to the CMHC. It also relied on cash from the Bank of Canada and financial support from the US Federal Reserve. There is a clear correlation between a bank's exposure to securitisation and its reliance on the CMHC programme. This is demonstrated in the cases of Bank of Montreal and Scotiabank. Neither bank relied heavily on securitisation or the CMRC programme. Bank of Montreal also had a smaller portfolio of mortgages, so there were fewer securitised mortgages (MacDonald 2012). At the other end of the scale, CIBC, Royal Bank of Canada and Toronto-Dominion Bank all relied heavily on securitisation and thus received a great deal of help from the CMHC scheme. Since it would be unrealistic for banks to reduce their exposure to securitisation, stress tests are crucial to micro-prudential regulation and financial stability.

Conclusion

Canadian banks were prepared when they entered the crisis since the traditional, conservative banking model used by most banks protected them from the US sub-prime crisis. In particular, the structure of the Canadian residential-mortgage market provided resilience to the Canadian economy. The Bank of Canada, as the central bank, provided minimal yet decisive, aggressive yet flexible support to banks during the financial crisis. The most successful assistance was from the CMHC. The extension of the CMHC programme to purchase government-insured mortgages also provided much needed liquidity in the financial market. The Canadian regulators worked well together during the financial crisis of 2007–9. The simple but modern regulatory architecture combined with clear mandates served Canada well. The ABCP crisis in the early stage of the financial crisis proved to be a challenge for the regulators, especially the OSFI. It was criticised for not regulating and supervising non-banks which created ABCP. Apart from this, the OSFI was commended and praised for its strict yet effective regulatory approach. The FCAC protected consumers well, and a number of cases mentioned above show that breaching market conduct rules will lead to enforcement.

At a macro-prudential level, it is apparent that the Canadian philosophy of prevention is better than cure can be found in the supervisory framework and the OSFI's style of supervision. The ABCP crisis demonstrated that the OSFI and provincial securities regulators lacked a co-ordinated response. Scholars, academics and politicians have discussed throughout the years whether Canada should have a single, national securities regulator to deal with systemic risks. Systemic risks are particularly prevalent in modern banking, largely because of the reliance on securitisation and the interconnectedness of banks. Further, Canadian banks are highly concentrated and there is a danger of too-big-to-fail. The advantages and disadvantages of a single, national securities regulator have been discussed. To date, there are five provinces which support a single federal regulator: Saskatchewan, New Brunswick, British Columbia, Prince Edward Island and Ontario. It will take political will and time for Canada to have a single regulator. Financial stability can be better served in Canada with an update of its insolvency law. The current legislation is archaic and it is important that depositors are adequately protected. When dealing with distressed banks, time is of the essence. Pre-stabilisation and special bank insolvency mechanisms need to be in place if a bank fails. Although bank insolvencies are rare in Canada, rescuing a bank is very much a political decision and having a suitable legislative framework in readiness for a potential crisis aligns with the Canadian philosophy of prevention is better than cure.

The best kept secret during in the financial crisis has to be the non-disclosure of US and Canadian financial support to Canadian banks. This has important macro- and micro-prudential ramifications for policymakers and scholars. At a micro-prudential level, a clear relationship between a bank's exposure to securitisation and its reliance on government support, especially the CMHC programme, was demonstrated. Although the World Economic Forum (2012) ranks Canada fifth in terms of financial stability, and Canada survived the global financial crisis well, it is evident that the Canadian financial regulatory framework can be improved in a number of areas.

Bibliography

Aintablian, S. and Roberts, G. (2005) 'Market Response to Announcements of Mergers of Canadian Financial Institutions', *Multinational Finance Journal*, 9(1), pp. 72–98.

Allen, J. and Engert, W. (2007) 'Efficiency and Competition in Canadian Banking', *Bank of Canada Review*, Summer, pp. 33–47.

Allen, J. and Liu, Y. (2007) *A Note on Contestability in the Canadian Banking Industry, Bank of Canada Working Paper 2007-7*, Canada: Bank of Canada.

Anand, A. (2010) 'Is Systemic Risk Relevant to Securities Regulation?', *University of Toronto Law Journal*, 60, pp. 941–81.

Argitis, T. (2014) 'Two Provinces Join Canada's National Securities Regulator', *Bloomberg*, 9 July 2014, available: http://www.bloomberg.com/news/articles/2014-07-08/two-provinces-join-canada-s-national-securities-regulator [accessed 17 May 2015].

Baron, J. (2012) 'How Regulating Risk and Eschewing Competition Can Ameliorate a Global Financial Crisis: Canada's Perspectives and Experiences', *The Antitrust Bulletin*, 58(4), pp. 597–615.

Beans, Kathleen M. (2008) 'Canadian Chief Risk Officers: Discuss Risk Management Issues and Lessons Learned from the Current Crisis', RMA Journal, 90(10), pp. 22–5.

Ben-Ishai, S. (2009) 'Bank Bankruptcy in Canada: A Comparative Perspective', *Banking and Finance Law Review*, 25(1), pp. 59–74.

Berger, A., DeYoung, R., Genay, R. and Udell, G. (2000) 'The Consolidation of the Financial Services Industry: Causes, Consequences, and Implications for the Future', *Journal of Bannking and Finance*, 23, pp. 135–94.

Bessler, W. and Murtagh, J. (2002) 'The Stock Market Reaction to Cross-border Acquisitions of Financial Services Forms: An Analysis of Canadian Banks', *Journal of International Financial Markets, Institutions and Money*, 12, pp. 419–40.

Bikker, J. and Haaf, K. (2002) 'Competition, Concentration and Their Relationship: An Empirical Analysis of the Banking Industry', *Journal of Banking and Finance*, 26(11), pp. 2191–214.

Black, L. and Hazelwood, L. (2013) 'The Effect of TARP on Bank Risk-Taking', in *International Finance Discussion IFDP 1043*, Washington D.C.

Blakely, K. (2008) 'Why Are Canadian Banks the Envy of the World?', *The RMA Journal*, 91(8), pp. 12–20.

Bordo, M., Redish, A. and Rockoff, H. (2015) 'Why Didn't Canada Have a Banking Crisis in 2008 (or in 1930, or 1907, or...)?', *The Economic History Review*, 68(1), pp. 218–43.

Brean, D., Kryzanowski, L. and Roberts, G. (2011) 'Canada and the United States: Different Roots, Different Routes to Financial Sector Regulation', *Business History*, 53(2), pp. 249–69.

Breydo, L. (2015) 'Structural Foundations of Financial Stability: What Canada Can Teach America about Building a Better Regulatory System', *University of Pennsylvania Journal of Business Law*, 17(3), pp. 973–1082.

Brzezinski, L. (2009) 'Canada's ABCP Crisis – The Aftermath', *Blaney McMurtry-Commercial Litigation Update* [online], pp. 1–4, available: http://www.blaney.com/articles/canadas-abcp-crisis-the-aftermath[accessed 25 May 2015].

Candian Bankers' Association (2014) *Banks and the Economy* [online], available: http://www.cba.ca/en/media-room/50-backgrounders-on-banking-issues/122-contributing-to-the-economy [accessed 24 May 2015].

Caprio, G., D'Aprice, V., Ferri, G. and Puopolo, G. (2014) 'Macro-financial Determinants of the Great Financial Crisis: Implications for Financial Regulation', *Journal of Banking & Finance*, 44, pp. 114–29.

Carpentier, C. and Suret, J. (2009) *Proposal for a Single Securities Commission: Comments and Discussion*, Montreal, Canada.

Choudhri, E. and Schembri, L. (2013) *A Tale of Two Countries and Two Booms, Canada and the United States in the 1920s and the 2000s: The Roles of Monetary and Financial Stability Policies*.

Claessens, S. and Laeven, L. (2004) 'What Drives Bank Competition? Some International Evidence', *Journal of Money, Credit, and Banking*, 36(3), pp. 563–99.

Dickson, J. (2010) 'Too Focused on the Rules: The Importance of Supervisory Oversight in Financial Regulation', *Cardozo Journal of International and Comparative Law*, 18, pp. 623–31.

Duchin, R. and Sosyura, D. (2014) 'Safer Ratios, Riskier Portfolios: Banks' Response to Government Aid', *Journal of Financial Economics*, 113, pp. 1–28.

Estey Commission (1986) *The Report of the Inquiry into the Collapse of the CCB and Northland Bank. Ottawa: Supply and Services Canada.*

Financial Consumer Agency Commission (2006) *General Survey on Consumers' Financial Awareness, Attitudes and Behaviour,* Montreal, Canada: Les etudes de marche createc.

Financial Consumer Agency Commission (2008) *Commissioner's Decision #104* [online], available: http://www.fcac-acfc.gc.ca/eng/forIndustry/publications/ commissionerDecisions/decisions/Pages/Commissi-Dcisions-99.aspx [accessed 1 May 2015].

Financial Consumer Agency Commission (2008) *Commissioner's Decision #102* [online], available: http://www.fcacacfc.gc.ca/eng/industry/CommDecisions2/ PDFs/102-eng.pdf [accessed 1 May 2015].

Financial Stability Board (2015) *2015 Update of List of Global Systemically Important Banks,* Switzerland: Financial Stability Board.

Focarelli, D. and Pozzolo, A. (2001) 'The Patterns of Cross-border Bank Mergers and Shareholdings in OECD Countries', *Journal of Banking & Finance,* 25, pp. 2305–37.

Ford, C. (2010) 'Principles-based Securities Regulation in the Wake of the Global Financial Crisis', *McGill Law Journal,* 55, pp. 257–307.

Government of Canada (2003) *Response of the Government to Large Bank Mergers in Canada: Safeguarding the Public Interest for Canadians and Canadian Businesses and Competition in the Public Interest: Large Bank Mergers in Canada* Canada: [online], available: http://www.parl.gc.ca/HousePublications/Publication. aspx?DocId=1028932&Language=E&Mode=1.

Government of Canada (2009) *Canada's Economic Action Plan,* Canada: Department of Finance.

Gropp, R., Gruendl, C. and Guenttler, A. (2014) 'The Impact of Public Guarantees on Bank Risk Taking: Evidence from a Natural Experiment', *Review of Finance,* 18, pp. 457–88

Gueyie, J.-P. (2013) 'The Impact of the Subprime Crisis on Canadian Banks' Stock Returns', *Frontiers in Finance and Economics,* 10(2), pp. 103–28.

Hockin (2009) *Expert Panel on Securities Regulation: Creating an Advantage in Gobal Capital Markets, Final Report and Recommendations,* Canada: Department of Finance.

International Monetary Fund (2014) *Canada: Financial Sector Assessment Program Crisis Management And Bank Resolution Framework – Technical Note,* Washington DC: International Monetary Fund.

International Monetary Fund (2015) *Canada Article IV Consultation,* Washington D.C.: International Monetary Fund.

Jackson, J. (2013) *Financial Market Supervision: Canada's Perspective,* 7–5700, United States of America.: Congressional Report Service Report for Congress.

Kiladze, T., Perkins, T., Robertson, G., Nelson, J., Erman, B., Slater, J., Jones, J., Waldie, P. and Keenan, G. (2013) 'The 2008 Financial Crisis: Through the Eyes of Some Major Players', *The Globe and Mail.*

Knight, M. (2012) 'Surmounting the Financial Crisis: Contrasts between Canadian and American Banks', *American Review of Canadian Studies,* 42(3), pp. 311–20.

Longworth, D. (2009) *Financial System Policy Responses to the Crisis,* Toronto, Canada.

Lortie, P. (2010) *The National Securities Commission Proposal: Challenging Conventional Wisdom,* Montreal.

Lui, A. (2012) 'Retail Ring-fencing and Its Implications', *Journal of Banking Regulation*, 13(4), pp. 336–48.

MacDonald, D. (2012) *The Big Banks' Big Secret Estimating Government Support for Canadian Banks during the Financial Crisis*, Canada.

Merton, R. C. (1995) 'A Functional Perspective of Financial Intermediation', *Financial Management*, pp. 23–41.

Merton, R. C. and Bodie, Z. (1995) 'A Conceptual Framework for Analyzing the Financial System', *The Global Financial System: A Functional Perspective*, pp. 3–31.

Mohsni, S. and Otchere, I. (2014) 'Financial Crisis, Liquidity Infusion and Risk-taking: The Case of Canadian Banks', *Journal of Banking Regulation*, 16(2), pp. 146–67.

Mohsni, S. and Otchere, I. (2015) 'Financial Crisis, Liquidity Infusion and Risk-taking: The Case of Canadian banks', *Journal of Banking Regulation*, 16(2), pp. 1–22.

Office of the Comptroller of the Currency (2013) *An International Review of OCC's Supervision of Large and Midsize Institutions: Recommendations to Improve Supervisory Effectiveness*, USA: US Treasury.

Office of the Superintendent of Financial Institutions (2009) *Annual Report 2009–2010 – The Importance of Managing Risk*, Canada: Office of the Superintendent of Financial Institutions.

Office of the Superintendent of Financial Institutions (2010) 'Supervisory Framework' [online], available: http://www.osfi-bsif.gc.ca/eng/fi-if/rai-eri/sp-ps/pages/sff.aspx [accessed 5 March 2015].

Office of the Superintendent of Financial Institutions (2012) *OSFI Annual Report 2011–2012*, Ottawa, Canada: Office of the Superintendent of Financial Institutions.

Office of the Superintendent of Financial Institutions (2013) *OSFI Annual Report 2012–2013*, Ottawa, Canada: Office of the Superintendent of Financial Institution.

Office of the Superintendent of Financial Institutions (2014) *OSFI Annual Report 2013–2014*, Ottawa, Canada: Office of the Superintendent of Financial Institutions.

Office of the Superintendent of Financial Institutions (2016) *Who We Regulate* [online], available: http://www.osfi-bsif.gc.ca/Eng/wt-ow/Pages/wwr-er.aspx-?sc=1&gc=1#WWRLink11 [accessed 20 January 2016].

Ontario Securities Commission (2007) *Notice 11–904, 'Request for Comment regarding the Proposed Passport System*, Ontario, Canada.

Panzar, J. and Rosse, J. (1982) *Structure, Conduct and Comparative Statistics* Internal Report, unpublished.

Porter, T. (2010) *Canadian Banks in the Financial and Economic Crisis*, Internal Report, unpublished.

Rosse, J. and Panzar, J. (1977) *Chamberlin versus Robinson: An Empirical Test for Monopoly Rents* Internal Report, unpublished.

Roy, J. (2005) 'The Canadian Financial System and Its International Dimensions', *Latin American Business Review*, 6(1), pp. 71–82.

Seccareccia, M. (2013) 'Financialisation and the Transformation of Commercial Banking: Understanding the Recent Canadian Experience before and during the International Financial Crisis', *Journal of Post Keynesian Economics*, 35(2), pp. 277–300.

Statistics Portal (2015) *Canada: National Debt from 2004 to 2014 in Relation to Gross Domestic Product (GDP)* [online], available: http://www.statista.com/statistics/271233/national-debt-of-canada-in-relation-to-gross-domestic-product-gdp/ [accessed 23 April 2015].

Telfer, T. and Welling, B. (2008) 'The Winding-up and Restructuring Act: Realigning Insolvency's Orphan to the Modern Law Reform Process', *Banking and Finance Law Review*, 24(1), pp. 233–69.

Thibodeau, M. (2012a) *Proposed Federal Securities Regulator 1: Economic Aspects*, Publication Number. 2012-28-E, Ottawa, Canada: Library of Parliament.

Thibodeau, M. (2012b) *Proposed Federal Securities Regulator 2. Constitutional Aspects*, Ottawa, Canada: Library of Parliament.

Turner, A. (2009) *The Turner Review: A Regulatory Response to the Global Banking Crisis*, London: Financial Services Authority.

World Economic Forum (2012) *The Financial Development Report 2012* [online], available: http://www.weforum.org/issues/financial-development [accessed 6 April 2015].

Yedlin, D. (2015) 'The Case for a Single Securities Regulator Has Not Diminished', *Calgary Herald, 17 February 2015*, 17 May 2015, available: http://calgaryherald.com/news/national/the-case-for-a-single-securities-regulator-has-not-diminshed [accessed 17 May 2015].

7 Germany

Introduction

The German Labour Minister Franz Müntefering sparked off a discussion on regulatory reform in Germany just before the global financial crisis. The debate has been named the 'locust debate' as he used the term to portray players in the shadow banking sector as avaricious. Müntefering's metaphor is represented in a model in Miniature Wonderland, Hamburg. In 2009 and 2013, Miniature Wonderland asked the six German political parties to represent their vision of Germany in the future in one square metre. The back of each model represents the party's vision in 2009 and the front is their vision four years later. At the back of the Social Democratic Party's model, a locust and a roulette wheel represent the shadow banking sector. There is also a large piggy bank highlighting the importance of saving for a rainy day. Finally, there is a broom sweeping away figurines of tax evaders.

In Germany, the size of the shadow banking industry is small relative to its economy (Zimmermann 2009). However, the metaphor of a locust is interesting for another reason. The chronophage is a clock with no hands or numbers outside Corpus Christi College, Cambridge. An insect, similar to a locust or a grasshopper, sits above the clock and eats away time as it slips by. It reminds us that the passing of time is inevitable. How appropriate this is when we apply it to financial regulation. Although the effects of the global financial crisis have stabilised since its onset, Western countries, including Germany, are still trying to rebuild their economies. At the time of writing, global stock markets are recovering after a week of panic selling due to a fall in oil prices and the slowdown of the Chinese economy (Kollewe 2016). The world is nervous of another financial crisis. The chronophage is a suitable analogy to remind us that we must act fast to ensure that we have learnt from past mistakes. The next financial crisis may be different to the global financial crisis but financial institutions should be ready to face such a challenge. Effective and reasonable legislation should thus be in place.

Germany is ranked 18th in relation to financial stability (World Economic Forum 2012). This is ahead of the US and the UK. Its stability is due to a decline in credit-default-swap spreads and thus a reduced risk of a sovereign-debt crisis. Overall, Germany is ranked 11th, behind the other four countries studied in this book (World Economic Forum 2012). Its weaknesses include an unstable currency system and weak equity-market development. Further, since the release of these statistics in 2012, Germany has become part of the European Banking Union. This has increased state regulation at both national and European levels. The global financial crisis revealed that German banks are the least profitable in the EU. In particular, the 'Landesbank problem' is currently a concern for national and European policymakers. The unique, fragmented German federal system, subsidiarity and regional principles which have shaped the German banking sector now face additional challenges. There is more political will than ever to reform the Landesbank structure. The previous style of self-regulation within the three distinct pillars of banking has been replaced by more government regulation.

The Bundesbank and institutional weaknesses during the financial crisis of 2007-9

The German financial regulatory and supervisory structure

In Germany, universal financial regulation was chosen as the best method to cope with the 'functional despecialisation' (Taylor 2009) of the financial market. As in the UK, a regulatory shift from an institutional regulatory approach to an integrated/functional approach was adopted by the German government. The Law on Integrated Financial Services Supervision of 2002 (Gesetz über die integrierte Finanzleistungsaufsicht) reflects such a regulatory shift. As a result of this, the single regulator, the Federal Financial Supervisory Authority (Bundesanstalt für Finanzdienstleistungsaufsicht (BaFin)), was created at federal level (Filipova 2007). As the micro-prudential regulator, BaFin regulates and supervises all financial services providers (sections 1(I) and 4(I) of the Act establishing the Federal Financial Supervisory Authority). Established in 2002, BaFin is based in Bonn and Frankfurt am Main. It is supervised by the Federal Ministry of Finance (Bundesfinanzministerium). According to section 6(1) of the Banking Act 1961 (Gesetz über das Kreditwesen), BaFin is the administrative authority responsible for the supervision of institutions under the Banking Act 1961. BaFin has to balance different regulatory objectives: financial stability – the overriding objective in banking regulation (section 6(II), Banking Act 1961) – and protecting consumers in insurance regulation (section 81(I), Insurance Supervision Act 1992). BaFin was established not because of a financial crisis. Rather, it was set up because of the Bundesbank's attempt to gain more supervisory powers after losing its monetary-policy role to the ECB. This sparked off a political debate, resulting in the compromise whereby the Bundesbank retained its supervisory role but BaFin was given micro-prudential regulatory powers (Zimmermann 2012). The Bundesrat (Upper Chamber of German Parliament) only agreed by default since the opposition-ruled Länder (German states) staged a walk-out over a new immigration law on the same day (Zimmermann 2012).

The Ministry of Finance has control over the federal fiscal budget and market supervision. It exercises legal and technical oversight over BaFin (Handke 2012). The Ministry of Finance provides the framework for stable and efficient financial markets at both national and international levels. The final federal financial regulator is the German Central Bank (Deutsche Bundesbank). The Bundesbank shares banking supervisory duties with BaFin. It is the macro-prudential regulator and its responsibilities include ongoing banking supervision and crisis management (Group of Thirty 2008). Besides these bodies on a federal level, there are supervisors at the level of the Länder. The Bundesbank and BaFin together form the two-pillar regulatory structure in Germany.

Section 7(1) of the Banking Act 1961 states that, as part of the ongoing supervision process, the Bundesbank has a number of responsibilities. These include analysing reports and returns which financial institutions have submitted and assessing whether the capital and risk-management procedures of banks are adequate (German Federal Financial Supervisory Authority 2014). Germany kept its dual system of financial supervision due to the federal form of state organisation and the dispersed landscape of German financial business (Filipova 2007). One of the strengths of the German financial regulatory system is the close co-operation between BaFin and the Bundesbank. Section 7(1) of the Banking Act 1961 and the Co-operation Agreement between the Deutsche Bundesbank and BaFin for Supervision of Credit and Financial Institutions sets out a clear division of labour between the two organisations. The Bundesbank has macro-prudential responsibility under section 7(1) Banking Act 1961. Section 7(2) of the Banking Act 1961 is important because it aims to prevent overlaps and ensure the consistency of the quality of supervision by the two regulatory authorities, as well as a clear division of responsibilities and good flow of information. Essentially, the Bundesbank has ongoing supervision duties and will report to BaFin on its findings and evaluations as quickly as possible.

The Bundesbank has wide powers under Article 2(1) of the Banking Act 1961 to provide information to banking institutions. This is an unusual power and emphasises the mutual duty of both regulator and regulatee to provide information. Further, under Article 2(1), the Bundesbank has powers to clarify with the institutions at its own discretion any discrepancies regarding the documents. It also has the right to demand information accordance to section 44(1) of the Banking Act 1961. Otherwise, under section 7(2)(4) of the Banking Act 1961, BaFin is the only authority which can make decisions and issue administrative acts. It bases its decisions upon the results and findings of the German Central Bank. However, BaFin is not confined to the Bundesbank's publications: it can conduct its own audits.

Co-operation is a key element of Article 2 and the Bundesbank supervises 'problem banking institutions' (Article 5), institutions of systemic importance

(Article 6) and institutions under intensified supervision (Article 7). These different levels of supervision reflect the risk levels of institutions under the Supervisory Review and Evaluation Process (SREP). The SREP is defined in Article 1 of the Banking Act 1961. Article 10 then provides details of the SREP risk profile. The SREP focuses on forward-looking risk assessment, taking into account current and potential risks. It also uses a risk-based supervision plan. These are similar to the UK PRA's Risk Assessment Framework. Articles 5 to 7 highlight the importance of close co-operation and co-ordination between the German central bank and BaFin in making the final assessment of the institution, especially with banks under intensified supervision. For banks which are classified as 'problem banks' or institutions of systemic importance under Articles 5 and 6, BaFin has the power to ask the Bundesbank to provide more facts and carry out deeper analysis. Article 9 provides more information on further principles of co-operation. Article 19 further states that the Bundesbank and BaFin should work closely together when conducting stress tests. These are commendable measures due to the importance attached to clear communication, co-operation and co-ordination between the regulatory bodies.

Article 3(2) of the Banking Act 1961 is fundamental in understanding the relationship between the Bundesbank and BaFin. The Article stipulates that 'the final assessment and decision-making power on all supervisory measures and questions of interpretation shall rest with BaFin'. BaFin is thus the supervisory agency responsible for micro-prudential regulation. Article 8 is interesting because it introduces the concept of a BaFin risk committee. The Bundesbank is a permanent member of the BaFin risk committee without voting rights. The Bundesbank has two members on the BaFin risk committee. The risk committee meets four times a year and its rationale is to act as a linchpin between the two supervisory bodies on both macro- and micro-prudential issues. Article 8(3) Banking Act 1961 then introduces the concept of an ongoing-supervision committee. This committee can meet at either the Bundesbank or BaFin. The frequency of its meeting is flexible. Although it has to meet at least four times a year, it can meet for informal purposes between these meetings (Article 8(3)). The establishment of the risk and ongoing-supervision committees aligns the two supervisory bodies with the principle of sharing information about banks.

Having examined the German legislation on banking regulation, research conducted by Paul *et al.* (2012) provides an interesting insight into the relationship between the Bundesbank and BaFin. Paul *et al.* (2012) conducted a survey in 2010 of 1,919 German banks. These banks included co-operative banks, savings banks, commercial banks and others. They conducted a similar survey in 2006. The survey of 2010 asked banks to rate statements from 1 (completely untrue) to 5 (completely true). Each grade of this scale was weighted with an index value, ranging from 0 points for the value of '1' to 100 points for the value of '5'. The response rate was 20 per cent. Paul *et al.*'s research is important because there was increased debate over the sharing of supervisory responsibilities between the Bundesbank and BaFin. Their survey in 2010 revealed that there were high scores for dialogues between the two supervisory agencies, especially for statements such as 'strong co-operation with supervisors' (score of 80), 'supervisors are familiar with the individual bank' (score of 75) and 'supervisors are familiar with the individual bank's business in general' (score of 74) (Paul *et al.* 2012). The scores for these statements in 2006 were similarly high.

Paul *et al.* (2012) then asked the banks for their opinions on both the Bundesbank and BaFin. The results showed that the supervisors at the Bundesbank are more competent and act more swiftly and pragmatically than the supervisors at BaFin. The difference in the quality of the supervisors is even starker in 2010 than 2006. Paul *et al.* (2012) thus cast doubt on the German Ministry's decision to keep the current division of supervisory authorities and increase the powers of BaFin. In Paul *et al.*'s opinion, 'the more promising strategy would be that the two authorities should not be played off against each other but represent themselves as one independent institution resisting all attempts of bank lobbyism' (Paul *et al.* 2012). The next sections will review the German financial regulators' strengths and weaknesses during the global financial crisis and whether the current single-regulator model should stay.

The policies of the Bundesbank and the ECB during the financial crisis 2007–9

Having lost its power to make monetary-policy decisions, the Bundesbank has merely implemented the ECB's decisions in this area since January 1999 under the European Economic and Monetary Union. The ECB's primary objective is to maintain price stability under Article 127 of the Treaty of the Functioning of the European Union (TFEU). Without prejudice to the primary objective, the ECB should support the aims of economic growth and high level of employment (TFEU: Articles 3, 119 and 146). Unlike the US Federal Reserve, the ECB does not have a mandate to pursue full employment. The ECB's fiscal measures during the financial crisis of 2007–9 can be described as bold, decisive and creative. Apart from the usual cuts in interest rates, the ECB created new rescue mechanisms, such as the Enhanced Credit Support and the Securities Markets Programme (European Central Bank 2011). As the lender of last resort, the ECB was decisive in dealing with the financial crisis. On 9 August 2007, it became clear to the ECB that the short-term money market was in trouble. It therefore provided almost €95 billion of overnight credit against collateral to banks in the Euro area, the largest amount of financial support from the ECB in nine years (Cecchetti 2009). The ECB was flexible and adaptive in its liquidity support. It adopted the use of shorter-term maturities of three to six months in its longer-term refinancing operations to increase the amount of liquidity in the financial system (European Central Bank 2011). After the collapse of Lehman Brothers

in September 2008, the ECB reacted swiftly again, this time cutting interest rates by 50 basis points. The ECB was not acting alone. Its decision to
slash interest rates was in line with other central banks, such as the Bank of
England, Federal Reserve and Bank of Canada. In pursuing its primary objective of price stability, the ECB communicated and co-operated with other
central banks.

As the economy weakened further, the ECB cut key interest rates to 1
per cent in the period October 2008 to May 2009 (European Central Bank
2011). The ECB was more decisive than EU finance ministers in reacting to
the financial crisis. The latter adopted the European Recovery Plan in 2008,
which, although it provided immediate fiscal stimulus, was too small in terms
of size and failed to share the fiscal burden amongst member states (Hodson
and Quaglia 2009). Meanwhile, to reduce the depth of the liquidity problem, the ECB bought €60 billion worth of debt securities backed by mortgages as well as covered bonds (Hodson and Quaglia 2009). This was part of
the unconventional support mechanism offered by the ECB: the Enhanced
Credit Support. Other measures include the conversion of a variable- to a
fixed-rate tender procedure for all refinancing operations, widening the range
and proportion of assets for use as collateral and currency-swap agreements
(European Central Bank 2011). Despite its boldness, decisiveness and creativity, the ECB needed assistance from the Federal Reserve. The Federal
Reserve provided support to the ECB by issuing swaps in return for Euros.
The ECB was then able to lend US dollars to a number of European banks,
where they could hold assets in dollars and make loans to support trade in
dollars (Bernanke 2013).

As the financial crisis continued, the ECB's Securities Markets Programme
aimed to keep the monetary-policy-transmission mechanism running
smoothly by purchasing sovereign debts and 'sterilising' them (Belke 2010).
The Securities Markets Programme worked by allowing commercial banks to
sell sovereign debts to the ECB and receive much needed liquidity in return.
The ECB had, till then, tried to separate its monetary policy from fiscal policy. Belke (2010) criticised the launch of the Securities Markets Programme
as bowing to pressure from industry players (such as the European Association of Traders) and driven by politics rather than markets. The fundamental
criticism against the ECB is that it bailed out government deficits (Belke
2010). In defence of the programme, the ECB intervened in the secondary
market only and thus did not breach Article 125(1) of the TFEU. Further,
the ECB sterilised the sovereign debts, so that its liquidity conditions were
not affected (Cour-Thimann and Winkler 2012). Belke (2010) submits that
the ECB breached the spirit of the TFEU by bailing out government deficits. Moreover, the ECB has become more politically dependent because
national fiscal policies could dominate monetary policy. This can been seen in
the ECB's purchase of Greek, Spanish and Portuguese debts. Belke (2010)
proclaimed that 'ECB will thus automatically transform into a quasi-fiscal
agent of euro area governments in times of crises'. Darvas (2012) agrees,

explaining that the purchase of Greek debts was flawed because Greece's fiscal position was unsustainable. In his view, the Securities Markets Programme was weak because it did not have clear guidelines. Nevertheless, he disagrees with the criticism that the ECB was financing national governments because, as mentioned above, the ECB only bought debts on the secondary markets, did not issue new bonds and fully sterilised the purchases. Interestingly, the Bundesbank opposed the Securities Markets Programme from the beginning, as it thought the programme was trying to circumvent Article 123 TFEU, namely the ban on central banks financing governments (Sester 2012).

In total, the ECB granted €467 billion to support banks in the Euro area (Sikka 2009). Trichet, President of the ECB, commented: 'The ECB and the Eurosystem, which responded decisively to the financial crisis, can be counted on to remain a reliable anchor of stability and confidence' (Trichet 2010). Given the unprecedented scale of the global financial crisis of 2007–9, the ECB had to act swiftly and decisively. The Enhanced Credit Support mechanism was creative and boosted liquidity in the global financial system in several ways. More controversial is the Securities Markets Programme due to its bailing out sovereign debts. Nevertheless, the ECB's Securities Markets Programme purchases were never as large as the quantitative-easing programmes conducted by other central banks. It was only at country level that the scale of the purchases under the Securities Markets Programme was larger than that of the Federal Reserve, and it was still smaller than the Bank of England's quantitative-easing scheme (Ghysels *et al.* 2014). Therefore, it would be unfair to compare the ECB's Securities Markets Programme with the large-scale asset-purchase schemes mentioned earlier. The closest and most suitable comparison to the ECB's intervention would be that of the Danish Central Bank during the 1960s and 70s (Ghysels *et al.* 2014).

Institutional regulatory weaknesses during the financial crisis 2007–9

Unlike the Federal Reserve, the ECB does not have supervisory or regulatory powers over banks in the Eurozone (Cassola *et al.* 2013). The Herculean task of supervising 6,000 banks in the Eurozone seems impossible (Tröger 2014). Rather, the Bundesbank retains the regulatory and supervisory role in Germany. As the macro-prudential regulator, the Bundesbank was criticised for failing in its supervisory role, especially in the near collapse of IKB Deutsche Industriebank (IKB) and Landesbank Sachsen Girozentrale (Sachsen LB) (Marinova 2009). Although the former is a small, niche public bank and the latter is a regional, state-owned bank, they had similar business models. IKB specialised in lending to the German Mittelstand (small- to medium-sized businesses). Despite its sound levels of capital between 1998 and 2007, it was unable to absorb the losses incurred in the US sub-prime market as approximately half of IKB's investments were in asset-backed securities (Marinova 2009). Without the support of BaFin and the Ministry of Finance, IKB would have collapsed (Forbes *et al.* 2015).

Sachsen LB increasingly built up an ambitious business model after the European Commission abolished state guarantees for public banks in July 2005. Similar to other Landesbanken, Sachsen LB felt compelled to increase its competitiveness once the safety net of state guarantees was removed. Its Dublin branch started to invest heavily in asset-backed securities. Sachsen LB encountered liquidity problems and the state of Saxony guaranteed €2.8 billion to save the bank. Bank failures often involve corporate governance and regulatory weaknesses. IKB and Sachsen LB are no exceptions. With the former, the board of directors failed to notice and act upon the large amount of securitised assets. Further, the board continued to use inappropriate risk measurements even after the financial crisis. Scholars such as Forbes *et al.* (2015), Hau and Thum (2009) and Kirkpatrick (2009) believe that weak governance due to lack of suitable industry experience played a big part in the demise of IKB. Similarly, Sachsen LB's board did not change its investment strategy despite the bank's large exposure to asset-backed securities. BaFin found the very high profitability figures unusual and asked its external auditor, KPMG, to conduct a special audit of Sachsen LB. KPMG found that Sachsen LB's management was unaware of the quantity of asset-backed securities its Dublin branch had purchased. Neither was Sachsen LB aware of the potential losses it could incur (Marinova 2009). Nonetheless, BaFin did not take any action after this special audit and failed to prevent Sachsen LB from collapse. BaFin's annual reports between 2004 and 2012 reveal that they were diligent in carrying out special audits under section 44 of the Banking Act 1961. On average, there were 285 special audits in 2004–12. It is noticeable that the figures dropped just before the financial crisis started and then rose again in 2009. The statistics would indicate the intensification of information flow (Fischer and Pfeil 2004) between the authorities during the financial crisis, but it is evident that BaFin failed to act upon early warnings and red flags when issues were raised, as in the Sachsen LB incident.

Ungeheuer (2009) and Hüfner (2010) describe the government's initial stabilisation as 'ad hoc', but the German Parliament's verdict on the performance of the German authorities is more positive in the rescue of Hypovereins Real Estate Aktiengesellschaft (HRE) (Deutscher Bundestag 2009a). After HRE bought the Dublin-based bank Depfa in 2007, it suffered liquidity problems. Its business model was heavily reliant on financing long-term wholesale investments by short-term interbank funding, and it had large exposure to collateralised debt obligations (Hopt *et al.* 2009). When liquidity dried up in the secondary market after Lehman Brothers collapsed, HRE faced imminent insolvency (Deutsche Bundesbank 2009). The rescue of HRE was driven predominantly by a political desire to save the reputation of covered bonds (Pfandbriefe). The German covered-bonds model has become a template in other European countries, and the collapse of HRE would have had serious repercussions throughout the European financial market.

The Bundesbank and BaFin reacted promptly. After a weekend's discussion, the two authorities offered the first rescue package of €35 billion, of which the Bundesbank injected €20 billion and a financial syndicate €15 billion. Both amounts were secured by a central-government guarantee. A month later, HRE's liquidity situation deteriorated and the authorities provided another injection of €50 billion, with collateral provided by HRE (Deutsche Bundesbank 2009). Still struggling despite two rescue packages, Parliament stepped in and passed the Financial Market Stabilisation Act (FMSA) on 17 October 2008 to assist HRE. Article 1 of the FMSA established the Financial Market Stabilisation Fund (Finanzmarktstabilisierungsgesetz) (FMSF), which is managed by the Financial Market Stabilisation Agency (Ungeheuer 2009; Sinn 2010). Article 2 gave the FMSF the ability to buy securities or derivatives from financial institutions as long as the FMSF acquired them before 30 October 2008 and the institution concerned had sufficient regulatory equity (Ungeheuer 2009). In return, the financial institution received debt instruments issued by the German government. As a result of the FMSA, HRE received a guarantee line of €52 billion in separate tranches (Deutsche Bundesbank 2009). In consideration of its support, the FMSF effectively took over HRE and owned all its shares. The guarantee provided under the FMSA is in line with EU competition laws, so no separate approval was needed (Ungeheuer 2009).

The FMSA is flexible because the rescue measures are optional. Financial institutions are not obliged to use them. Further, financial institutions can decide which type of rescue mechanism and what conditions will apply. This is different to the Emergency Economic Stabilisation Act in the US. Section 102(3) of the Emergency Economic Stabilisation Act states that the US Secretary of State will determine the terms and conditions of the guarantee. The flexibility under the FMSA, however, is mutual. Therefore, under section 4(1) of the FMSA, financial institutions do not have a right to receive assistance. Certain conditions are attached to the use of the stabilisation mechanism, with two being rather controversial. First, annual executive pay of over €500,000 is considered unreasonable under section 5(2)(4) of the Regulation implementing the Financial Market Stabilization Fund Act 2008 (Verordnung zur Durchführung des Finanzmarktstabilisierungsfondsgesetzes). Not surprisingly, private commercial banks were reluctant to take up the offer in light of this. Second, dividends and profit distributions cannot be paid out to shareholders other than the FMSF (Benzler and Breilmann 2009). The rationale of the latter is to keep monies received from the rescue package within the financial institution in order to boost its equity position. The prohibition is reasonable to the extent that it is lifted once the rescue package no longer applies.

The takeover of HRE was possible under the Supplementary Financial Market Stabilisation Act of March 2009. Despite opposition and criticism from some shareholders such as J.C. Flowers, a US investor who had a 24 per cent shareholding in HRE, the German government managed to acquire HRE through two tender procedures in March and April 2009. Following the European Commission's approval of the acquisition, the government called a shareholders' meeting to increase the capital. The FMSF was the sole purchaser of new shares and increased its shareholding to over 90 per cent, thus squeezing out minority shareholders. HRE was nationalised without resorting to nationalisation, known as the expropriation method in German law. Legally, this is possible under section 12 of the Supplementary Financial Market Stabilisation Act. Nonetheless, claims have been brought by share-holders contesting the constitutional validity of the Supplementary Financial Market Stabilisation Act (Hopt *et al.* 2009). Hopt *et al.* (2009) question the compatibility of this Act with the principle of the right to property under German constitutional law. Their main concern is that minority shareholders with less than a third of the share capital can be squeezed out under the Sup-plementary Financial Market Stabilisation Act. If the German government did not lower the requirement to exclude shareholders' pre-emption rights to 90 per cent, J.C. Flowers could have vetoed the capital increase with his 24 per cent shareholding in HRE, since he wanted to stay as a shareholder (Ker-sting 2012). Time is of the essence in crises, so section 12, paragraph 4 of the Financial Market Stabilization Acceleration Act can be justified in exceptional circumstances, such as the global financial crisis.

The German Parliament (Bundestag) produced its report into the HRE episode in September 2009. In the report, employees of the Bundesbank and BaFin defended the relationship between the authorities, stating that 'they worked together decently and respectably' (Deutscher Bundestag 2009a). In particular, they highlighted the Bundesbank's excellent supervisory role. Wit-nesses described the close relationship between the Bundesbank and BaFin in monitoring the liquidity position of HRE between February and March (the Bundesbank's reports increased in frequency from monthly to weekly during this period (Deutscher Bundestag 2009a)). Some German politicians, how-ever, were more critical about the effectiveness of the two-pillar regulatory system. In the Parliamentary Commission's report on HRE in August 2009 (Deutscher Bundestag–Das Parlament 2009), the Christian Democratic Union and the Free Democratic Party wanted the Bundesbank to have all the supervisory powers in order to avoid overlapping of duties. The opposi-tion Social Democratic Party and the Greens strongly opposed the Bundes-bank having more power. Insurance giants, such as Allianz and Münchner Rück, supported the opposition's argument, saying that the Bundesbank did not have the necessary experience in supervising the insurance industry (Zimmermann 2012). The government ultimately backed down due to pres-sure from industry players.

A common denominator of the failure of IKB, Sachsen LB and HRE is the heavy reliance on securitised products. The Bundesbank initially retained its conservative approach to the use of securitisation in banks' business models till the early 1990s. This is demonstrated by its strong opposition to the gov-ernment and private organisations issuing securitised instruments (Fischer and Pfeil 2004). The Bundesbank warned of the short-term nature of such financial products and its impact on interest rates. Germany's past history of wars and hyperinflation in the Weimar Republic led to a very strong desire for the Bundesbank to be independent, separating its monetary policy from its regulatory role. Harmonisation at the European level left the Bundesbank with Hobson's choice: it was compelled eventually to allow the use of money-market funds by German banks under the Undertakings for Collective Investment in Transferable Securities and Investmentfonds (Organismen für gemeinsame Anlagen in Wertpapieren) 2009/65/EG. It would be unreasonable to blame the Bundesbank for yielding to securitisation, due to the global competitive banking environment. However, its role as a supervisor can be improved. Annual reports of the Bundesbank in the period 2004–12 showed that the Bundesbank conducted on average 158 on-site supervisions of financial institutions. There was an increase in the number of site visits after the beginning of the financial crisis in late 2007, which indicates heightened monitoring. However, this did not necessarily result in the Bundesbank acting upon the risks detected. Similar to the FSA in the UK, the Bundesbank and BaFin could have done better as supervisors (Marinova 2009).

Whilst the performance of the Bundesbank and BaFin was mixed, the Ministry of Finance was criticised for its weak performance (Handke 2012). Handke (2012) describes the Ministry of Finance's performance as poor and ill-prepared for a serious, unexpected crisis, such as the HRE incident (Deutscher Bundestag 2009a). It had to outsource some of its policy tasks to private companies since the Ministry of Finance lacked the requisite resources. Besides, the Ministry of Finance is very dependent on BaFin, even for daily operations (Deutscher Bundestag 2009b). Bearing in mind that the Ministry of Finance is 'the supreme official authority' for BaFin's management and can issue orders to BaFin on a range of organisational issues, the Ministry of Finance's performance during the HRE episode is disappointing. As we saw in Chapter 3, lack of resources, especially human resources, affected the performance of the FSA in the UK. Recruitment of qualified and skilled personnel in the UK has subsequently resolved this issue. The German government ought to invest more in human resources (Hüfner 2010). It is ironic to note that the Bundesbank had too many employees after losing its monetary role to the ECB (Frach 2008). Better allocation of resources is needed amongst German financial regulatory authorities.

After the initial stage of firefighting, the German government shifted its focus to crisis management, namely removing toxic assets from the balance sheets of banks. In May 2009, Parliament adopted the Act to Develop Financial Market Stabilisation ('Bad Bank Act'). Under the Bad Bank Act, Special Purchase Vehicles (SPV) can buy toxic assets at a discount of approximately 10 per cent of their book value, thus removing them from banks' balance sheets. SPVs can issue bonds with repayments guaranteed by SoFFin (Benzler and Breilmann 2009). Although a good idea in theory, only one bank has used this scheme (Hüfner 2010). The scheme is voluntary, and there are uncertainties as to how the value of future liabilities arising from the toxic assets is calculated (Hüfner 2010). Therefore, the scheme merely buys time and does not encourage investors to provide new capital in the short term (Ungeheuer 2009). Besides, financial institutions must cover their losses for 20 years. This condition does not appeal to potential investors. The fact that only one bank participated is worrying, and the inability to raise new capital is a handicap. Therefore, Hüfner (2010) suggested that BaFin and the Bundesbank should have tried to prevent banks from getting into difficulties by performing regular stress tests, closely monitoring capital adequacy and taking requisite actions swiftly.

To conclude, the three German financial regulatory authorities and the ECB tried to contain and limit the systemic risks at the onset of the financial crisis. Although German banks were originally conservative and self-regulation dominated till the early 1990s, the financial regulatory landscape changed when the Bundesbank permitted banks to use securitised products in their business models. There was more government intervention and regulation, although it is clear that the Bundesbank, BaFin and the Ministry of Finance made errors in their respective roles. The ECB was bold, decisive and creative in its monetary policies. Apart from utilising its conventional tools, such as cutting interest rates, it created new rescue mechanisms, such as the Enhanced Credit Support and the Securities Markets Programme. The latter was criticised for bailing out sovereign debts. Nonetheless, the ECB acted legally and the scale of the Securities Markets Programme is not the same as the Bank of England's. The Bundestag passed a number of important pieces of legislation to, first, stabilise the financial market and, second, to remove toxic assets from banks' balance sheets. Yet the rescues of IKB, Sachsen LB and HRE all revealed institutional weaknesses at BaFin, the Bundesbank and Ministry of Finance. The two-pillar regulatory structure was criticised for such failures and some politicians called for structural reform. It is evident that the authorities should have been more proactive and taken more supervisory interventions when red flags were raised. Yet politicians and industry players will ultimately decide the fate of BaFin and Bundesbank.

Macro- and micro-prudential regulatory frameworks in Germany during the financial crisis of 2007–9

Macro-prudential regulatory framework

Germany felt the full impact of the global financial crisis in 2007–9, which came as a surprise to many Germans, since there was a degree of complacency about the soundness of its financial system (Zimmermann 2012). The HRE rescue and the bailouts of other Landesbanken highlight a serious regulatory weakness in the German financial system: an inefficient and political regulatory framework for regulating state-owned, savings and co-operative banks. This is a pertinent issue for regulators, policymakers and academics, as German state-owned banks accumulated a third of all losses amongst German banks, even though they make up only a fifth of the German banking sector

(Hüfner 2010). German banks are the least profitable in Europe (Wilson and Wiesmann 2010), so improving the state-owned banks' performance will contribute to better financial performance and financial stability in both Germany and Europe. Europe's 'weakest financial link' needs to be addressed urgently. This section will feature the two macro-prudential regulatory questions. First, is it likely that the German state-owned banks will merge with the pillar of savings/co-operative banks? Second, if this is the case and the de facto boundaries within the pillars disappear, what are the implications for German regulators to ensure financial stability?

An analysis of the German banking system is necessary before we can answer these questions. Many authors (Fischer and Pfeil 2004; Hackethal 2004; Hüfner 2010) have described the financial system as 'fragmented'. This is because the total combined assets of the top five banks is less than 20 per cent (Hackethal 2004). Germany's three-pillar model has provided the basis for regulators' supervisory policies. The three pillars are private commercial banks, state-owned banks (savings banks, with Landesbanken at the apex) and co-operative banks. State-owned savings banks are essentially public credit institutions. They are subject to the important principle of serving the public interest and not maximising profits. An example of this is section 3(2) of the Bremisches Sparkassengesetz (savings banks law of the State of Bremen). Further, they are under no pressure to distribute dividends (Simpson 2013). The savings banks' main clients are the Mittelstand. German savings banks are a hybrid: they are regional and avoid competing with each other, but savings banks situated in cities compete with private, commercial banks (Hackethal 2004). Smaller savings banks compete with co-operative banks. This 'regional principle' leads to inter-pillar competition, predominantly in retail banking. Savings banks are therefore highly competitive since they cannot subsidise their services from other regions.

Savings banks have no owners since they are legally and economically independent institutions. They are privately managed by the municipality, the municipality principle ensuring that the public mandate is fulfilled. Landesbanken are owned by the federal states and savings banks in individual states (Hackethal 2004; Deutscher Sparkassen- und Giroverband 2015). They are wholesale banks and also act as service providers and lenders to savings banks in their state. Public ownership of Landesbanken is not a problem per se, since the pursuance of the public-interest maxim implies a conservative, risk-averse approach. Empirical evidence, however, reveals that weak corporate-governance practice, especially at the supervisory board level, contributed to the weak performances of public banks. Literature on the relationship between bank losses and governance of German public banks is scarce, but recent research by Hau and Thum (2009) shows that the financial and managerial competence of the public banks' supervisory boards led to lower profits in the period 2000–7. In particular, the average pre-tax return on equity over the period 2000–7 was 4 per cent for Landesbanken and the central institutions of co-operative banks. This is in comparison to 10 per cent for the savings banks and co-operative banks and 7.5 per cent for the private banks (Hüfner 2010).

The other piece of research on this topic is by Beck *et al.* (2009). Their results contrasted with Hau and Thum's. Beck *et al.* (2009) showed that co-operative banks were the most stable, followed by savings banks and then private banks. Co-operative banks are more stable than savings banks due to lower volatility of profits. Private banks are the least stable because their business models are the riskiest, with a heavy reliance on the wholesale market (Deutsche Bundesbank 2015). However, their capital levels and profitability are higher at the same time. The different results can be attributed to the research methodology. Beck *et al.*'s research did not include the five large private banks, Landesbanken and two central co-operative institutions. Further, their data stop at 2007, so the impact of the financial crisis of 2007–9 has not been taken into account.

Sitting at the top of the savings-banks pillar, Landesbanken act as central institutions to these banks and provide liquidity. The subsidiarity principle (Subsidiaritätsprinzip) restricts the ability of Landesbanken to provide retail services because the primary provider of this type of service is savings banks. Landesbanken only step in if it is inefficient for savings banks to provide certain retail activities to customers, such as capital-markets products (Reid and Lister 2006). Landesbanken also compete with large, private banks in a range of financial services, including wholesale banking and capital-market services. The traditional public-interest business model has been replaced by an international, universal-banking model, but the governance structure remains public-centred, with employees and politicians acting as shareholder representatives. Securitised debt forms a bigger part of liabilities in Landesbanken than in private banks. Meanwhile, debt securities and other fixed-interest securities form a more significant portion of their assets than in private banks. Retail deposits form a small part of the funding profile of Landesbanken. The final trigger for fragility in the Landesbanken sector was the removal of the state guarantee by the European Commission in 2005 (Sinn 2010; Wilson and Wiesmann 2010). The guarantee offered repayment claims against the German federal states to the creditors of public banks. Refinancing was therefore on favourable terms. But ratings agencies reclassified the banks when the guarantee was removed and, due to market pressure, Landesbanken creditors were offered higher interest rates, thus wiping out the banks' profit margins.

To protect profitability, Landesbanken took greater risks and invested heavily in securitisation (Sinn 2010). This proved to be a disastrous tactic and cost Landesbanken heavily. Profitability in Landesbanken was negative in 2007–9 (Wilson and Wiesmann 2010). The introduction of the financial-market transaction tax (Finanztransaktionssteuer) on speculative and technical trading (Buchler and Thies 2013) and the higher regulatory burden under Basle III have prompted a debate as to whether the public–private business model of Landesbanken is here to stay. There is also more political will to reform the Landesbank problem than ever (Wilson and Wiesmann 2010).

The financial crisis of 2007–9 revealed shortcomings in German banking supervision. Information exchange between BaFin and Bundesbank is very important to efficient co-operation as part of the crisis-prevention mechanism. BaFin and Bundesbank operate a very close information flow, which helps them to carry out their supervisory duties. However, neither supervisor had their own in-house auditing staff preparing audit reports till recently (Fischer and Pfeil 2004). Expenditure on external auditors by both supervisors is therefore most probably reflected in the supervisors' fees. Statistics on this information are unavailable, so it is hoped that the supervisors can publish this information in the future (Fischer and Pfeil 2004). The fees will then be passed on to the banks. Another weakness on this issue is a lack of auditor independence amongst the pillars of state-owned banks and co-operative banks. These banks are subject to the Banking Act 1961 just as other banks are. Due to the subsidiarity principle, they are jointly supervised by both BaFin and the banks' respective associations, namely the Deutscher Sparkassen- und Giroverband and the Bundesverband der Deutschen Volksbanken und Raiffeisenbanken (Paul *et al.* 2008). In contrast to the private commercial banks, which utilise independent external auditors, the regional associations of savings banks and those of co-operative banks are audited by internal auditing staff.

The most intriguing feature of auditing is that, in most cases, BaFin appoints the same auditor for both the state-owned banks and their respective regional associations. The same applies to co-operative banks (Fischer and Pfeil 2004). Landesbanken such as Bremer Landesbank and Norddeutsche Landesbank have maintained their declarations of independence and avoided conflicts of interest in their financial statements (Bremer Landesbank 2013; Norddeutsche Landesbank Girozentrale 2014). Further, they submit that their internal audit committees (appointed by the Supervisory Board) have a 'risk-oriented' and 'process-independent' monitoring process (Bremer Landesbank 2013; Norddeutsche Landesbank Girozentrale 2014). The audit committee audits the entire bank and reports directly to the Managing Board. Since regional savings-banks associations and Landesbanken fund the Deutscher Sparkassen- und Giroverband and the latter represents the funders' interests, the use of external auditors would possibly reduce opacity and cosiness.

External auditors audit the annual financial statements and reports of Landesbanken but do not produce external auditors' reports. External auditors' reports are particularly beneficial since they provide an assessment of a bank's risk profile (Fischer and Pfeil 2004). Other reports do not. A comparison of the auditors' reports for Deutsche Bank and Landesbank Baden-Württemberg confirm this: the former auditor's report contains an assessment of risk but the latter's does not. This raises questions about the quality of audits. Since the business model of Landesbanken is very similar to private, commercial banks, there is a case for arguing that Landesbanken should produce externally audited reports so that their risk profiles can be scrutinised. This would be particularly valuable in light of the poor performance of most Landesbanken during and for some time after the financial crisis of 2007–9.

A number of authors (Fischer and Pfeil 2004; Reid and Lister 2006; Wilson and Wiesmann 2010) argue that Landesbanken can either be privatised or merge with savings banks in order to stay competitive. Before both options are discussed, it is important to review the weaknesses of the current supervisory and regulatory framework in relation to state-owned banks and savings banks. The global financial crisis highlighted, first, that the business model of Landesbanken is unsustainable for the reasons given above. Most Landesbanken are still struggling to produce healthy profits. Landesbank Berlin was bought by its member savings banks and West Landesbank was liquidated. HSH Nordbank lost €800 million in 2013 and poor-quality shipping loans cost the bank €185 million in the first nine months of 2014 (*The Economist* 2015). Only seven Landesbanken survived the financial crisis of 2007–9.

There are certain constraints within the current German financial landscape which indicate that Landesbanken could consolidate by merging with savings banks rather than by privatisation. This is due to three reasons: first, the subsidiarity principle will largely deter Landesbanken from competing with savings banks by branching into retail services. Without much experience in retail banking, it would be difficult for them to generate huge profits. Second, recent statistics show that there was a contraction of 25 per cent between 1995 and 2005 in the savings-banks sector (Reid and Lister 2006). Finally, extreme changes to the German financial landscape are unlikely due to the fact that state-owned banks are subject to state law and local politicians generally support the public-ownership concept (Reid and Lister 2006).

Politics plays an inevitable part in finance due to the importance of financial institutions. This is particularly so in Germany, where state politicians sit on the supervisory boards of Landesbanken. This raises both regulatory and corporate-governance issues, such as the qualifications and experience of these politicians. Since the global financial crisis, Germany has revised the German Corporate Governance Code (Deutscher Corporate Governance Kodex) (GCGC). Similar to that in the UK, the GCGC is not legally binding on non-listed public companies, and Landesbanken use their own corporate-governance guidelines (Kohler 2010). Although most Landesbanken adapt the GCGC to suit their own business model, there is little uniformity in corporate governance. Some banks, such as Bayern LB, state that their own corporate-governance guidelines go beyond the GCGC in certain areas (Bayern Landesbank 2015). This is demonstrated in the qualifications, expertise and training of supervisory members. Clause 5.4.1 of the GCGC states that supervisory board members will have 'the knowledge, ability and expert experience required to properly complete its tasks' (Regierungskommission Deutscher Corporate Governance Kodex 2015). Clause 5.4.5 requires supervisory members to devote sufficient time to fulfil their mandates. Further, they should 'undertake the necessary training and further education measures required for their tasks'. The employer will support the training costs.

Bayern Landesbank's corporate-governance guidelines are very similar in this area. They do, however, under clause 2(c), include induction training for new supervisory board members (Bayern Landesbank 2015). All the other Landesbanken generally comply with the GCGC, with some variations of certain issues, such as compensation at HSH Nordbank.

As seen earlier, HSH Nordbank suffered terrible financial losses during and after the global financial crisis. Despite their declaration of conformity to the GCGC, there appears to be corporate-governance, regulatory and political issues with Landesbanken. Politics is embedded in Landesbanken as part of German banking culture. This is demonstrated by the fact that HSH Nordbank has to keep a second office in Kiel despite its heavy financial losses (*The Economist* 2015). The irony is that most Landesbanken ticked all the boxes of corporate governance and regulation. HSH Nordbank complied with the GCGC and even passed the stress tests in October 2014 (*The Economist* 2015). Observing the spirit of the law, therefore, is as important as observing the letter of the law. The board of directors at HSH Nordbank has taken positive steps in corporate governance to move on. These include, first, getting rid of all senators or ministers from the affected federal states, Hamburg and Schleswig-Holstein (Bundesanstalt fur Finanzdienstleistung-saufsicht (BaFin) 2014). Second, the Supervisory Board appointed the Chief Risk Officer to the Managing Board (Bundesanstalt fur Finanzdienstleistung-saufsicht (BaFin) 2014). Both are excellent steps to reduce the influence of politics and add expertise on financial risks to the Managing Board. It would be most encouraging to see other Landesbanken follow suit.

German banks will be subject to more regulation at the European level. The European Commission provided state aid to Landesbanken such as Bayern LB, HSH Nordbank and Landesbank Baden-Württemberg, some of which is ongoing. As part of the financial aid package, the European Commission laid down certain requirements, such as decreasing foreign business activities and significantly reducing total assets, as well as risk-weighted assets (Bundesanstalt fur Finanzdienstleistungsaufsicht (BaFin) 2014). Germany has been part of the Single Supervisory Mechanism (a pillar of the European Banking Union) since November 2014. Supervision of 'significant institutions' is shared between the ECB and national supervisor. The definition of 'significant institutions' can be found in the Single Supervisory Mechanism Regulation (Council Regulation 1024/2013) and the Single Supervisory Framework Regulation (Council Regulation 468/2014). Landesbanken fall under the definition of 'significant institutions', so the ECB has more supervisory control over Landesbanken (European Central Bank 2014c). The ECB is the macro-prudential supervisor and has worked closely with the Bundesbank so far to try and achieve a harmonised supervisory approach at the European level. Early indications are that the Single Supervisory Mechanism is positive, although there are some ongoing challenges.

The Bundesbank has made some organisational changes in order to adapt. First, it has established three new units. One unit is specifically for staff to co-ordinate with colleagues from the Bundesbank who work in the joint supervisory teams. The joint supervisory teams are led by the ECB but staff are mainly from the Bundesbank. Second, there is a new unit for analysing foreign banks under the supervision of the ECB. Finally, a secretariat has been established, which will prepare meetings for the Supervisory Board. The Supervisory Board is the decision-making branch of the European Banking Union (Dombret 2015). The Bundesbank is trying to achieve the principle of proportionality in its organisational reforms. The principle aims to be efficient so that larger banks and larger tasks have bigger teams of staff to supervise. Currently, the joint supervisory teams vary from 5-70 staff (Dombret 2015), a discrepancy which subsequently affects the workload and quality of supervision. Throughout this book, it has been highlighted several times how important it is to have adequate and qualified supervisory staff. As such, sufficient human resources must be allocated to Landesbanken, as both the size of the banks and the complexity of the work justify this. The joint supervisory team will need to improve communication with the savings banks' regional associations to avoid duplication.

In relation to the problem of costs encountered by savings banks, it is difficult to see how the Single Supervisory Mechanism will improve the situation. This is because, according to the ECB's Guide to Banking Supervision (European Central Bank 2014b), the team carrying out on-site inspections has to be headed by someone from the ECB. The rest of the team will consist of joint-supervisory-team members. In the case of Landesbanken, supervision is already shared between BaFin and the regional banks' associations. Therefore, harmonisation of supervision has actually increased the number of supervisors involved. This will most likely lead to higher costs and increased inefficiency. From a practical perspective, better communication internally within the supervisory team is necessary to avoid misunderstandings and duplication of responsibilities. Otherwise, Landesbanken will have to bear even higher costs than previously. Given that the business models of Landesbanken are similar to private commercial banks, it is only fair that there are more supervisory dialogues between the joint supervisory team and Landesbanken.

To answer the first of the two macro-prudential questions asked at the beginning of this section, mergers between savings banks and Landesbanken are more likely than privatisation of Landesbanken due to the subsidiarity principle, the regional principle, contraction in the savings-banks sector and political support for the public ownership and mandate of Landesbanken. Landesbanken ticked the boxes for corporate-governance compliance and stress tests, but most of them performed poorly in the global financial crisis. To answer the other question, then, whilst internal self-regulatory measures, such as the ones taken by HSH Nordbank, have been bold and encouraging, since the financial crisis there has been more state intervention and regulation. In light of the increased vertical supervisory scrutiny at both national and European levels (under the European Banking Union), it is important that the Bundesbank allocates adequate numbers of skilled staff to supervise Landesbanken. The latest report from the ECB reveals that around 960 staff were recruited in 2014 to carry out supervisory duties. Seventy-three per cent of the staff were recruited from the national supervisory organisations of EU member states (European Central Bank 2014a). Particularly encouraging is the fact that all the staff are highly qualified and some are at manager level. The ECB intended to recruit the remaining 40 positions in 2015 (European Central Bank 2014a). Clear, frequent and timely information flow between the Bundesbank, BaFin and the regional savings associations, especially the Deutscher Sparkassen- und Giroverband, as the umbrella organisation for savings banks, is crucial. Crisis prevention is important to preserve financial stability. The current opaque nature of auditing and the use of same the auditors in the pillar of state-owned banks is unsatisfactory. Since the business model of Landesbanken is very similar to that of private, commercial banks, external auditors should audit Landesbanken to better scrutinise the risk profile.

Micro-prudential regulatory framework

There have been a number of national and European changes to micro-prudential regulation and supervision in Germany since the global financial crisis. BaFin's micro-prudential supervisory powers have been strengthened. These powers are in capital and liquidity requirements. Both German and European legislation require a higher level of capital to improve a bank's stability (Deutsche Bundesbank 2015). It is interesting to note that amongst the countries studied in this book Germany had the second lowest capital-to-assets ratio (World Bank 2015). Efficient and effective supervision requires rules which target specific problems. The revised section 10(b) of the Banking Act 1961 provides more flexibility to BaFin since there are four circumstances in which it can ask a financial institution to raise its capital. An example is the ability to raise a newly formed organisation's capital level to counter additional risks associated with the new business. The same applies to liquidity in that BaFin can ask for an additional liquidity buffer under section 11(2) of the Banking Act 1961. These sections allow BaFin to intervene earlier and with more flexibility. Under section 45(1) of the Banking Act 1961, BaFin has powers to help a weak bank earlier when they have insufficient funds or liquidity. A bank's net financial assets or financial reports will suffice, rather than relying on its failure to meet capital or liquidity requirements. There is also a new prohibition on payments of own funds if they are not adequately covered by the year's net income (Bundesanstalt für Finanzdienstleistungsaufsicht (BaFin) 2009).

The Solvency Regulation 2007 (Solvabilitätsverordnung) requires German banks to produce a quarterly report on minimum capital levels, and the Liquidity Regulation 2006 (Liquiditätsverordnung) requires a monthly report on liquidity and asset quality. Particular attention should be paid to the asset quality of loans from German banks. Statistics reveal that during 2004–14, Germany had the worst non-performing-to-performing-loan ratio amongst the five countries studied in this book (World Bank 2015). This can be explained by banks' exposure to the real-estate sector and to the sovereign-debt crisis. Germany had outstanding loans of €323 billion to the PIIGS countries (Portugal, Ireland, Italy, Greece and Spain) at the end of 2011 (Bowman 2012). In the ECB stress-test report, Germany had the highest exposure to sovereign debt (European Banking Authority 2014). Sovereign debts are not risk-free, so these debts need to be backed up by capital (Weidmann 2015). Although the state moved bad-quality assets from Hypovereins Real Estate to FMS Wertmanagement and Erste Abwicklungsanstalt in October 2010, selling bad-quality real-estate loans was not appealing to most banks during the financial crisis due to the erosion of prices. However, since the global financial crisis, Basle III changes and Germany's own legislative reforms, it has been suggested that some German banks may feel that it is best to sell poor-quality loans rather than extend them (Rottke 2012).

In its monthly report of March 2015, the Bundesbank was still concerned about the impact of the sovereign-debt crisis on German banks. The Financial Stability Committee, formed in 2013 to enhance macro-prudential regulation in Germany, agreed in its annual report of 2015 that it is concerned with low interest rates fuelling the residential-property market, and external risks from countries such as Greece. There is empirical evidence showing that a negative correlation exists between non-performing real-estate loans and economic growth (Beck *et al.* 2013). The Bundesbank's research in 2014 shows that severe stress scenarios can significantly increase losses from domestic credit institutions arising from residential mortgages (Deutsche Bundesbank 2014). The Financial Stability Committee (2015) therefore made some recommendations to give BaFin powers to regulate residential-property loans. These recommendations included a cap on loan-to-value and debt-to-income ratios as well as compulsory amortisation requirements. These seem sensible as low interest rates look likely to stay for a while, and we must learn from the debt-fuelled problems exhibited in the global financial crisis.

At a European level, the single rulebook of the European Banking Union implements Basel III. The single rulebook aims to provide a single set of harmonised prudential rules, which both 'significant' and 'less significant' institutions throughout the EU must respect. It contains three Directives on crisis prevention and management: the Capital Requirements Directive (Council Directive 2013/36/EU), Capital Requirements Regulation (EU Regulation 575/2013) and the Bank Recovery and Resolution Directive (Council Directive 2014/59/EU). This trio of legislation aims to address the importance of having sufficient capital, especially counter-cyclical capital to act as a buffer to external shocks. It also provides a new legal framework to rescue banks in trouble by a 'bail-in' mechanism. The bail-in mechanism is a better and fairer way of resolving a bank in trouble because it reduces social costs. The Bank Recovery and Resolution Directive (BRRD) is flexible since it only sets the minimum rules. Member states can add their own rules in addition to those in the BRRD and in the technical standards of the Directive as long as the new rules do not conflict with the BRRD. These Directives are appropriate since it has been established that higher capital ratio is required to better absorb externalities and reduce risks, since it increases shareholders' liability. These measures attempt to increase safety, which is crucial for financial stability.

Germany has implemented the counter-cyclical capital buffer stated in the Capital Requirements Directive (Council Directive 2013/36/EU) via section 10d of the German Banking Act (Kreditwesengesetz). BaFin decides the counter-cyclical capital buffer rate, which will be between 0 per cent and 2.5 per cent. This rate incorporates the credit-to-GDP gap (German Federal Financial Supervisory Authority 2015). The strengths and weaknesses of the credit-to-GDP gap was analysed in Chapter Two. Since BaFin decides the buffer rate, there is flexibility given to national supervisors. This flexibility is important to reflect the diverse and individual culture of financial institutions in each country. Germany has also implemented the BRRD through its Act on the Recovery and Resolution of Credit Institutions 2015 (Gesetz zur Sanierung und Abwicklung von Kreditinstituten), which incorporates a number of key elements, such as the bail-in mechanism, a recovery plan and cross-border co-operation with national supervisory authorities. The bail-in mechanism applies to financial institutions which have a minimum level of liabilities. This level is specific and tailor-made for each financial institution (Buscher and Link 2015).

The European Banking Union has not been entirely popular with the Germans for two reasons. First, some Germans believe that Landesbanken are smaller than international banks and so the former should be excluded from European supervision (Elliott 2012). This argument is weak since we have seen that some Landesbanken had ambitious business models similar to those of big, international banks. Second, since local politicians often sit on the boards of Landesbanken, some Germans are concerned that supervision at a European level would reduce the cosy relationship between politicians and bank directors of Landesbanken (Elliott 2012). Given that weak corporate governance at certain Landesbanken contributed towards the global financial crisis, increased supervision at European level is one way of reducing this cosy relationship. Despite these objections, BaFin has been co-operating with the European Supervisory Authorities since 1 January 2011, when the European financial supervisory framework came into force. BaFin is still responsible for day-to-day supervision of financial institutions but it works with the European Supervisory Authorities (ESAs) to ensure that there is greater harmonisation of financial supervision in the EU. The ESAs have wide-ranging powers which include drafting specific rules and guidelines for national authorities and financial institutions in the form of technical standards, guidelines and recommendations; monitoring how rules are being enforced by national regulators (they are able in some circumstances to give binding instructions to national regulators and financial institutions); taking action in emergencies, including the banning of certain products; and mediating and settling disputes between national supervisors. Member states can decline to comply with a recommendation or guideline, but technical standards will be binding as an EU regulation or decision.

Early indications from the Supervisory Convergence Report of the European Banking Authority bode well for the future. There has been convergence of supervisory frameworks but more work needs to be done to achieve convergence in supervisory methodologies, practices and outcomes (European Banking Authority 2015). In particular, there are two fundamental approaches to determining capital buffers and additional capital requirements. The first approach envisages that these requirements should be fully covered by a bank's own eligible funds, whilst the second allows the use of other instruments, albeit only in specific circumstances (European Banking Authority 2015). The European Banking Authority issued its 'Guidelines for Common Procedures and Methodologies for the Supervisory Review and Evaluation Process' in 2014, which should facilitate further harmonisation in capital requirements.

Conclusion

In Hamburg's Miniature Wonderland, the only other political-party model to refer to financial reforms is that of the Christian Democratic Union. The party's main concern is the high level of debt and this is reflected in the debt clock shown in the model. Debt is necessary in a modern economy to finance wealth creation, but mismanagement of debt, clearly demonstrated in the global financial crisis, is a concern for all. Managing debt safely has been the challenge for all countries involved in the crisis. In Germany, the financial crisis came as a surprise to most people since the reputation of German banks had been solid and robust. Yet private, commercial banks in Germany met a similar fate to those in the US and the UK, although the proportion of such banks is smaller in Germany. Besides, profitability and earnings ratios are higher in private banks than in state-owned or co-operative banks. A high earnings ratio indicates better capacity to generate capital internally. It would be safe to state that higher capital requirements are vital to sustain a healthy bank business model. Solvency, especially the asset quality of loans, is equally important. In Germany, the quality of real-estate loans is important because of the fear of another debt-fuelled property boom. Basel III, the Solvency and Liquidity Regulations and the Banking Act 1961 have all targeted important areas of prudential regulation.

National and European politics play important roles in Germany. The Landesbank business model was discussed before the financial crisis, but there is now more political will, especially at the European level, to make changes to the model. Landesbanken are in a unique position since they combine the principles of subsidiarity and regional commitment to help the Mittelstand; and local politicians sit on their supervisory boards. Yet the business model of Landesbanken is very similar to that of private, commercial banks. The unusual combination is not *the* problem. Rather, the supervisory arrangements for Landesbanken were inadequate. Given these banks' heavy reliance on securitised products, there should have been more frequent dialogues, audits and on-site visits by BaFin. Most Landesbanken are still struggling to produce profits. Coupled with the Basel III requirements and the financial-market transaction tax, Landesbanken are feeling the strain. It appears that mergers with savings banks are more likely to happen than the privatisation of state-owned banks due to the regional and subsidiarity principles. Drastic changes are unlikely due to the influence of state law and politicians. The prudential implication of mergers between state-owned and savings banks is that the Bundesbank allocate adequate numbers of skilled staff to supervise Landesbanken. The weak performances of Landesbanken have increased vertical supervisory scrutiny at both national and European levels (under the European Banking Union).

Structurally, the HRE incident revealed weaknesses in the relationship between the Bundesbank and BaFin. Criticisms have been made with regards to this supervisory structure. Yet the division of macro- and micro-prudential power has survived the criticisms, and the financial crisis, largely due to the influence of political and industry players. It seems therefore that the single regulator is here to stay for the foreseeable future. The increased vertical co-operation with European regulators seems to be working well in Germany so far. The day-to-day management of implementing macro- and micro-prudential regulation still lies with the German regulators. Increased harmonisation has increased the number of staff involved in supervision. This is particularly problematic for Landesbanken and co-operative banks, since they are also supervised by their regional associations. Therefore, to avoid these banks facing prohibitive costs, it is important that BaFin, regional associations and European regulators communicate and co-operate effectively.

Bibliography

Bayern Landesbank (2015) *Corporate Governance Principles*, Germany: Bayern Landesbank [online], available: https://www.bayernlb.de/internet/en/content/metanav/presse/konzinf_1/corpgov_3/corpgov.jsp [accessed 8 September 2015].

Beck, R., Jakubik, P. and Piloiu, A. (2013) *Non-performing Loans: What Matters in Addition to the Economic Cycle?*, Internal Report, unpublished.

Beck, T., Hesse, H. and von Westernhagen, N. (2009) 'Bank Ownership and Stability: Evidence from Germany', Deutsche Bundesbank Working Paper Series [online], available: www.voxeu.org/index.php?q=node/3549.

Belke, A. (2010) 'Driven by the Markets? ECB Sovereign Bond Purchases and the Securities Markets Programme', *Intereconomics*, 45(6), pp. 357–63.

Benzler, M. and Breilmann, A. (2009) 'M & A, Restructuring and Liquidation of Financial Institutions: Germany' in Bruno, E., ed., *Global Financial Crisis – Navigating and Understanding the Legal and Regulatory Aspects*, Globe Business Publishing Limited.

Bernanke, B. S. (2013) *The Federal Researve and the Financial Crisis*, Princeton University Press.

Bowman, L. (2012) 'Europe's Bad Debt Goliath', *Euromoney Magazine* [online], available: http://www.euromoney.com/Article/3111102/Germany-Europes-bad-debt-Goliath.html?p=3 [accessed 31 August 2015].

Bremer Landesbank (2013) *2013 Reports and Financial Statements* [online], available: https://www.bremerlandesbank.com/uploads/tx_auwdownloadmanager/Reports_and_financial_statements_2013_en.pdf [accessed 12 September 2015].

Buchler, F. and Thies, H. (2013) 'Germany' in Campbell, D., ed., *Regulation of Financial Services, The Comparative Law Yearbook of International Business*, Kluwer Law International.

Bundesanstalt fur Finanzdienstleistungsaufsicht (BaFin) (2009) *Annual Report*, Germany: BaFin.

Bundesanstalt fur Finanzdienstleistungsaufsicht (BaFin) (2014) *Annual Report*, Germany: BaFin.

Buscher, A. and Link, V. (2015) *Recovery and Resolution: Implementing Act for European Directive Now in Force* [online], available: http://www.bafin.de/SharedDocs/Veroeffentlichungen/EN/Fachartikel/2015/fa_bj_1501_sanierungs-abwicklungsgesetz_en.html [accessed 19 January 2016].

Cassola, N., Hortaçsu, A. and Kastl, J. (2013) 'The 2007 Subprime Market Crisis through the Lens of European Central Bank Auctions for Short-term Funds', *Econometrica*, 81(4), pp. 1309–45.

Cecchetti, S. (2009) 'Crisis and Responses: The Federal Reserve in the Early Stages of the Financial Crisis', *The Journal of Economic Perspectives*, 23(1), pp. 51–76.

Cour-Thimann, P. and Winkler, B. (2012) 'The ECB's Non-standard Monetary Policy Measures: The Role of Institutional Factors and Financial Structure', *Oxford Review of Economic Policy*, 28(4), pp. 765–803.

Darvas, Z. (2012) 'The ECB's Magic Wand', *Intereconomics*, 47(5), pp. 266–7.

Deutsche Bundesbank (2009) *Financial Stability Review*, Frankfurt-am-Main: Deutsche Bundesbank.

Deutsche Bundesbank (2014) *Financial Stability Review*, Frankfurt-am-Main: Deutsche Bundesbank.

Deutsche Bundesbank (2015) *Monthly Report, Structural Developments in the German Banking Sector*, Germany: Deutsche Bundesbank.

Deutscher Bundestag–Das Parlament (2009) *Kaum Kompetenzen fur die Kontrolleure*, 36–7, Germany: Deutscher Bundestag.

Deutscher Bundestag (2009a) *Beschlussempfehlung und Bericht des 2. Untersuchungsausschusses nach Artikel 44 des Grundgesetzes*, Berlin, Germany: Deutscher Bundestag.

Deutscher Bundestag (2009b) *Mitarbeit von Privaten an Gesetzentwurfen und Arbeitsfahigkeit der Bundesministerien. Antwort der Bundesregierung auf die Kleine Anfrage der Fraktion Die Linke 16/14025*, Berlin, Germany: Deutscher Bundestag.

Deutscher Sparkassen- und Giroverband (2015) *Inside the Savings Banks Finance Group*, Germany: Deutscher Sparkassen- und Giroverband.

Dombret, A. (2015) *The First Six Months of European Banking Supervision – An NCA's Perspective*, Frankfurt-am-Main, Germany: Deutsche Bundesbank.

The Economist (2015) 'Lost a Fortune, Seeking a Role' [online], available: http://www.economist.com/news/finance-and-economics/21638143-seven-german-landesbanken-survived-financial-crisis-are-still [accessed 16 September 2015].

Elliott, D. (2012) *Key Issues on European Banking Union: Trade-offs and Some Recommendations*, New York, United States of America.

European Banking Authority (2014) *Results of 2014 EU-wide Stress Test: Aggregate Results*, Germany.

European Banking Authority (2015) 'EBA Report on Convergence of Supervisory Practices' [online], available: http://www.eba.europa.eu/supervisory-convergence;jsessionid=C4710DF6F0F9482C7C2DEA760E2AB7CE [accessed 27 December 2015].

European Central Bank (2011) *The Montary Policy of the European Central Bank*, Frankfurt, Germany: European Central Bank.

European Central Bank (2014a) *ECB Annual Report on Supervisory Activities*, Germany [online], available: https://www.bankingsupervision.europa.eu/ecb/pub/pdf/ssmar2014.en.pdf?a88c90797b71eea2e8c133ef20a370d1 [accessed 2 September 2015].

European Central Bank (2014b) *Guide to Banking Supervision*, Germany: European Central Bank.

European Central Bank (2014c) *The List of Significant Supervised Entities and the List of Less Significant Institutions*, Germany: European Central Bank.

Filipova, T. (2007) *The Concept of Integrated Financial Supervision and Regulation of Financial Conglomerates in Germany and the United Kingdom*, Munich, Germany: C.H. Beck.

Financial Stability Committee (2015) *Recommendation of 30 June 2015 on New Instruments for Regulating Loans for the Construction or Purchase of Residential Real Estate*, AFS/2015/1, Germany: Bundesanstalt für Finanzdienstleistungsaufsicht.

Fischer, K.-H. and Pfeil, C. (2004) 'Regulation and Competition in German Banking: An Assessment' in Krahnen, J. and Schmidt, R., eds., *The German Financial System*, New York: Oxford University Press.

Forbes, W., Donohoe, S., Prokop, J. and Buchanan, B. (2015) 'Financial Regulation, Collective Cognition, and Nation State Crisis Management: A Multiple Case Study of Bank Failures in Germany, Ireland, and the UK', *The Journal of Risk Finance*, 16(3), pp. 284–302.

Frach, L. (2008) *Finanzaufsicht in Deutschland und Grossbritannien*, Wiesbaden: VS Verlag.

German Federal Financial Supervisory Authority (2014) *Banking Supervision* [online], available: http://www.bafin.de/EN/BaFin/FunctionsHistory/BankingSupervision/bankingsupervision_node.html [accessed 20 September 2015].

German Federal Financial Supervisory Authority (2015) *Counter-cyclical Capital Buffer* [online], available: http://www.bafin.de/EN/Supervision/BanksFinancialServicesProviders/CapitalRequirements/CCB/ccb_artikel.html [accessed 19 January 2016].

Ghysels, E., Idier, J., Manganelli, S. and Vergote, O. (2014) 'A High Frequency Assessment of the ECB Securities Markets Programme', *European Central Bank Working Paper 1642* [online], available: doi: http://papers.ssrn.com/sol3/papers.cfm?abstract_id=2393376 [accessed 11 August 2015].

Group of Thirty (2008) *The Structure of Financial Supervision: Approaches and Challenges in a Global Marketplace* Washington, DC: The Group of Thirty.

Hackethal, A. (2004) 'German Banks and Banking Structure' in Krahnen, J. and Schmidt, R., eds., *The German Financial System*, United States: Oxford University Press.

Handke, S. (2012) 'Political Deadlock in German Financial Market Policy', *German Policy Studies*, 8(1), pp. 43–80.

Hau, H. and Thum, M. (2009) 'Subprime Crisis and Board (In-)Competence: Private versus Public Banks in Germany', *Economic Policy*, 24, pp. 701–52.

Hodson, D. and Quaglia, L. (2009) 'European Perspectives on the Global Financial Crisis: Introduction*', *Journal of Common Market Studies*, 47(5), pp. 939–53.

Hopt, K., Kumpan, C. and Steffek, F. (2009) 'Preventing Bank Insolvencies in the Financial Crisis: The German Financial Market Stabilisation Acts', *European Business Organization Law Review*, 10(4), pp. 515–54.

Hüfner, F. (2010) *The German Banking System: Lessons from the Financial Crisis*, Internal Report, unpublished.

Kersting, C. (2012) 'Combating the Financial Crisis: European and German Corporate and Securities Laws and the Case for Abolishing Sovereign Debtors' Privileges', *Texas International Law Journal*, 48(2), pp. 270–301.

Kirkpatrick, G. (2009) 'The Corporate Governance Lessons from the Financial Crisis', *OECD Journal: Financial Market Trends*, 1, pp. 61–87.

Kohler, M. (2010) *Corporate Governance and Current Regulation in the German Banking Sector: An Overview and Assessment*, Internal Centre for European Economic Research Report, unpublished.

Kollewe, J. (2016) 'World Stock Markets Bounce Back after Turbulent Week', *The Guardian* [online], available: http://www.theguardian.com/business/2016/jan/22/world-stock-markets-bounce-back-nikkei-ecb-draghi [accessed 22 January 2016].

Marinova, M. (2009) 'Can Capital Ratios be the Centre of Banking Regulation – A Case Study', *European Financial and Accounting Journal*, 4(4), pp. 8–34.

Norddeutsche Landesbank Girozentrale (2014) *Annual Report* [online], available: https://www.nordlb.com/fileadmin/redaktion_en/branchen/investorrelations/geschaeftsberichte/2014/NORDLB_AoeR_Annual_Report_2014.pdf?sword_list[]=auditors&no_cache=1 [accessed 10 September 2015].

Paul, S., Stein, S. and Uhde, A. (2008) 'Measuring the Relationship between Supervisory Authorities and Banks: An Assessment of the German Banking Sector', *Journal of Risk Management in Financial Institutions*, 2(1), pp. 69–87.

Paul, S., Stein, S. and Uhde, A. (2012) 'Measuring the Quality of Banking Supervision Revisited Assessments by German Banks before and during the Financial Crisis', *Journal of Governance and Regulation*, pp. 93–115.

Regierungskommission Deutscher Corporate Governance Kodex (2015) *Deutscher Corporate Governance Kodex* Germany: Regierungskommission Deutscher Corporate Governance Kodex.

Reid, A. and Lister, R. (2006) *German Landesbanken: Analytical Background and Methodology*, Internal Report, unpublished.

Rottke, N. (2012) *The German Market for Distressed Real Estate Assets in 2012 Investor Opportunities and Threats*, Wiesbaden, Germany.

Sester, P. (2012) 'The ECB's Controversial Securities Market Programme (SMP) and Its Role in Relation to the Modified EFSF and the Future ESM', *European Company & Financial Law Review*, 9(2), pp. 156–78.

Sikka, P. (2009) 'Financial Crisis and the Silence of the Auditors', *Accounting, Organisations and Society*, 34(6–7), pp. 868–73.

Simpson, C. (2013) *The German Sparkassen (Savings Banks) – A Commentary and Case Study*, Internal Civitas Report, unpublished.

Sinn, H.-W. (2010) *Casino Capitalism – How the Financial Crisis Came About and What Needs to be Done Now*, Oxford: Oxford University Press.

Taylor, M. (2009) 'Blurring the Boundaries in Financial Stability.' in Bruni, F. and Llewellyn, D. T., eds., *The Failure of Northern Rock: A Multi-dimensional Case Study*, Vienna: SUERF – The European Money and Finance Forum.

Trichet, J.-C. (2010) 'State of the Union: The Financial Crisis and the ECB's Response between 2007 and 2009', *Journal of Common Market Studies*, 48(1), pp. 7–19.

Tröger, T. H. (2014) 'The Single Supervisory Mechanism – Panacea or Quack Banking Regulation? Preliminary Assessment of the New Regime for the Prudential Supervision of Banks with ECB Involvement', *European Business Organization Law Review*, 15(4), pp. 449–97.

Ungeheuer, C. (2009) 'The Current Financial Crisis and Rescue Packages in Germany' in Bruno, E., ed., *Global Financial Crisis, Navigating and Understanding the Legal and Regulatory Aspects*, Globe Business Publishing Limited.

Weidmann, J. (2015) 'The Way to Make Debt Safer', *Deutsche Bundesbank Publications* [online], available: http://www.bundesbank.de/Redaktion/EN/Standardartikel/Press/Contributions/2015 [accessed 22 June 2015].

Wilson, J. and Wiesmann, G. (2010) 'Finance: Germany's Weak Link', *Financial Times* [online], available: http://www.ft.com/cms/s/0/482e3c24-ca6e-11df-a860-00144feab49a.html#axzz3jGeJ88Tq [accessed 18 August 2015].

World Bank (2015) *World Development Indicators* [online], available: http://data.worldbank.org/data-catalog/world-development-indicators [accessed 25 August 2015].

World Economic Forum (2012) *The Financial Development Report 2012* [online], available: http://www.weforum.org/issues/financial-development [accessed 6 April 2015].

Zimmermann, H. (2009) 'Varieties of Global Financial Governance? British and German Approaches to Financial Market Regulation' in Helleiner, E., Pagliari, P. and Zimmermann, H., eds., *Global Finance in Crisis*, London: Routledge.

Zimmermann, H. (2012) 'No Country for the Market: The Regulation of Finance in Germany after the Crisis', *German Politics*, 21(4), pp. 484–501.

8   Conclusion and recommendations

Introduction

'Events in the recent global financial crisis have changed central banking forever' (Mishkin 2012). Central banks' challenges have become more complicated and their powers have increased in turn to cope with the challenges. Without the right tools to deal with excessive leverage and a credit-fuelled asset bubble, central banks felt vulnerable. Entering the global financial crisis, the policy framework and Bagehot's rule proved to be too restrictive. This meant that central banks such as the Bank of England, ECB and the Federal Reserve had to be creative and bold in their crisis-management policies. Using the Bank of England as a case study in this chapter, the author will analyse how it has carried out its mandate of financial stability since the global financial crisis. Recommendations will be made based on the experiences and lessons learnt from Australia, the US, Canada, Germany and the EU. With the Bank of Japan imposing a negative interest rate, emerging threats to financial stability from the UK leaving the EU, the buy-to-let market, cyber attacks, a decrease in oil prices and volatility in the global stock markets, it is a fascinating time to conduct research into financial stability.

New tools for financial stability: tackling moral hazard

Moral hazard is a potential problem if banks know for certain that the Bank of England will provide liquidity support as the 'lender of last resort' (Shafik 2015). Banks will have less incentive to monitor their liquidity positions. The Bank of England has reduced this problem by asking banks to hold more liquid assets and introducing a resolution regime to wind down ailing banks. The Basel III liquidity coverage ratio has been implemented since October 2015. This replaced the individual liquidity guidance, although the two are similar. Banks will have to provide information about their liquidity-risk position and management. Although it is too early to assess the impact of the liquidity coverage ratio on banks, a study by Banerjee and Mio (2015) showed that the individual liquidity guidance did not lead to tightening of banks' balance sheets or to reduced lending to the non-financial sector. Stricter liquidity regulation did not have a negative impact on banks.

Stricter capital requirements, however, appear to have a negative consequence in that they lead to higher costs for borrowers. Pre-emption is a key characteristic of the Financial Policy Committee's (FPC) prudential supervisory style. Therefore, it has implemented the counter-cyclical capital buffer and is currently keeping it at 0 per cent as the economy is still recovering. The FPC intends to increase the buffer gradually to 1 per cent. The aim is to raise sufficient capital during a strong economy so that banks can use their reserves to write down the value of loans and have sufficient capital to absorb losses in stress. The estimated cost of the counter-cyclical capital buffer at its peak of 1 per cent is approximately 0.1 per cent of GDP. This cost will most likely be passed onto borrowers who will pay higher interest rates (Mustoe 2015). Despite the higher cost, implementing a counter-cyclical capital buffer will help with financial stability. It is a useful preventative tool that the Bank of England can use during a bull market. Together with other capital buffers, such as the capital-conservation buffer, the global systemic-importance buffer for global systemically important banks (G-SIB) and the systemic-risk buffer for ring-fenced banks and large building societies, it should make banks more resilient to shocks in the financial system (Bank of England 2015d). To reduce systemic risks nationally, the domestic systemic-risk buffer focuses on the impact of failing banks on the UK economy. Leverage requirements are also important in the new capital framework. These requirements do not use risk-weighted assets. Instead, the leverage ratio is the amount of Tier 1 capital relative to total assets. The reasons for having a leverage ratio are twofold. First, it limits a bank's ability to increase its exposures relative to its capacity to absorb losses. Second, since the leverage ratio does not use risk-weighted assets in its calculation, it avoids the uncertainties attached to the latter (Bank of England 2009). Essentially, the leverage ratio provides another way of ensuring that banks have sufficient capital since risk-weighting or stress-testing may have underestimated the amount of capital required (Rule 2015).

Using a comparative approach, the UK's leverage requirements for G-SIBs in 2015 are arguably reasonable to other countries such as the US and Germany. In the US, the G-SIB leverage ratio is 5 per cent at holding company level and 6 per cent for insured deposit-taking subsidiaries. In the UK, the G-SIB leverage ratio is 3.4 per cent-3.9 per cent although the UK operates a counter-cyclical leverage buffer as well (Bank of England 2015d). Australia and Canada do not have any global systemically important banks, whilst Deutsche Bank is the only global systemically important bank in Germany, and its leverage ratio is 3.6 per cent in 2015 (Deutsche Bank 2015). Germany and the UK have implemented the Basel III G-SIB standards via the Capital Requirements Directive IV along with other European Economic Area countries. The G-SIB standards are based on an internationally agreed method and aim to reduce moral hazard linked to the problem of 'too big to fail' banks (Australia Prudential Regulatory Authority 2013). Five factors are taken into account when calculating the G-SIB standards: size, interconnectedness, cross-jurisdictional activity, substitutability and complexity. Although the UK G-SIB leverage ratio is fairly low, it has a counter-cyclical leverage buffer which should provide additional protection to banks against shocks. The current counter-cyclical leverage ratio is 35 per cent of a firm's institution-specific counter-cyclical capital-buffer rate (Prudential Regulatory Authority 2015). Time will tell whether this works. In contrast to the prescriptive nature of the G-SIB standards, the rules for domestic systemically important banks (D-SIBs) are more flexible, since national regulatory authorities decide the assessment and application of the D-SIB rules. The D-SIB rules will be implemented by phases, with annual increments starting in January 2016 till full implementation in 2019. The new UK capital framework also focuses on micro-prudential regulation. Two new requirements target specific banks with capital weaknesses. First, the additional minimum Pillar 2A capital requirements will make adjustments to take into account risks currently not reflected or insufficiently reflected in Pillar 1 of the capital framework (Bank of England 2015d). The second additional requirement is the Prudential Regulatory Authority buffer. This ensures that banks with weak governance and risk management will have more capital than other banks to deal with adverse situations.

Measuring risks in securitisation is difficult because securitisation takes advantage of the weaknesses in risk weightings by allowing banks to reduce their capital whilst increasing their revenues (Rule 2015). The global financial crisis revealed that not all credit ratings in assessing the quality of securitised products were reliable. Therefore, the Basel Committee worked with the International Organisation for Securities Commissions and published a set of simple, transparent and comparable criteria on securitisation for consultation. They called for more transparency and alignment of issuers' incentives with those of investors. The EU Commission has also circulated a proposal on developing a high-quality, sustainable securitisation framework. The framework includes asset-backed commercial paper, which created regulatory problems in Canada. Rule (2015) believes that these proposals should achieve the macro- and micro-prudential regulatory aims of a sustainable securitisation market. The simple, transparent and comparable criteria sound sensible. It has been established earlier in this book that securitisation has its benefits, even though the mismanagement and lack of understanding of securitised products contributed to the global financial crisis. If managed well, securitisation can diversify funding sources and allocate risks efficiently in the financial system (European Commission 2015). Since the global financial crisis, the EU Commission has implemented a number of reforms regarding securitisation to restore financial stability. Examples include the Capital Requirements Directive IV and compulsory checks by EU banks, acting as investors, that originating banks have retained an interest of at least 5 per cent in securitised assets (European Commission 2015). Simplification of securitisation and more transparency should increase financial stability.

Tackling emerging risks in the UK with new regulatory tools

Armed with its new regulatory tools, the Bank of England has been tackling emerging risks well. To avoid another credit bubble, the Bank of England is targeting the buy-to-let market, which it believes could pose a threat to financial stability. The disparity between lending in the buy-to-let market and the owner-occupier market is stark. In the third quarter of 2015, the stock of lending in the buy-to-let sector rose by 10 per cent compared to only 0.3 per cent growth in the stock of lending to owner-occupiers (Bank of England 2015a). The Bank of England has already put several measures in place to deal with the increase in lending in the buy-to-let market. The Prudential Regulation Authority (PRA) will review lenders' underwriting standards. Second, the FPC currently has powers of direction in relation to towner-occupier-mortgage lending under the Bank of England Act 1998 (Macro-prudential Measures) Order 2015. This enables the FPC to set limits to the loan-to-income ratio and the debt-to-income ratio. The Treasury plans to give similar powers of direction to the FPC in relation to the buy-to-let mortgage-lending sector. The German Bundesbank has similar concerns. The Financial Stability Committee in Germany therefore made some recommendations to give the Federal Financial Supervisory Authority powers to regulate residential-property loans. These recommendations include a cap on the loan-to-value and debt-to-income ratios, as well as compulsory amortisation requirements. Germany had a population of 80,709,056 in 2015, whilst the UK had 64,643,370 (European Commission 2014). However, due to a low birth rate and an ageing population in Germany, the UK's population is forecast to overtake Germany's by 2050 (European Commission 2014). The UK government has already promised to supply 400,000 new houses by 2020 (Chan 2015). Therefore, in January 2016, the government announced that it will directly commission 13,000 new starter homes for first-time buyers in southern England (Perraudin 2016). However, house prices are forecast to increase faster than earnings by 2020, thus making it difficult for individuals to afford houses. Home ownership in the UK has decreased from 73 per cent in 2007 to 65 per cent in 2015 due to high property and mortgage costs (Chan 2015). Targeting the buy-to-let market will hopefully reduce the number of investor buyers and the rise in house prices (Evans 2015).

Chapters 2 and 6 have shown that effective regulation of the Canadian residential-mortgage market is a crucial factor in the robustness of its financial system. In particular, the fact that all mortgages with a loan-to-value ratio of more than 80 per cent had to be insured for the whole amount

(Ratnovski and Huang 2009). Financial stability in the residential-property market can be further enhanced by regulation of credit products, including investor-housing mortgages, by soft law. In Australia, the National Consumer Credit Code encourages responsible lending and has a compulsory External Dispute Resolution-scheme membership. The National Consumer Credit Code is part of the National Consumer Credit Protection Act 2009 ('the NCCP Act'). The NCCP Act created a single, national consumer-credit regime. The regulatory coverage of credit products under the National Consumer Credit Code has been expanded to include investor-housing mortgages (Australian Securities and Investments Commission 2013a). The Australian Securities and Investments Commission regulates the conduct of lenders and brokers (Australian Securities and Investments Commission 2013b). The FCA should consider adopting a similar code to strengthen consumer protection and financial stability. In the meantime, the FPC has powers of recommendation which it can use to carry out its mandate of financial stability (Bank of England 2015a). The counter-cyclical capital and leverage buffers can assist here. Since investors can increase leverage by buying several properties to make capital gains (Dyson 2014), increasing the counter-cyclical buffers in a strong economy will provide banks with more reserves to absorb losses and preserve financial stability. The combination of stricter lending requirements to investor landlords and the counter-cyclical buffers should provide the Bank of England and UK banks with better tools to maintain financial stability.

The FPC is also monitoring the UK commercial-property market and cyber risks. Commercial-property prices have risen significantly recently (Bank of England 2015a). Although the use of leverage dropped after the global financial crisis, it rose in 2015 (Bank of England 2015a). Around 75 per cent of small- to medium-sized business rely on commercial property as collateral to support their bank loans. If there is a downturn in the commercial-property market, this could create problems for these businesses when accessing finance. Finally, a recent survey by the Bank of England revealed that 46 per cent of banks are concerned about cyber risks (Bank of England 2015a). Royal Bank of Scotland and NatWest were victims of cyber attacks in 2015 (Collinson 2015). Both banks have been attacked five times in the last three years. Cyber attacks are usually temporary in nature and targeted at individual banks. They can create panic amongst customers because their personal details may have been compromised and they cannot access cash. As a result of this, the Bank of England conducted a cyber exercise in November 2015 with the US. The Bank of England has also made good progress with the 'CBEST' testing of banks' resilience to cyber attacks. From July to December 2015, five more firms undertook the CBEST tests, bringing the total of firms which have completed the tests to 10 (Bank of England 2015a). Overall, early indications of the Bank of England's ability to tackle emerging risks with new tools are positive, and it will be interesting to see the impact of the counter-cyclical capital and leverage buffers in practice.

Tackling the danger of power concentration in the Bank of England

Independence and accountability are important at the Bank of England for two reasons. First, central banks are government bodies: accountability and independence are important to avoid abuse of power and democratic deficit. Second, this book has mentioned the concerns of some scholars who believe that the Bank of England may become too powerful due to the 'twin-peaks' model. This section will reveal that, although the Monetary Policy Committee (MPC) is transparent and operates on the principle of personal accountability, the oversight and supervisory aspects of the Bank of England need to be more transparent and accountable. The MPC sets interest rates at the Bank of England. One of the strengths of the MPC is its accountability. The Bank of England has traditionally been praised for both its independence and its accountability to Parliament (Gerlach-Kristen 2004; Blinder *et al.* 2008). Gerlach-Kristen's research reveals that dissent in MPC meetings from June 1997 to February 2003 was common, with almost two thirds of meetings containing dissenting votes (Gerlach-Kristen 2004). Minutes from March 2003 to December 2005 were unavailable on the Bank of England's website, but this book has found that dissenting votes between January 2005 and November 2015 made up 44.2 per cent of total votes. There was no extreme divergence of members' opinions on interest rates, although there were two occasions in 2005 and one occasion in 2007 where the voting result was 5–4. Divergence in voting is important for future policy since it encourages challenges and debate.

An interesting pattern worth noting is the continuous period of unanimous decision between July 2011 and August 2014. A possible explanation is the desire of the MPC to keep interest rates low whilst the asset-purchase programme was still running against a background of weak recovery. Blinder *et al.* (2010) opine that the MPC's culture is 'individualistic', whilst the ECB's Governing Council is 'genuinely collegial' and the Federal Reserve's Financial Open Market Committee (FOMC) under Alan Greenspan 'autocratically collegial'. Whalen (2011) submits that Alan Greenspan, who was Chairman for 19 years, essentially controlled the Federal Reserve's Board of Governors and focused primarily on monetary policy. Whalen (2011) added that central banks tend to be 'authoritarian and regressive in thinking' and suffer from a 'superman' syndrome. This view seems to be challenged now by the Obama government, which has appointed experts other than economists to the Federal Reserve. Although Janet Yellen, the current Chair of the Federal Reserve, is an economist, there is little to date to suggest that she runs a 'superwoman' Federal Reserve. A speech she gave in 2015 highlights the fact that the Federal Reserve is absolutely committed to its dual mandates of maximum employment and stable prices (monetary policy is not the sole purpose of the Federal Reserve) (Yellen 2015). Further, the September 2015 minutes of the FOMC reflect a very thorough and detailed discussion of whether it should raise the interest rate. Issues such as employment-market conditions, emerging countries' financial situations, the inflation outlook and domestic and foreign economic conditions were discussed (Board of Governors of the Federal Reserve Board System 2015).

The voting results reveal that the majority of the FOMC was cautious and did not feel that it was the right time to raise the interest rate. One member objected on the grounds that keeping interest rates very low for such a long period is not appropriate for the US economy, which is strong on consumption. Interestingly, the frequency and number of members dissenting in FOMC meetings have increased since Yellen became the Chair. Since April 2014, there have been dissenting votes fairly regularly, with two dissenters in September 2014 and even three dissenters in December 2014. This contrasts with the history of dissenting votes in FOMC meetings when Bernanke was Chairman. The increase in dissenting votes is to be welcomed because disagreements promote scrutiny, avoid rubber-stamping decisions and encourage independence of mind. Should this trend continue, it would be difficult to associate the Federal Reserve with the 'superman' image (Whalen 2011). The voting results are similar to those of the MPC in October 2015, where, by a majority of 8–1, it was agreed to keep the interest rate at 0.5 per cent. However, Andrew Sentance, a former member of the MPC, encouraged existing members of the MPC to be more courageous and raise the interest rate. He believes that since MPC members are meant to exercise independence, they should grasp the nettle and raise the interest rate before it is too late (BBC 2015b).

Sentance's concern that interest rate should be raised is valid, since this was discussed in the FMOC meeting of October 2015. The minutes reveal that leaving interest rates between 0 per cent and 0.25 per cent for too long could lead to financial instability due to increased corporate borrowing in the US (Fleming and Wigglesworth 2015). The FMOC voted 9–1 in favour of keeping the interest rate the same but indicated that there is likely to be a rise in December 2015 if economic activity continues to improve and there are no 'unanticipated shocks... adversely affecting the economic outlook' (Federal Reserve Bank 2015a). In other words, the October meeting was important because the Federal Reserve made a clear announcement to global markets that raising the interest rate is a real possibility. Indeed, the Federal Reserve increased its interest rate by 0.25 per cent in December 2015. This is the first interest-rate rise in ten years (Morris 2015). However, after careful consideration, the MPC did not raise the interest rate in January 2016. Inflation has slowed due to a decrease in oil prices (Bank of England 2016). Overall, there is clear evidence of independence at the MPC through the dissenting-voting patterns. In the period 2005–15, there was a reduction of dissenting votes, although this should not cause real alarm since it can be attributed primarily to the gradual economic recovery and asset-purchase programme following the global financial crisis.

Accountability is also strong at the MPC. Not only does it publish minutes with votes recorded, it has also implemented the recommendation made by the Warsh Review, led by Kevin Warsh (former Federal Reserve Governor). Since March 2015, the Bank of England has published minutes with an eight-year lag. Issing (2015) believes that the combination of personal accountability and the publication of votes can lead to the public attaching more importance to individual members than to the reasons behind their decisions. He continues that this is potentially a problem in the EU, where different national interests are represented. However, personal accountability is not a hindrance in the UK. In fact, it is very much a positive aspect of the independence and general accountability of the Bank of England. Every month, after its Council meeting, the ECB holds press conferences. at which the media can ask questions, encouraging public access and transparency; but the decision not to publish minutes or voting results has been criticised for not being transparent (Eijffinger and De Haan 2000). Although the MPC does not give monthly media interviews, it gives regular press interviews. MPC members also appear before Parliament to answer questions (Bank of England 2015b). Therefore, it is submitted that the Bank of England's mandate of monetary policy is transparent, with personal accountability making an important contribution to independence and general accountability. This is particularly important in light of the Bank of England's increased macro-prudential powers to perform the mandates of prudential regulation and financial stability.

This book predicts that there will be more vertical co-operation between the Bank of England, the European Supervisory Authorities and the ECB due to the centralisation of monetary policy and supervision. Although the Bank of England still retains the mandate of monetary policy, more co-operation with the European Supervisory Authorities means more information sharing. It has been argued that the ECB should publish its minutes and voting records within eight weeks of its meetings so that the Bank of England has more information on the ECB's monetary policy (Transparency International 2012). Further, there should be more frequent reports from the ECB to national parliaments of member states on the Single Supervisory Mechanism. Between November 2013 and November 2014, the ECB submitted quarterly reports to the European Parliament, EU Council and European Commission regarding its progress on the Single Supervisory Mechanism. This complies with paragraph 1 of the Interinstitutional Agreement between the European Parliament and the ECB on the practical modalities of the exercise of democratic accountability and oversight over the exercise of the tasks conferred on the ECB within the framework of the Single Supervisory Mechanism (2013/694/EU). Yet it does not appear that national parliaments of member states were kept informed. As Chapter 2 of this book made clear, the ECB can apply higher capital buffers to credit institutions and impose stricter requirements, subject to close co-operation with the national supervisors under the Capital Requirements Directive (2013/36/EU) and Article 5 of the Single Supervisory Mechanism Regulation. It is therefore important that the ECB and the national supervisors, such as the Bank of England, frequently share information. Currently, the ECB's transparency in this issue is lacking. It is hoped that the ECB will act on this matter. Otherwise, the information cascade to the Bank of England will be weak compared to the upward information flow to the ECB. A potential difficulty is how this information can be shared in a safe manner. There are provisions in the Inter-institutional Agreement concerning professional secrecy and confidentiality (paragraphs H, I, J, L, N and sections 2, 4 and 5). Transparency may have to be balanced with competing interests such as the ECB's roles in macro- and micro-prudential supervision. This is an area which the author of this book intends to research.

Internal oversight and supervision at the Bank of England

Although the MPC at the Bank of England carries out the mandate of monetary policy in a transparent way, we saw in Chapter 2 that the Serious Fraud Office is currently investigating the Bank of England's role as lender of last resort during the financial crisis. The allegation is that the Bank of England was involved in manipulating money-market auctions. Having discovered 50 examples of market manipulation, the Bank of England admitted that it did not have a proper channel to raise the alarm. Despite the implementation of an 'attestation and escalation policy', the outcome of the Serious Fraud Office could tarnish the reputation of the Bank of England as a supervisor. The PRA has set out its whistleblowing policy on its website but this is only the first step to improve accountability. Legislation should be enacted to increase accountability and transparency by imposing accountability on *regulatory agencies* if they breach any whistleblowing laws, such as the Public Interest Disclosure Act 1998. This is the position with the Federal Reserve in the US. The Notification and Federal Employee Anti-discrimination and Retaliation Act of 2002 ('the No FEAR Act') not only requires federal agencies in the US to comply with anti-discrimination and whistleblowing legislation, it also imposes positive duties on federal agencies. Such duties include providing an annual report to Congress and the Department of Justice with details about the status of complaints and how the regulatory agency is improving compliance with whistleblowing law. The Federal Reserve's website publishes statistical data of equal-opportunity complaints on its website (Federal Reserve Bank 2015b). Borak (2004) believes that the No FEAR Act increases governmental accountability because the attention is on the quality of the information provided by the whistleblower rather than on the whistleblower. Anonymity might help: if the whistle-blower's identity is unknown, full attention can be given to the quality of information. However, anonymity does not seem to be available for public employees in the US. Anonymity is available under section 806 of the Sarbanes–Oxley Act for employees working in publicly traded companies and under section 15 of the Dodd–Frank Wall Street Reform and Consumer Protection Act 2010 ('the Dodd–Frank Act') in relation to information regarding a violation of securities laws if they are represented by a counsel. However, when whistleblowers claim a reward under the Dodd–Frank Act, they have to reveal their identities. The Public Interest Disclosure Act 1998 in the UK encourages whistleblowers to raise their concerns openly rather than anonymously. Anonymity may raise questions about the credibility of the whistleblower and impede further questions arising from the whistleblower's information.

Public-sector employees may face the dilemma of revealing potentially sensitive information or even an issue of national security. In the US case of Garcetti v Ceballos 547 US 410 (2006), the Supreme Court, by a majority of 5–4, held that most public employees are not protected from whistleblowing under the First Amendment. This case concerns a memorandum written by a deputy district attorney with an allegation of governmental misconduct. The Supreme Court explained that 'exposing governmental inefficiency and misconduct is a matter of considerable significance' and that employees who blow the whistle 'pursuant to their professional duties' may face disciplinary action. Ceballos's memorandum, therefore, did not constitute protected speech and his demotion did not breach any law. This case has attracted negative opinions (Nahmod 2008; Secunda 2008) primarily because taxpayers do not have a choice of leaving a government when they are dissatisfied. Unhappy shareholders in a company can exit by selling shares. Legislation is thus needed to protect public-sector employees as well as impose duties on government to increase accountability. The Public Interest Disclosure Act 1998 does not encourage individual whistleblowers to raise the alarm, nor does it improve organisational accountability. It merely provides whistleblowers with protection from unfair dismissal and discrimination after they blew the whistle. In most cases, this protection is insufficient since whistleblowers are often made 'redundant' and are forced to sign gagging clauses to prevent them from publicly revealing the information. Therefore, a similar version of the No FEAR Act should be considered in the UK to increase the Bank of England's accountability. The new whistleblowing rules in the UK imposed on private firms have encouraged private-sector whistleblowers to speak up. In 2014–15, there was a 28 per cent increase in disclosures to the FCA, and the FCA foresees a similar pattern in the future (Whiteley *et al.* 2015). The new whistleblowing rules offer private-sector employees more protection, with obligations imposed on relevant firms to inform employees of internal whistleblowing policies, production of an annual report by the 'whistleblowing champion' to the board of directors and notification to the FCA if the firm was unsuccessful in a whistleblowing claim (Whiteley *et al.* 2015). These are all positive steps to increase accountability of private firms, but similar rules should apply to regulatory agencies.

Regulatory capture

Lobbying by pressure groups is one way of undermining the governance and independence of central banks and regulatory authorities. On occasions prior to the global financial crisis, supervisors bowed to pressure groups and lobbyists, fearing that the economy would suffer if regulation and supervision were too strict. Lobbying is a form of 'regulatory capture', also known as the private-interest approach (Stigler 1971). Regulation is perceived as a product, enhancing the power of bankers and politicians. Competing interest groups such as bankers, politicians and consumers try to influence national policies towards banks in ways that favour themselves even if these policies do not maximise social welfare. According to Mervyn King: 'The sheer weight of resources, time and legal effort put in by banks to try to persuade regulators that what they were doing was compliant with the rules made life extraordinarily difficult for the regulators' (Joint Committee on the draft Financial Services Bill 2011). In his view, regulatory capture has been a serious issue for the past 20 years.

Critics of regulatory capture argue that the causal relationship in regulatory capture is unclear in analysing the performance of regulators. Just because Parliament has adopted a policy supported by a group of bankers does not necessarily imply that there is something wrong (Carpenter 2010). Yet Baxter (2011) argues that regulatory capture can be seen in the US financial industry. For example, the Office of the Comptroller of the Currency has utilised its powers to enable national banks to avoid restrictions on their activities. Further, the SEC adopted a 'consolidated supervised entities' policy which meant that large banks were able to increase their leverage ratios to very high levels (Baxter 2011). In the US, the five leading US investment banks lobbied hard to weaken capital requirements and insisted that their own sophisticated computer models could predict bankruptcy risks (Sinn 2010). In Germany, the Bundesbank resisted the use of securitised products for a long time. It was compelled eventually to allow the use of money-market funds by German banks under the Undertakings for Collective Investment in Transferable Securities and Investment (Organismen für gemeinsame Anlagen in Wertpapieren) 2009/65/EG due to European harmonisation. In the UK, evidence of regulatory capture was manifested in the FSA's light-touch regulatory style with banks, the use of individual banks' computer models rather than the FSA's risk-assessment framework and the reliance on rating agencies to assess important risks as financial products became increasingly complicated (Warwick Commission 2012; Watson 2013). Watson (2013) is of the opinion that regulatory capture and the 'intellectual or moral failure' to deal with risk concentration in Northern Rock and some Irish banks played a role in the financial crisis.

These examples illustrate that industry players and stakeholders can wield very powerful forces against the regulators. Indeed, the pressure exerted by lobbyists can be excessive. Before Sir Mervyn King stepped down as Governor of the Bank of England in 2013, he warned that some bankers in the UK had pressurised politicians to relax capital requirements after the global financial crisis. Sir Mervyn raised his concern by speaking about the dangers of lobbying in front of the House of Commons Treasury Select Committee. The Banking Commission (House of Commons Treasury Committee 2013) has since recommended that the Governor of the Bank of England should have a personal responsibility to sound the alarm to Parliament or the public if bank lobbying of government becomes a concern. 'Bad lobbying is a deliberate attempt to deceive or distort. Because of the iterative nature of the policy engagement process, this ultimately destroys trust between the regulator and the regulated' (James 2014). The Governor's personal responsibility to raise the alarm when bank lobbying becomes excessive is a good idea, although the banking industry should also curb its lobbying and work with the regulator. Robert Jenkins, formerly a lobbyist and an ex-member of the FPC, said that bank lobbyists' argument that prudence is bad for the economy is mistaken: 'For the truth is that banks can strengthen their balance sheets without harming the economy. They can do so by cutting bonuses, by curtailing intra-financial risk-taking and by raising term debt and equity' (Jenkins 2011).

According to Transparency International (2012), one way of reducing bank lobbying is for central banks to sign up to the Transparency Register. The Transparency Register was set up in 2011 by the European Parliament and the European Commission. It records contact between interest groups and the European Parliament and Commission. However, it does not provide a list of meetings between the respective parties. It has been suggested that signing up to the Transparency Register will show the commitment of a central bank to increasing transparency. The Bank of England may wish to consider joining the Transparency Register and, additionally, record its meetings with interest groups.

The Warwick Commission (2012) believes that 'regulatory capture substantially contributed to the regulatory failure'. Boyer and Ponce (2012) opine that concentration of supervisory authority within a single supervisor, such as a central bank, increases the likelihood of regulatory capture where bank supervisors are likely to pursue their own self interests. This reduces the social-welfare function of a central bank. The Warwick Commission (2012) recommended two ways to reduce regulatory capture. First, macro-prudential regulation of liquidity, leverage and capital should adopt a risk-based, counter-cyclical approach, so that the regulator is strict in a bull market and more lenient in a bear market. In theory, the wide discretionary powers enjoyed by the FPC to direct and make recommendations and the PRA's judgement-based supervisory style could lead to regulatory capture. Yet evidence to date shows that the PRA is monitoring and supervising banks well. At a micro-prudential level, the PRA scrutinises closely banks' compliance with capital requirements. As part of the stress-test exercise, it can send an unstructured data request to all banks detailing specific information if banks have kept inadequate records of such information. Further, banks need to provide written justification if they need third-party capital injections, such as from parent institutions. All this information will be used in the supervisory dialogues between the PRA and individual banks (Bank of England 2015c). Supervisory dialogues can promote exchanges in information, and enforcement can be avoided since supervisors can make the necessary changes (Andenas and Chiu 2014). Annual cyclical stress-test scenarios will be conducted by the PRA every two years. There will also be a biennial exploratory scenario to test emerging or latent risks such as buy-to-let mortgages (Bank of England 2015e).

Having weighed the pros and cons of including UK investment-banking subsidiaries of foreign-owned banks in the stress-testing framework, the Bank of England decided against including them. This is because it believes that the stress-test results of a UK subsidiary that is only a part of the bigger group are of limited value. Rather, the Bank of England's supervisory approach focuses on working with the home regulators of these banks. This involves sharing group-level test results with the Bank of England. The UK's co-operative, information-sharing supervisory style differs from the Federal Reserve's supervisory approach, since investment-banking subsidiaries of foreign-owned banks are included in the Federal Reserve's stress-testing framework (Bank of England 2015e). From the UK's perspective, the Bank of England is trying to keep regulatory costs down as much as possible. It based its decision on the knowledge that the UK have a sound resolution mechanism for UK subsidiaries. This is found in the Banking Act 2009, where the Special Resolution Regime (SRR) applies to UK subsidiaries of foreign-owned banks. The SRR would thus be able to deal with the UK subsidiary of Lehman Brothers should a scenario similar to that in 2008 take place. The SRR allows foreign authorities to ring-fence local assets of UK bank branches (not subsidiaries) of foreign banks. Hence, if Bank of America's UK branch is in distress, US authorities have full power to ring-fence the assets of the UK branch. This seems sensible in theory given that branches are part of the parent company, whereas subsidiaries are separate legal entities and locally incorporated (Lui 2012). The Vickers Report in 2011 recommended ring-fencing retail banking from investment-banking activities and a 10 per cent equity baseline (Vickers 2011b). The government has since adopted retail ring-fencing and 'electrified' it, thus giving the regulator enforcement power. Sections 71–80 of the Financial Services (Banking Reform) Act 2013 incorporates the electrification of retail ring-fencing. The PRA also has to review proprietary trading by relevant persons and produce a written report to the Treasury (Financial Services (Banking Reform) Act 2013: section 9). Prescription in the form of legislation is thus a good way to reduce regulatory capture by the regulator, since this is not dependent on the regulator's judgement. Ring-fencing should make banks more resilient to external shocks and improve financial stability.

The second recommendation made by the Warwick Commission on reducing regulatory capture is that the host regulator should have more power than the home regulator to deal quickly with potential issues in relation to UK branches of foreign-owned banks. When Icelandic banks such as Glitnir, Landsbanki and Kaupthing ran into financial trouble in 2008, the Icelandic government did not have sufficient financial resources to compensate UK depositors. The UK government (host country) had to step in and provide compensation to UK depositors even though the FSA only had secondary responsibility for regulating and supervising the branches of these Icelandic banks. The primary responsibility for supervision was with the Icelandic regulator: under the EU Second Banking Directive 1989, the home state has primary responsibility for prudential regulation of branches. With the collapse of Lehman Brothers International European, the UK again bore the brunt of the financial disaster. Therefore, it is only logical that the host-country regulator should take a leading role in the regulation and supervision of cross-border bank branches.

Since the UK is not part of the European Banking Union, neither the Single Supervisory Mechanism nor the Single Resolution Mechanism applies. The Bank Resolution and Recovery Directive (2014/59/EU) applies to the UK and is an attempt to harmonise the resolution regime across the EU. The Bank Resolution and Recovery Directive (BRRD) contains improvements to resolve EU cross-border bank issues, such as a range of legal powers enjoyed by relevant authorities to resolve failing banks (section 84), a bail-in mechanism and the requirement of joint decisions from the College of Supervisors on recovery plans. However, the BRRD does not apply to branches of foreign-owned banks. In fact, member states have the right to reject third-country resolution proceedings relating to third-country branches in the EU under section 102 of the BRRD. Therefore, it appears that the UK could reject resolution proceedings from a branch of Lehman Brothers or from banks such as Glitnir. The BRRD improves the resolution procedure but oversight of branches of foreign-owned banks remains a problem. This is particularly problematic since a unique feature of the UK banking sector is the international dimension. There are 150 deposit-taking foreign subsidiaries and 98 deposit-taking foreign branches from 56 different countries (Bush *et al.* 2014). Foreign branches constitute 29 per cent of UK-resident banking assets, compared to 16 per cent in Belgium and 14 per cent in the US. Articles 21, 26 and 27 of the Capital Requirements Directive IV should therefore be amended so that the host (not the home) supervisor has more supervisory powers in a crisis. In particular, Article 27 should be broadened so that the host supervisor can intervene and resolve banks in an emergency. Merely allowing the host supervisor to take 'precautionary emergency measures' is not enough in light of the FSA's experience with Icelandic banks and Lehman Brothers. This is necessary if we want to encourage foreign banks to provide retail banking in the UK (Lui 2012).

Better enforcement by the PRA and FCA

Effective enforcement powers, like clear objectives, sufficient resources and independence, are important to the success of a regulator. After the global financial crisis, the PRA and FCA bolstered their enforcement strategies by pursuing a 'credible deterrence' policy (Teasdale 2011; Wilson and Wilson 2014). Credible deterrence relies on proactive enforcement and publicity of successful convictions, judgements and decisions (Teasdale 2011). It applies to both criminal and civil breaches by financial organisations. The PRA and FCA pursued separate investigations into the near collapse of the Co-operative Group under section 77 of the Financial Services Act 2012. The investigation was necessary since there was a financial capital shortfall of £1.5bn in May 2013, which was largely a result of the acquisition of the Britannia Building Society in 2009 (Goff and Gray 2014). Sir Christopher Kelly's report into the capital shortfall of the Co-operative Bank found nine governance and management failures (Kelly 2014). Only one of them, the economic climate, was outside the control of the Co-operative Bank. The Kelly report found that the merger with the Britannia Society was a major contributor to the Co-operative Bank's failure because the due diligence carried out into the riskiest parts of Britannia Society (corporate loan books and commercial-real-estate lending) were not thorough. Further, the senior management team lacked experience in banking and the culture was 'fallible' (Kelly 2014). The board directors did not welcome challenges and did not take advice from regulators seriously.

Despite its 'Co-operative' name, the FCA and PRA found that the bank did not co-operate with regulators. In particular, it breached Principle 11 of the Principles for Businesses because it did not notify the regulators of changes to two senior positions between April 2012 and May 2013 nor the reasons behind the changes (Financial Conduct Authority 2015b). The PRA separately found that the Co-operative Bank failed to comply with Principle 3 of the Principles for Businesses between July 2009 and December 2013. The Co-operative Bank's risk-management model, which had three lines of defence, was seriously flawed in theory and practice. The PRA and FCA ultimately issued a public censure against the Co-operative Bank. Although the Co-operative Bank's offences were serious and a financial penalty would have been imposed under normal circumstances, the PRA and FCA took into consideration that a financial penalty would not promote the safety and soundness of banks under the PRA's statutory objective set out in section 2 of the Financial Services and Markets Act 2000.

A recent example of the FCA using credible deterrence is the imposition of a £72,069,400 fine on Barclays for its failure to minimise financial-crime risks (Financial Conduct Authority 2015a). Although the FCA did not find that Barclays was involved or assisted in financial crime, Barclays failed to carry out enhanced due diligence and monitoring risks on politically exposed persons. In particular, the FCA found five specific failings: the failure of senior management to oversee financial-crime risks in relation to the business relationship with the clients ('the Business Relationship'); failure to address certain characteristics of the Business Relationship that indicated a high risk of financial crime; failure to monitor ongoing risks in relation to the Business Relationship; failure to ascertain the nature of the transaction with the clients, as well as failure to verify the client's stated source of funds against the funding sources for the transaction (Financial Conduct Authority 2015a).

Another recent example of successful enforcement action by the twin-peaks model is that against Standard Chartered Bank ('SC Bank'). In December 2013, the PRA told SC Bank to dismiss Richard Meddings, a former Group Finance Director of SC Bank. The PRA was worried about the potential conflict between Meddings's duty to oversee risk operations and his responsibility in finance (Wilson 2013). The FCA also imposed a fine of £8.75m on Coutts for failing to take reasonable care to establish and maintain effective anti-money-laundering systems and controls relating to high-risk customers, including politically exposed persons.

The Courts are also showing signs of being tougher on financial crimes. In December 2015, the Court of Appeal considered the mitigating circumstances of Tom Hayes, the first trader convicted for manipulating Libor, and reduced his sentence from 14 to 11 years. Despite the reduction of sentence, it appears that the Courts now view financial crime as seriously as other types of crime (BBC 2015c). Following a heavier crackdown on financial crime, the FCA has abandoned an industry review into the culture of banks. Instead, it launched a review in January 2016 into Lloyds Banking Group to determine whether it has manipulated the price of government bonds (Treanor 2016). The shadow chancellor has criticised this move. In his view, the FCA is softening its approach towards banks (BBC 2015a). The Walker Review of 2010 investigated banks' corporate-governance weaknesses after the global financial crisis and made 39 recommendations. It would be nice to have an up-to-date industry review of banking culture to see if banks have made improvements since the Walker Review. It is hoped that the FCA will remain robust and thorough in adopting an individualistic style in reviewing bank culture.

The interventionist, proactive styles of both the PRA and FCA are most encouraging. It is hoped that they will adopt the same styles with regulation and supervision of UK banks. The challenge is, as Ferran (2011) argues, 'to maintain an aggressively judgmental style when economic conditions improve and political sentiment moves on'. A considerable challenge indeed. Early indications are positive, though, and it is envisaged that the credible-deterrence policy is here to stay. In 2013, the FCA published 76 final notices and imposed total fines of £423.2 million. Further, in the year 2012–13, the FCA took more actions against individuals than firms. This is illustrated by 55 actions against individuals, which included more than £5m in fines, 43 prohibitions and 13 criminal convictions. Meanwhile, the FCA took action against 38 firms, resulting in total fines of £418m (McDermott 2013). Tracey McDermott (2013), Director of Enforcement and Financial Crime at the FCA, made it clear in her speech that the credible-deterrence strategy will continue.

Consumer protection will be further enhanced by the Senior Managers and Certification Regime, which came into force in March 2016. The Financial Services (Banking Reform) Act 2013 introduces the Senior Managers and Certification Regime ('SMCR'). Under the SMCR, there is a statutory duty for senior managers to take reasonable steps to prevent regulatory breaches by the firms in which they work (HM Treasury 2015). Further, senior managers' qualifications and conduct will be subject to stricter scrutiny since the firms which the senior managers work for have to submit documents outlining their responsibilities. Senior managers will also have to comply with the Rules of Conduct. The SMCR is to be welcomed since it will raise the standard and conduct of senior managers. Several banks in the UK, notably the ones which required governmental assistance, had senior managers who were not qualified in finance or economics. Senior bankers are professionals and they should be subject to conduct rules similar to those of other professions. The removal of the reverse burden of proof means that regulators have the onus of proving that senior managers failed to take reasonable steps to prevent regulatory breaches in their areas of responsibility. This burden of proof is in line with other regulatory enforcement actions. The original reverse burden of proof can be understood against the background of public anger. However, the reversal seems to demonstrate the Treasury's attempt to dilute the personal accountability of senior managers. Bailey at the PRA said that the change is merely procedural rather than substantive (Treanor 2015). It is argued that regulators will need more time and resources to deal with investigations into personal accountability with the reversal in the burden of proof. If the approval procedure of senior managers and high standards are observed, there is less likelihood of misconduct. However, when misconduct does take place, it is important that regulators have sufficient resources for fair and thorough investigations. It would be a shame to introduce a new offence for senior managers only for it to be difficult and expensive to operate.

Conclusion

Stiglitz (2015) described the financial crisis of 2007–9 as the 'Long Slump'. Although Lagarde of the IMF has praised the UK's economic recovery to date, uncertainties remain in relation to the UK leaving the EU and its potential impact on the UK's economy. Already, Lagarde has indicated that the UK's departure from the EU would pose a risk to the UK's economy (Elliott and Allen 2015). Financial stability is fundamental to a recovering economy, not just for the UK but for other countries affected by the global financial crisis, such as the ones studied in this book. Banks are a form of utility – their role in lending to individuals and businesses is the lifeblood of society. This is a very important aspect of banking and it is time that banks and financial institutions were managed and supervised well. Poor corporate governance contributed to the collapse and near collapse of several banks in the UK, US and Germany. This book has discussed some of the failures in corporate governance. However, the primary aim of this book is to focus on macro- and micro-prudential regulatory failures, as well as the architecture of regulatory agencies and central banks.

In terms of regulatory architecture, individuality is here to stay. Each country is unique because of its heritage, history, geography, culture and law. The type of regulatory architecture that works best is ultimately a national and often a political decision. Indeed, it has never been the author's objective to find the ideal model, because there is no such concept. This is further compounded by the fact that there is little empirical evidence of correlation between regulatory architecture and supervisory effectiveness. While the regulatory architecture can facilitate more effective supervision, it is equally important for regulators to have sufficient resources, clear mandates, good communication and co-operation. An interesting observation is that the EU Single Supervisory Mechanism resembles the US regulatory system more closely than the UK's twin-peaks model (Breydo 2015). If the Single Supervisory Mechanism proves to be a success then the suggestion of integrating the Office of the Comptroller of the Currency with the Federal Reserve will not seem too far-fetched (Breydo 2015). Nonetheless, US scholars have concerns about conflicts of interest, in particular that between monetary policy and financial stability, when it comes to integrating the two regulatory agencies (Calomiris and Litan 2000).

A clear trend is that central banks' role in prudential supervision has increased since the global financial crisis. Monetary policy and prudential supervision, especially micro-prudential supervision, are important in times of crises. The centralisation of supervision in the European System of Financial Supervision means that there should be clear communication and co-operation between supervisory authorities and national regulators. The success of the Australian and Canadian financial systems reinforces the importance of communication and co-operation, be it horizontally with other national regulators and central banks or vertically with federal regulators. With increased demands for transparency and accountability due to the re-centralisation of financial supervision, further research needs to be undertaken into what kind of information can be shared in a safe environment, as well as public access to documents.

The use of the Bank of England as a case study is useful because it illustrates how it has been using its new regulatory tools in practice. To date, the UK's new capital framework and the FPC's focus on monitoring the buy-to-let market seems to be working well. Germany, Canada and Australia are also targeting the buy-to-let market. Australia's National Consumer Credit Code provides borrowers with another layer of protection. This includes investors in the buy-to-let market. The UK might wish to consider adopting a similar code to protect consumers. The UK financial sector is the most international in the world. As a result of this, supervision and resolution of foreign branches of banks are of particular importance. Appropriate changes to Articles 21, 26 and 27 of the Capital Requirements Directive IV should therefore be made so that the host (not the home) supervisor has more powers in a crisis.

Other areas where improvement has been made include the use of credible deterrence by the PRA and FCA in recent actions, such as those against the Co-operative Bank and Barclays Bank. The Court of Appeal's sentence of

11 years for Tom Hayes, the first trader convicted of manipulating Libor, is also very encouraging. A more interventionist and proactive regulatory style in micro-prudential supervision is also welcome. The stress tests and CREST tests on banks' ability to deal with cyber risks are all examples of the PRA's new regulatory style.

There is no room for complacency, though. Although the Bank of England's MPC is transparent with its minutes and voting records, the role of lender of last resort in the global financial crisis may tarnish the Bank of England's reputation pending the outcome of the Serious Fraud Office's investigation. Consideration should be given to the No FEAR Act in the US, so that regulatory agencies can be held accountable for their actions. Finally, the ongoing issue of regulatory capture in the form of lobbying remains a conundrum. Proposals to tackle this issue include the use of a Transparency Register, stricter macro-prudential regulation and amending the law on cross-border insolvency. To conclude, the progress made by regulators and central banks to date has been good but more needs to be done. Industry players too have to take responsibility to shape the future of financial institutions before the next financial crisis arrives.

Bibliography

Andenas, M. and Chiu, I. eds. (2014) *The Rise of Macro-prudential Supervision*, United Kingdom: Routledge.

Australia Prudential Regulatory Authority (2013) *Information Paper: Domestic Systemically Important Banks in Australia*, Australia: Australia Prudential Regulatory Authority.

Australian Securities and Investments Commission (2013a) *National Credit Code* [online], available: http://www.asic.gov.au/asic/asic.nsf/byheadline/Consumer-Credit-Code [accessed 6 December 2015].

Australian Securities and Investments Commission (2013b) *Regulatory Guide 166 Licensing: Financial requirements*, Australia: Australian Securities and Investments Commission.

Banerjee, R. and Mio, H. (2015) *Staff Working Paper No. 536 The Impact of Liquidity Regulation on Banks*, London: Bank of England.

Bank of England (2009) *Financial Stability Report*, 26, London: Bank of England.

Bank of England (2015a) *Financial Stability Report 2015*, London: Bank of England.

Bank of England (2015b) *Monetary Policy Committee* [online], available: http://www.bankofengland.co.uk/monetarypolicy/Pages/overview.aspx [accessed 18 November 2015].

Bank of England (2015c) *Stress Testing the UK Banking System: Guidance for Participating Banks and Building Societies*, London: Bank of England.

Bank of England (2015d) *Supplement to the December 2015 Financial Stability Report: The Framework of Capital Requirements for UK Banks*, London: Bank of England.

Bank of England (2015e) *The Bank of England's Approach to Stress Testing the UK Banking System*, London: Bank of England.

Bank of England (2016) *Bank of England Maintains Bank Rate at 0.5 per cent and the Size of the Asset Purchase Programme at £375 billion* [online], available: http://www.bankofengland.co.uk/publications/Pages/news/2016/001.aspx [accessed 25 January 2016].

Baxter, L. (2011) 'Capture in Financial Regulation' Can We Channel It Toward the Common Good?', *Cornell Journal of Law and Public Policy*, 21, pp. 175–200.

BBC (2015a) 'Banking Culture Inquiry Shelved by Regulator FCA' [online], available: http://www.bbc.co.uk/news/uk-35204010 [accessed 10 January 2016].

BBC (2015b) 'Central Banks Need to Be Courageous on Rates, Sentance Says' [online], available: http://www.bbc.co.uk/news/uk-35204010 http://www.bbc.co.uk/news/business-34483861 [accessed 17/11/2015].

BBC (2015c) 'Trader Tom Hayes Has Libor Rate-rigging Sentence Cut to 11 Years' [online], available: http://www.bbc.co.uk/news/business-35152839 [accessed 21 December 2015].

Blinder, A. (2010) 'How Central Should the Central Bank Be?', *Journal of Economic Literature*, 48(1), pp. 123–33.

Blinder, A., Ehrmann, M., Fratzscher, M., De Haan, K. and Jansen, D.-J. (2008) 'Central Bank Communication and Monetary Policy: A Survey of Theory and Evidence', *Journal of Economic Literature*, 46(4), pp. 910–45.

Board of Governors of the Federal Reserve Board System (2015) *Minutes of the Federal Open Market Committee*, United States of America: Board of Governors of the Federal Reserve System.

Borak, S. (2004) 'Legacy of Deep Throat: The Disclosure Process of the Whistleblower Protection Act Amendments of 1994 and the No FEAR Act of 2002', *The University of Miami Law Review*, 59(4), pp. 617–60.

Boyer, P. C. and Ponce, J. (2012) 'Regulatory Capture and Banking Supervision Reform', *Journal of Financial Stability*, 8(3), pp. 206–17.

Breydo, L. (2015) 'Structural Foundations of Financial Stability: What Canada can Teach America about Building a Better Regulatory System', *University of Pennsylvania Journal of Business Law*, 17(3), pp. 973–1082.

Bush, O., Knott, S. and Peacock, C. (2014) *Why is the UK Banking Sector So Big and Is That a Problem?*, 54, United Kingdom: Bank of England.

Calomiris, C. and Litan, R. (2000) 'Financial Regulation in a Global Marketplace', *Brookings-Wharton Papers on Financial Services 283, 304*.

Carpenter, D. (2010) 'Confidence Games: How Does Regulation Constitute Markets?' in Balleisen, E. and Moss, D., eds., *Government and Markets: Toward a New Theory of Regulation* pp. 170–3.

Chan, S. (2015) *Millions Give Up on Home Ownership as House Prices Soar, The Telegraph* [online], available: http://www.telegraph.co.uk/finance/property/house-prices/12057861/Millions-give-up-on-home-ownership-as-house-prices-soar.html [accessed 19 December 2015].

Collinson, P. (2015) 'Cyber Attack Hits RBS and NatWest Online Customers on Payday', *The Guardian* [online], available: https://www.theguardian.com/business/2015/jul/31/rbs-and-natwest-customers-complain-of-online-problems [accessed 14 December 2015].

Deutsche Bank (2015) *Deutsche Bank Reports Third Quarter 2015 Net Loss of EUR 6.0 Billion after Specific Items* [online], available: https://www.db.com/ir/en/content/ir_releases_2015_5066.htm [accessed 11 December 2015].

Dyson, R. (2014) 'My Top 10 Tips for Buy-to-let Success', *The Telegraph* [online], available: http://www.telegraph.co.uk/finance/personalfinance/investing/buy-to-let/11161497/Buy-to-let-my-top-ten-tips.html [accessed 5 January 2016].

Eijffinger, S. and De Haan, J. (2000) *European Monetary and Fiscal Policy*, United Kingdom: Oxford University Press.

Elliott, L. and Allen, K. (2015) 'IMF Boss Christine Lagarde Says She Wants Britain to Stay in EU', *The Guardian* [online], available: http://www.theguardian.com/business/2015/dec/11/imf-lagarde-wants-britain-stay-in-eu-osborne [accessed 22 December 2015].

European Commission (2014) *Population (Demography, Migration and Projections)* [online], available: http://ec.europa.eu/eurostat/web/population-demography-migration-projections/population-projections-data [accessed 12 January 2016].

European Commission (2015) *An EU Framework for Simple, Transparent and Standardised Securitisation*, Brussels: European Commission.

Evans, J. (2015) 'Buy-to-let Set to Dip as UK Landlords Feel Sting of Custs', *Financial Times*, 18 December 2015.

Federal Reserve Bank (2015a) *Minutes of the Federal Open Market Committee, October 27–28, 2015*, United States of America: Federal Open Market Committee.

Federal Reserve Bank (2015b) *No FEAR Data* [online], available: http://www.federalreserve.gov/eeo.htm [accessed 2 December 2015].

Ferran, E. (2011) 'The Break-up of the Financial Services Authority', *Oxford J Legal Studies*, 31(3), pp. 455–80.

Financial Conduct Authority (2015a) *FCA Fines Barclays £72 Million for Poor Handling of Financial Crime Risks* [press release], available: [accessed 12 December 2015].

Financial Conduct Authority (2015b) *The Financial Conduct Authority Censures the Co-operative Bank for Listing Rules Breaches and Failing to Be Open with the Regulator* [online], available: http://www.fca.org.uk/news/fca-censures-the-co-operative-bank-for-listing-rules-breaches [accessed 17 December 2015].

Fleming, S. and Wigglesworth, R. (2015) 'Fed Minutes Point to December Rate Rise', *Financial Times* [online], available: http://www.ft.com/cms/s/0/344f275a-8e26-11e5-8be4-3506bf20cc2b.html?siteedition=uk#axzz3rwhnQxbZ [accessed 18 November 2015].

Gerlach-Kristen, P. (2004) 'Is the MPC's Voting Record Informative about Future UK Monetary Policy?', *The Scandinavian Journal of Economics*, 106(2), pp. 299–313.

Goff, S. and Gray, A. (2014) 'Regulators to Probe Co-op's Finances in a Fresh Blow to Bank', *Financial Times* [online], available: http://www.ft.com/cms/s/0/772a98d2-81af-11e3-87d5-00144feab7de.html#axzz2set9PgCS [accessed 5 February 2014].

HM Treasury (2015) *Senior Managers and Certification Regime: Extension to All FSMA Authorised Persons*, United Kingdom: HM Treasury.

House of Commons Treasury Committee (2013) *Changing Banking for Good: First Report of Session 2013–14*, I: Summary, and Conclusions and Recommendations, London: House of Commons, The Stationery Office Limited.

Issing, O. (2015) 'Communication, Transparency, Accountability: Monetary Policy in the Twenty-First Century', *Federal Reserve Bank of St. Louis Review*, 87(2), pp. 65–83.

James, S. (2014) *A Report on Lessons Learnt from the Negotiation of the Alternative Investment Fund Managers' Directive*, United Kingdom: King's College London.

Jenkins, R. (2011) 'Lessons in Lobbying', at the third Gordon Midgley Memorial Debate, London.

Joint Committee on the Draft Financial Services Bill (2011) *Uncorrected Transcript of Oral Evidence*, HC 1447–xi, London: HMSO.

Kelly, C. (2014) *Failings in Management and Governance: Report of the Independent Review into the Events Leading to the Co-operative Bank's Capital Shortfall* [online], available: http://www.co-operative.coop/PageFiles/989442031/kelly-review.pdf [accessed 20 December 2015].

Lui, A. (2012) 'Retail Ring-fencing and Its Implications', *Journal of Banking Regulation*, 13(4), pp. 336–48.

McDermott, T. (2013) *Enforcement and Credible Deterrence in the FCA*, London: Financial Conduct Authority.

Mishkin, F. (2012) 'Central Banking after the Crisis', in *Central Bank of Chile, Monetary Policy and Financial Stability, Sixteenth Annual Conference of the Central Bank of Chile*.

Morris, B. (2015) *US Rate Rise: Why It Matters*, BBC [online], available: http://www.bbc.co.uk/news/business-35105299 [accessed 17 December 2015].

Mustoe, H. (2015) 'RBS and Standard Chartered Weakest in Bank Stress Test', *BBC*.

Nahmod, S. (2008) 'Public Employer Speech, Categorical Balancing and Section 1983: A Critique of Garcetti v Ceballos', *University of Richmond Law Review*, 42, pp. 569–81.

Perraudin, F. (2016) 'No 10 Hails Building of 13,000 New Homes in Southern England', *The Guardian* [online], available: https://www.theguardian.com/society/2016/jan/04/13000-homes-in-south-east-to-solve-housing-crisis [accessed 8 January 2016].

Prudential Regulatory Authority (2015) *Implementing a UK Leverage Ratio Framework – PS27/15* [press release], available: [accessed 15 December 2015].

Ratnovski, L. and Huang, R. (2009) *Why Are Canadian Banks More Resilient?*, Washington, United States of America: International Monetary Fundhttp://papers.ssrn.com/sol3/papers.cfm?abstract_id=1442254 [accessed 9 December 2015].

Rule, D. (2015) *What Is Left to Do on the Post-crisis Bank Capital Framework?* [press release], available: [accessed 14 December 2015].

Secunda, P. (2008) 'Garcetti's Impact on the First Amendment Speech Rights of Federal Employees', *First Amendment Law Review*, 7, pp. 117–44.

Shafik, M. (2015) *Goodbye Ambiguity, Hello Clarity: The Bank of England's Relationship with Financial Markets*, London: Bank of England.

Sinn, H.-W. (2010) *Casino Capitalism- How the Financial Crisis Came About and What Needs to be Done Now*, Oxford: Oxford University Press.

Stigler, G. (1971) 'The Theory of Economic Regulation', *The Bell Journal of Economics and Management Science*, 2(1), pp. 3–21.

Stiglitz, J. (2015) *The Great Divide – Unequal Societies and What We Can Do About Them*, United Kingdom: Penguin Books Limited.

Teasdale, S. (2011) 'FSA to FCA: Recent Trends in UK Financial Conduct Regulation', *Journal of International Banking Law and Regulation*, 26(12), pp. 583–6.

Transparency International (2012) *Improving the Accountability and Transparency of the European Central Bank*, Brussels.

Treanor, J. (2015) 'UK Government Waters Down Financial Regulation Regime', *The Guardian* [online], available: https://www.theguardian.com/business/2015/oct/15/financial-accountability-regime-will-not-be-fully-operational-until-2018 [accessed 3 January 2016].

Treanor, J. (2016) 'Lloyds under Investigation by FCA over Possible Market Rigging', *The Guardian* [online], available: https://www.theguardian.com/business/2016/jan/06/lloyds-under-investigation-fca-market-rigging [accessed 8 January 2016].

Vickers, J. (2011b) *The Independent Commission on Banking Final Report Recommendations*, London: Independent Commission on Banking.

Warwick Commission (2012) 'Regulatory Capture', [online], pp. 27–32, available: http://www2.warwick.ac.uk/research/warwickcommission/financialreform/report/chapter_5.pdf [accessed 20 February 2014].

Watson, M. (2013) *From Regulatory Capture to Regulatory Space?*, Oxford: The Foundation for Law, Justice and Society.

Whalen, C. (2011) 'I Am Superman: The Federal Reserve Board and the Neverending Crisis' in Tatom, J., ed., *Financial Market Regulation, Legislation and Implications*, United States of America: Springer.

Whiteley, N., Perry, M. and Easter, R. (2015) 'On My Whistle: Are You Ready to Meet the FCA/PRA's New Whistleblowing Requirements?', *Lexology Online* [online], available: http://www.lexology.com/library/detail.aspx?g=27f80444-18b4-4070-9d37-2acb8bd20b9c [accessed 2 December 2015].

Wilson, G. and Wilson, S. (2014) 'The FSA, "Credible deterrence" and Criminal Enforcement – A "Hapzard Pursuit"?', *Journal of Financial Crime*, 21(1), pp. 4–28.

Wilson, H. (2013) 'Standard Chartered Forced by Bank to Strip Top Executive of Risk Role', *The Telegraph*, 5 February 2014.

Yellen, J. (2015) 'Inflation Dynamics and Monetary Policy', at the Philip Gamble Memorial Lecture, University of Massachusetts, Amherst, Massachusetts, 24 September 2015.

Index